End Time Signs

Kurt B. Bakley

authorHOUSE®

AuthorHouse™
1663 Liberty Drive
Bloomington, IN 47403
www.authorhouse.com
Phone: 1-800-839-8640

Published by AuthorHouse   7/25/2012

ISBN: 978-1-4772-3701-4 (sc)
ISBN: 978-1-4772-3702-1 (e)

Table of Contents

Introduction

In this book I will show how coded messages in the Bible, Nostradamus and ancient Egypt art predicts future events for the years 2012-2019 and beyond. Appendix G: *Codes* of my book *The Experiment at Philadelphia* shows how and where I get these many codes for the predictions from 2012-2019 and beyond.

The predictions made in this book are sometimes based on Chinese astrology. In Chinese astrology there are 12 signs that rule one year every 12 years. Unlike our astrology that rules one month every year. The cycle of every 12 years means that predictions can be based on those yearly cycles. In another words the year 2015 minus cycles of 12 years backwards can tell us what will happen in 2015. Ecclesiastes 1:9 states that things that now happen happened in the past the same as the ancient Egyptians and Mayans believed.

Another difference of Chinese astrology is that it rules two hour time periods each day. Since there are 12 signs this covers a 24 hour time period of a day that each sign rules. The signs in our astrology don't do that. And in Chinese astrology the 12 signs also rule our 12 signs and 12 months. The polar opposites of these signs, Chinese, or ours, are connected to the same date and time and event. If an event in July-August of 2015 is predicted, then in January-February of 2015 or 2018- 2019, the polar opposite, is when the same event or another event may happen.

Chinese astrology begins its New Year of its certain signs on the second new moon after the winter solstice. This means New Year's Day is different each year and begins sometime in January or February each year. This makes our past year go into January-February by Chinese New Year's settings.

I also use in this book year/chapter codes of the Bible told of in Appendix G: *Codes* in my book *The Experiment at Philadelphia*. This is where a chapter in the Bible means a certain modern day year plus or minus the Chinese 12 yearly cycle. Times given in this book and my others can be Eastern Standard time, Eastern Daylight Savings time, Israeli time or the time at the place of the event.

Read *About the Author* at the end of this book for all my other books you may want to read. It tells you where you can buy them because they are only available at the web sites given. It will also tell you which ones to read first and how to read them, which is very important. If you haven't read my books entitled *The Experiment at Philadelphia, The Antichrist, The Nativity, Prophecies that have, will, or didn't happen and The boy who could predict earthquakes*, then read them first before this one because they give further documentation of the time of the end that may be in January of 2019 or beyond.

This book gives many different dates and events based on Bible prophecies and Nostradamus, Mayan, Egyptian and other sources. Matthew 24:20,32,38 and Luke 21:29-30 predicts end time signs as happening in the Spring, the Summer, the Fall (=winter in Greek) and the Winter. That is confusing but that's what it does. Isaac Newton, Kenneth Ring and Michael Drosnin may explain this in their books and theories as prophecies that have several futures written in code in them and only one comes true. See the books *The Bible Code I* and II and III by Michael Drosnin, *Heading toward Omega*, by Kenneth Ring and *Chaos: Making a new science*, by James Gleick. In fact, the Bible and other prophecies sometimes gives names, birthdays of leaders, exact dates, times and places of great events and they all come true except for the end time event. I Corinthians chapter 13 tells us that prophecy is written in part which meant sometimes parts of prophecies come true and sometimes parts fail. You must remember these things as you read this book and don't say it's a bunch of guesses and coincidences.

Ancient prophecies in the Bible can have past, present and future fulfillments over thousands of years with some or parts on the same date, place, time, name and event exactly alike or similar. It's like the *Twiligth Zone* show called *The Parallel* This is why it is written in multiple ways. You also must remember that parts of these ancient prophecies over thousands of years, now, our near or far future can give exact names, places, events and times and parts come true, but the rest fails both now, or in our near future, and in our far future.

I heard from many preachers preaching on just how much date setting for the end, Rapture or Second Coming of Christ is silly and foolish, but did you know that the Bible claims not knowing the day and hour and even the minute is foolish. The parable of Matthew 25:1-13 actually uses the word "foolish" as certain virgins who fell asleep and missed the Lord's Coming because they didn't know the minute He would return and fell asleep. The parable actually says they will be left behind and not aloud into the marriage supper and wedding of God. Other places in the Bible predict the same thing like Matthew 24:42- 51 predicts that no one can know the day and hour yet in that same chapter it predicts people to mock God's delay and go party and He comes and they are left behind to be thrown into hell. Matthew 22:2-14 also predicts the wedding of God and people not being ready because they are asleep and naked or in pajamas and the Lord's comes and they are left behind or in heaven without proper dress or suites and they are thrown out. It also says that the people who were invited (Christians) to the wedding of God at the end are not called, but servants of the Lord go out into the highways and invite many good and bad to the wedding of God and they are gathered up and make it to heaven while the other good people invited weren't ready and left behind and end up in hell at the end because they weren't ready and ashamed of the wedding of God as a joining of Christ and His Bride as a she/male, which is why they didn't come and weren't ready. Matthew 24:45-47 prediction of the good servant giving meat and food to his famnily and friends at this time might mean a supper time apperaance of Christ for the wedding. Matthew 25:1-13 predicts a midnight appearance. Israel is 6-7 hours difference in time to the Eastern U.S. making supper time (=the marriage supper of the Lamb in the U.S.) be midnight in Israel. Many Bible prophecies point to times of when people are sleeping when Christ returns and many as times when they are eating dinner. That's why we are told to watch because if we are asleep we are not watching and if we are eating we are not watching, but it is what we should be doing at that time surving food or meat when Jesus comes back.

The TV preachers and writers of Bible prophecy make these mistakes often and teach them often. Wasn't it silly and foolish to say the Common Market that turned into the EU as having ten kings or nations to it as the end time fulfillment of Bible prophecy foolish when it went to eleven. They then said well a little horn plus 10 equals 11 nations. Then when it went to thirteen they said well then little horn subdues three kings to make 13 be 10 again. That is silly and foolish too if you want to say that. It is now at 20-30 nations in the EU. Setting many dates is foolish to them. But it is not. Things change and dates change and events change as Bible prophecy predicts. That's why there are so many dates, times, places and events and leaders given in Bible prophecy. As I Corinthians chapter 13 predicts some prophecies and knowledge of the Bible fails and some come true. My book *Prophecies that have, will or didn't happen* shows that very point out very clearly.

Another thing that happens are that prophecies sometimes were fulfill already and/or are fulfilled many different times, places, ways, and people over the thousands of years since they were written down. What you say is a Bible prophecy may have been fulfilled hundreds to thousands of years ago. What you say is prophecies of the past may come true in our future. And what they say the antichrist is may also be wrong according to Bible prophecy. Ecclesiastes 11:2 predicts in the end that you would not know what evil shall come. Satan is a Trinity too as God and knows good, evil and neutral. The antichrist could well be a true born again Christian under full law and not a cult or heretic either when he comes. He also could be neutral or lawless. We just don't know as Ecclesiastes predicts and Daniel 9:27 predicts the antichrist to be greatly angered at the overspreading (many people) doing abominations (=sins). If he were lawless he would love them doing sins and teach them to do sins. Satan is not only the great adversary of the law, but a great adversary of lawlessness and lukewarm or neutralism. So beware of just who is the antichrist. See my book entitled *The Experiment at Philadelphia*.

The many different dates given in this book and my others are anniversaries of past events and dates of future events. They don't all happen at one event, date and place. Over the many years they may just all come true or have already. Things you think didn't happen have already happened on the exact date, place, time and event. For example, the Waco fire disaster on April 19, 1993, then two years to that date the Oklahoma City bombing on the exact anniversary of the first event. Here a little there a little just as Isaiah chapter 28 predicts. If a event happened in the past it is still a prophecy because the Bible is thousands of years old. Remember Ecclesiastes 1:9 that things of old will happen now and in our future.

See the publisher, if still in business, Willmann-Bell,Inc. P.O. Box 35025, Richmond, Virginia 23235 for books on astormony and planet and moon positions and phases for the future and past and solar and lunar eclipses for the future and the past. Look in *Astronomy* and *Sky and Telescope* magazines for ads for books and computer software for star and planet locations and moons phases for the future. Also look in them for calendars of different cultures from long past to long future along with moons phases, lunar and solar eclipses, holidays and feasts days and New Year's Days and Chinese signs and New Year's Days. See Office Depot for computer software on stars over long periods of time.

I am not Christ, God, the Holy Ghost, a prophet, the false prophet, the antichrist, the beast, satan, a demon, a false prophet, a false teacher, a heritic, a psyhic, a new ager, a astrologyer, a cult leader, but just a research-writer.

A wise man once said that he thought God created the Universe as one giant coded puzzle for man to figure out and put together.

June 12, 2012

Kurt B. Bakley

Chapter One

End Time Signs 1

II Samuel 11:1-2, Song of Solomon 2:7-13 And Luke 21:29 predicts when the year expires and/ or spring comes kings go to war. Some Bible translations puts this verses in II Samuel 11:1-2 as mentioning spring when Kings go to war. Spring comes on March 20-21. The Old Julian Calendar expires on that date meaning the year has ended and a new one begins. The date of March 1 and 24-25 also are times when the year expires to the Old Julian Calendar. Will on those dates we see war and attacks on Iran and Israel and the U.S. with possibly Russia becoming involved. People don't realize it that if Israel and the U.S. attack Iran Russia may count that as an attack on Russia and counter attack both Israel and the U.S. and Israel and the U.S. counter attacks Russia and possibly Syria and Iran. The latest news in 2012 was that President Putin in Russia is going to sign a covenant with Iran that if they are attack they will considered it an attack on Russia. Daniel chapter 10 predicts Israel attacking Iran (Persia) then returning to attack it again three weeks or years later. And Ezekiel chapters 38-39 predict a nation far north of Israel to attack Israel with Iran and Turkey and maybe others and God greatly destroys them on the mountains of Israel by Divine intervention or by Israel nuclear attack on the invading armies. In Jeremiah chapter 6 warns Benjamin Netanyahu (current Prime Minister of Israel on April 30, 2012) to be aware of a foreign army to the North that might attack or invade. Russia is directly North of Israel. President Putin of Russia was born October 7, 1952, which was the Chinese Year of the Dragon the same as 2012 is the Chinese Year of the Dragon. Was Revelation chapter 12 prediction of President Putin (Dragon) to fire three nuclear bombs at Israel after Israel attacks Iran as the third of the stars (=three bombs) falling from heaven drawn down by the Dragon (=Putin)? Or is the third of the stars 2000-3000 scud missiles fired by Syria with chemical and biological warheads? See the Bible's Isaiah 17:1,14. Does the chemical and biological weapons cause animals to have weird babies as Isaiah chapter 13 predicts. And Revelation chapter 13 predicts a beast as a lamb, but speaks as a dragon or satan. The current (April 2012) President of Iran Mahmound Ahmadinejad was born October 28, 1956 making him a Scorpio. The Scorpio sign is after the serpent or dragon in the garden of Eden that was satan and tempted Adam and Eve. See the book *As Above, So Below*, by Alan Oken. The President of Iran is a Dragon birth sign and is a lamb, or religious supposedly, but speaks as a dragon with great words against Israel and the U.S. This man born then is Revelation's fourth beast and final antichrist to start this war born in the cusp of the star time of Virgo, which is an earth sign. His belief's is to do just that. Revelation chapter 13 predicts this lamb to come up out of the earth (=Virgo). Both President Putin of Russia and Iran's President Ahmadinejad have birth signs of coming up out of the earth (=Virgo star time or cusp=earth) and like a lamb believe in God, but act and speak as a Dragon or devil or serpent and are connected to the Chinese Dragon in Year (=1952=Putin) and in sign (=Scorpio=dragon=Ahmadinejad). President Putin said he believe there is a creator, which is great difference coming from a former communist nation that are hard core atheists. But since Israel is 82-92 secular Jews at this time (2012) and the U.S. falling away into apostasy and becoming mostly a secular (=non-Christian) then God may just withdraw his hand from both nations (=U.S. and Israel) and the Harbinger happens destroying part or all of the U.S. and Israel in these wars and/or by tidal waves on the U.S. East Coast and/or West Coast then or later along with a Mount Saint Helens eruption or Yellowstone super volcano eruption then or later. Three great earthquakes and/or volcano eruptions and tidal waves may strike the U.S. on the East Coast and West Coast (Northwest Coast=Seattle and Mount Saint Helens) and one from the volcano eruption off of Africa in the Canary Islands to cause a tidal wave on the East Coast of the U.S. and the third would be a great earthquake in New Madrid, Missouri and/or Yellowstone Park super volcano ending the great U.S. existence.

The other dates of these events are January 1, 16-17, 24, February 1, 11, 14, 26-28, and April 1, 6-10, 12-17, 19-20, 25, 29-30, 2013 after the year expires and other prophecies given for these dates as this book documents. October 31 and November 1-2, 11, 2012 are also possible dates for these events as when the Anglo-Saxon calendar expires, the day of the dead (November 1-2) and the Old Halloween on November 11. Other dates are Spring, Summer, Fall and Winter on new moons; full moons; feast days, holidays, anniversaries; Chinese New Year; and the dream of red December 24-25 and a lake with many people in boats. The upcoming dates for 2012 or 2013-2019 can be for 2020-2060 or later. Every time a date or year is given in this book it maybe for those dates in other years in the future when they happen. So as Colossians 2:16-17 predicts watch and be ready on those dates or the anniversary of those dates years into the future. Don't begin to mock or scoff at them and people who write and preach them.

I had a dream in 2011-2012 of a piece of red paper with December 24 or 25 written on it then I saw the summer time and a great lake with many people in boats going about it. Was this the sooner and later Nostradamus predicted would change from the end in December 24-25, 2012 to the summer of 2012 on the ninth of AV or in July-August-September of 2012 or 2013. At that time is when many people travel for summer vacations by cars and boats on lakes, rivers and seas just as Daniel 12:4 predicted. He predicted that time is when knowledge of end times happens. This is recorded in my 14 books told of in *About the Author* at the end of this book who the angels speak of to these people on earth at this time about. Will angels be sent out then when many (=20,000) travel by car, plane, train or boat as chariots upon the mountains and hills and lakes, rivers and oceans? The constellation Auriga, The Charioteer, appears over head at early morning before dawn in late July and into August. See the Bible's Psalms 68:17, Song of Solomon 8:13-14, Revelation 2:29 and Proverbs 6:9-11. Those verses in Proverbs predicts work on a vineyard (books=publisher=wine harvest=July-August-September) as Song of Solomon chapter 8 predicts the angel voice is heard when people travelleth as Daniel 12:4 predicts. It also predicts these events as a time of an armed man as President Putin or Iran, Israel and U.S. trade attacks on each other. The "armed man" can also mean the date of the ninth of Av when two times the Jewish temple was destroyed on that exact date in 585-586 B.C. and 70 A.D. The fasting of the fifth month for 70 years from when the Temple was destroyed till its dedication in 515 B.C. (=Dog=Dragon) is recorded in Daniel chapters 9:1-3,26 (=flood=hurricane, tidal wave or Nor'Easter) and 10:2-4,13,20 and Zechariah 7:1-7 and 8:19. That date may come up again in 2012-2013 or other years when wars and attacks happen on Israel, U.S., Russian and other nations. Are these prophecies that of travel by many and the voice of an angel (spirit) speaks to 20,000 of them at this time of July-August of 2012? The angel and the moon when horrible vengeance's occurs in Nostradamus' quatrain might be a new moon or a full moon and the date of September 26-27, 2003 when Rosh Hashanah began on a new moon and was a Friday into Saturday=Jewish Sabbath. Nothing happen then but maybe what Colossians 2:16-17 predicts to watch for as a anniversary of that date or the others in this book as the time of the end or the signs of events showing the time of the end then or much later as shown in chapter 24 and 31 of this book about Isaac Newton prediction. II Peter 3:2-18 predicts people mock and scoff at this date setting. By that time if Israel and the U.S. survives the wars and attacks and tidal waves there could be between now and then three great earthquakes, three great volcano eruptions, three great tidal waves and three great wars in Israel and the U.S. happens and most of the other parts of the world maybe left in intact for generations to come. Then that is why they say they trusted in God and He didn't save them and they died (feel asleep) and mock an scoff them and their God, Bible and church. The Christian Church during these wars, attacks and natural disasters won't repent of their sins and humble themselves and turn to God but in each time like 9- 11 they will become proud and say we will build again and go on without God. Sometimes when there is a family tragedy or trouble in the world some people turn to God for strength and faith while many turn away from Him and are bitter and angry at Him and the Church and Bible. This may be what happens to Israel and the U.S. during these days and many years to come. The world may blame the U.S. and Israel for all their troubles. This is not to say the rest of the world won't have great wars, attacks, volcano eruptions, earthquakes and other man made and natural troubles, but that Israel, the U.S. and Christians and Jews will be the target for a long time to come even after or if their nations are destroyed or partially destroyed. The three volcanoes eruptions and earthquakes could be in the Canary islands off the west coast of Africa. Another in the Pacific or Mount Saint Helens and the last but worst the super volcano in Yellowstone Park if it erupts would destroy the entire U.S. causing great famines there and all over the world. This is because of the smoke and darkness it would cause would destroy all crops and the U.S. The U.S. unlike other nations exports foods to many or all of the world's people in one way or another.

Every time you see a date and year in this book not only look for that date and year for those events, but if nothing happens look to the other dates and years and other years not given on those dates for these events to happen. Also look for that date in this book for future events on that date or that date in the Bible's calendar and/or the Jewish Civil Calendar. For events and dates that failed see my books *The boy who could predict earthquakes* and *Prophecies that have, will, or didn't happen*.

The next two chapters tell of predictions of Joel and Acts chapters 2 in the Bible about prophecies of the last days. In those prophecies is that people in the last days would dream dreams that were prophetic. That prophecy directly came true with a dream I had recorded and interpreted in Chapter 3. But as Chapter 2 predicts the end time signs come in May-November of 2012, which may be true or not. It's possible those events predicted come true in July-August-September of 2012 and/or January-April of 2013. Nostradamus' quatrain C1:Q56 predicts times changing two times, sooner and later. Is the first time of a change or a date set for the end time signs that of May- November or December of 2012? Is it changed to July-August- September of 2012, sooner then expected as Psalms 90:14 predicts "early". The later changes in times of dates is not January 20-21, 2019 when the end may come, but December 24-25, 2060 when the end will come, which is later than expected. There is also another interpretation of these events and when they might happen before the end, which is they may not happen in July-August or September of 2012, but in January-April of 2013 as documented in this chapter. That same quatrain predicts when an angel and the moon (new or full moon?) is approaching the balance, which is the Libra sign great vengeances happen. The date of September 26-27, 2003 is the cusp of Libra the balances and was a new moon, Sabbath Day (=Saturday) and a holyday of Rosh Hashanah when the year expires and kings go to war. This alignment only happens once in a great while. But nothing happened then yet as Colossians 2:16-17 predicts it is a foreshadow of things to come. That means a Holiday, on or near, a new moon and Jewish Sabbath Day when end time events happen on.

The date of November 11 given in this book is after the Old Halloween date, which today is 10 days earlier on October 31 into November 1, which is also called All Saint's Day and The Day of the Dead in Mexico, probably given from the Mayans on November 1 or 2. November 11 is Veteran's that was set after the end of World War I when an agreement was sign in the 11th month (=November) on the 11th day and in the 11th hour in 1918. The Lord's prayer says: Hallowed by thy name, thy kingdom come… Could the "Hallowed" be the Halloween date of old or new when the events happen on and the kingdom of God comes? Will the Muslims pick that date for their Kingdom? And the name of God spelled backwards is Dog which is the Chinese Year of the Dog or its polar opposite the Year of the Dragon in the years 2012, 2018 and 2060.

The DVD called *Watchers 3* by L.A. Marzulli tell of the sun seen double as Nostradamus C2:Q41 predicted with strange things going around it and the moon changing degrees and the stars being places they should be might just be the prediction of Luke 21:11, 25, 26 that predicts signs in the sun, moon and stars and fearful and great signs from heaven when the seas and waves roaring (=tidal waves, Nor'Easters, Hurricanes). These reports were made in 2011 by L.A. Marzulli in DVD's called *The Watchers 1-3* which website WWW.lamarzulli.net can be found. He went to NASA or some other organizations and they slamed their doors shout in his face. He reorted that they had the same evidence and brushed them out because they thought it would scare people just as Luke 21:11, 25-26 predicted. Greenland has exactly 30 days of darkness till the sun comes up each year. Recently the sun came up two days earlier. The Bible Code predicted the moon would be changing in 2011, which was doucmented in those DVD's. They also reported the moon changed degrees, phases and places. The magnetic North Pole shown on compasss has changed the past few years annouced by Brian Williams on NBC news at about 40 miles a year. Other interpretations of these same prophecies are also mention in upcoming chapters as to what they might mean and be.

The President of Iran Ahmadinejad at this time (May 12, 2012) every time he speaks he prays a prayer for the last antichrist or god to come and kill and destroy all of Israel and the U.S. and Jews and Americans and infidels all over the world and usher in a new world with Islam as it new leader. The lady on *60 minutes* even asked him why he says that prayer every time he speaks. Nostradamus in quatrain C9:Q83 predicts a great earthquake in the theater (=Los Angeles=Hollywood= movie theaters), darkness and trouble in the air, in the sky, on earth (=land) when the infidels calls upon God and the Saints. These things could be volcano eruptions as smoke and darkness in the air and sky and attacks and wars as trouble on earth and sky when Iran, Russia, Syria, Turkey and others attacks. They seek to wipe out all the U.S. and Israel the infidels (=non-Muslims) who call themselves Saint or martyrs for doing so and kill the real Saints at a time in the evening when the theaters are full and there's a great earthqquake in Los Angeles and/or attacks, wars, volcano eruptions and tidal waves. These events could happen in May 9-10 or June 9-12 of 2013-2019 or beyond and leave ghost towns of Israel and the U.S. and as Mark 13:9-13 and Luke 21:12-19 predicts. The true Saints who are Christians and Jews left from this or these first holocausts, or natural disasters, will be persecuted and put into prison and killed if they don't deny Christ and convert to Islam. John 16:1-2 and Revelation 20:4-6 predicts this as they kill you thinking they do God service to do that horrible thing. If these wars and disasters happen early such as 2012-2013-2019, then those Saints remaining will have to be very patience and faithful till death for a long time just as Isaiah 6:11 and Revelation 6:9-11 predicts. Matthew chapter 24 predicts these things must happen before the end comes so there is many yet to be fulfilled before the end comes just as Joel and Acts chapter 2 both predicts these events are before the great and terrible Day of the Lord just as Matthew chapter 24, Mark 13 and Luke 17 and 21 predicted. These events seem like the end but are not. They are end time signs before the Day of the Lord exactly as Joel and Acts chapter 2 predicted.

Daniel chapters 9,11 and 12 were all written in 539-538 B.C. which were the Chinese Dog and Pig Years. The polar opposites those years are 2012 and 2013 A.D. And those years are 2018-2019 A.D. all times of when some of these events may happen to Israel and America. Daniel chapter 10 was written by 536-535 B.C. which was the Chinese Years of the Ox and Tiger, which today is polar opposite our 2015-2016 A.D. Daniel 9:26 predicts a "flood" during these times from 2012-2019 A.D. and a prince being Iran and/or Russia and other nations to attack Israel. The antichrist may come during these times or much later and make a seven year period peace plan and that all follow the full law and no more abominations (Muslim's law in Islam?) or sin committed by Christians or the secular. If you do he gives orders to kill you and put you in prison and torture and kill you unless you stop or the Muslims kill you unless you deny Jesus Christ and convert to Islam. Remember the very first of the 10 commandments: "have no other gods beside me."

Perry Stone in his *Unusual Prophecies Being Fulfilled* Prophetic Series Book Eight by Perry Stone Page 111 suggests that part of the 666 numbers in Revelation 13:16-18 maybe the name Allah the god of the Muslims who in that chapter and that name kills and makes war with the Saints as other parts of the book Revelation predicts for the end times. Order that books and other material at V.O.E. P.O. Box 3595, Cleveland, TN 37320. Other books put Hitler's name as 666 and the title of the Pope as 666 and even former leader of Russian Gorbachev having a red birth mark on his forehead symbolizing the mark of the beast on his forehead. One TV preacher named Irvin Baxter and his ministry called *End Time Ministries* at 1-800-363-8463 has one DVD that documents how Pope John Paul the II had a deal with Gorbachev of Russia to join the Catholic Church with his government of evil communism. He also called the newest Pope Benedict the XVI is also very corrupt and trying something similar. The news show *60 minutes* show told how many NAZI war criminals escaped Germany at the end of the war with help every time by the Catholic Church. Is the blood in the cup of the whore in Revelation chapter 17 that of the Saints or Jews killed with the help the Catholic church? Italy was Germany ally in World War II. The Catholic Church is also responsible for many Saints brutal deaths over the past 1600 years. They may join again with communism of Russia, China, EU and Muslims to again wipe out all Jews and any Americans left. See Mark 13:9-13 and Luke 21:12-19. The great Catholic church alone is already accused of killing any where from 2-62 millions Saints just because they weren't Catholic. See Ellen White's books and the books *Handwriting on the wall* and *Escape the coming night* by Dr. David Jeremiah.

Revelation 16:13-14 prediction of three frogs flying out from the mouths of the dragon, beast and false prophet at the end times maybe these three together joined in a one world domination to kill any true Christian and Jew. A frog is first formed as a tadpole and changes into a frog. Will these three Communism, Catholic and Muslims join in the end and change each other into one great evil form never seen before and go after the Americans and Jews they blame for all the worlds problems on? They are the trinity of the 666 and fly in the sky in many planes and possibly by UFOs and they reveal themselves to many and have books revealing the deepest darkest secrets of the Universe that perverts all the earth just as Revelation chapter 17-18 predicts of the whore to do that sits on seven hills of Rome, Italy. That place may become very rich during these many years after Israel and U.S. are destroyed just as those same chapters predicts along with the revealing of the UFOs. The UFOs came before the flood and after the flood to Babylon or Babel and took women before the flood and men after the flood had sex with them and started the Gentiles children of devils and all the ancient cultures and buildings of stones which the book of Revelation chapter 17 calls MYSTERY BABYLON THE GREAT MOTHER OF HARLOTS AND ABOMINATIONS OF THE EARTH. The women devils in UFOs are harlots or whores and they built or help build and teach the ancient Gentiles all their wisdom which we now call ancient astronauts or ancient aliens with all their seducing powers. The stones and monuments they built long ago are the abominations of the earth (=stones) that seduce just like a very sexy whore just as Revelation chapter 17 predicted. The books the UFOs bring are predicted in I Timothy 4:1-3 that predicted a church with forbidding to eat meats (=on Fridays) and forbidding to marry (=Catholic Priests) just as the Roman Catholic church does. Will a former or reigning pope now or in our future be raised from the dead and come back from a UFO? Will the Pope now, or the next one, write those books? Those doctrines of devils or ancient astronauts are the gods of the Gentiles will be filled with old fables, wive's tales and legends as I Timothy 1:4, 4:7; II Timothy 4:4; Titus 1:14; and II Peter 1:16 predicted. Or will the UFOs bring them that information that my two books entitled *The Antichrist* and *The Experiment at Philadelphia* tell of. Will the UFOs reveal themselves in our future as they did to our ancestors long ago before and after Noah's flood making the phrase to what the "the days of Noah" mean? The problem with those books and TV shows is that they call the UFO beings good, God, Jesus, Holy Ghost, angels. Not one time have I heard them called demons and devils and satan which they truly are. That's the great trick and delusion that II Thessalonians chapter 2 and other prophecies tell of. The author Arthur E. Bloomfield predicted it is not Russia we should fear in the end times but UFOs and science. Those books and wisdom the UFOs may bring are the first 14 chapters of my book entitled *The Experiment at Philadelphia* and my book *The antichrist* also shows how they will deceive and how its documented in the Bible. And what maybe confusing is that Revelation chapter 16 predicts a trinity of satan, which means and stands for the great full law, neutral and full lawlessness. Or will be these three remaining enemies of each other join for a long time ending in war with each other as Revelation chapter 17 predicts? In the 1800's the author Ellen White wrote and predicted for the last days that the antichrist would rule for a long time not the short three and a half years the Bible predicts. If these wars and natural disasters happen in 2012-2019 and 2026-2030 and the U.S. and Israel are destroyed then 48-30 years later after the long reign of these three antichrists the end comes it would be a long time rule of them.

At the end Daniel chapter 11 and Revelation chapters 17-19 predict the king of the North (=Russia? EU?) hates the whore (Catholic Church and UFOs and their joining with them and Muslims) and kills her and burns her with fire (=nuclear?)

The next chapters are taken from my other books. They have not been changed except for some deletions and a few additions. Remember if the dates and years fail to have the events happen at that time then look for future years on those dates for those events. You can replace any year with 2020-2060 on the dates given for earlier years as to when those events happen in the future.

The Chinese Snake rules our Taurus sign and month of May. The city of Los Angeles is in the Taurus zone as told in chapter 7 of my other book *Predictions for 2013-2014* and is ruled by Leo. The Leo sign (lion) runs from July 21-23 to August 21-23 and with its cusp of seven goes to August 28-30. Does the term "Babylon the great is fallen, is fallen," in the book of Revelation 14:8 and 18:2 mean two times Los Angeles is hit by an earthquake? Are those two earthquakes the one on January 17, 1994 that hit Northridge and the other "one hour" away as Revelation 18:17 predicts? Change the hour to a day of 24 hours and then change to years added to 1994 and it equals 2018 into 2019 when the second earthquake happens in the great city of Los Angeles. See also Revelation chapter 6. Or is Babylon, a spiritual name for the United States and especially Los Angeles, fallen twice once in 1994 and then again in 2018- 2019 right when the sun goes into a supernova and causes the earth to shake and be utterly destroyed just like Revelation 6:12-17 predicted? The "one hour" Babylon the great is fallen, is fallen that the book of Revelation 18:2-3,6,10 predicts in one hour or 60 minutes changed to six years added to 2013, counting each year or not, equals the years 2018-2019. The "wine of the wrath of her fornication" in (verse 3), could mean the wine harvest, which is July-August-September of 2015 and 2018-2019. Those months are in the fifth month (July-August) of the Bible's calendar as Zechariah 7:3,5, 8:19 predicts for a fast to help stop very bad events from happening in August to September, which is the wine harvest of very ripe grapes.

Revelation chapter 14 predicts in verse 8 that "Babylon is fallen, is fallen" by the middle angel of three. Could that be the half hour (=middle) of Revelation 8:1? Or is it three years as three angels trouble occurs for the U.S. (Babylon) on August 10, 2013, August 10, 2014, August 10, 2015? Or is Revelation six angels three more angels from August 10, 2016, August 10, 2017 and August 10, 2018, plus or minus three days or July-August of 2013-2018 as the first three angels then three more angels as years in the vine or grape harvest (=July- August) or wrath of God's winepress for those times and years that Revelation chapter 14 predicts? In Revelation chapter 14 predicts three angels then three more angels to make six angels or years. That equals six angels translated as six years plus the half a year as a half an hour (Revelation 8:1) from August 10, 2013 equals January 2019. It also could mean the three angels are the three woes on August 10, 2013, August 10, 2014, August 10, 2015, plus three and a half years from August 10, 2015 to January 21, 2019. That equals the three angels, plus three and a half angels as Revelation chapter 14 predicted. They all could mean trouble for Babylon (=U.S.) on all those exact dates, or on August 10, 2015 then on January 21, 2019. The second angel of three in Revelation chapter 14 is two or half of three added to three equals three and a half angels, or years, plus three more angels to make three more years. When you divide you always divide by two making two the half a year. Will the U.S. as Babylon is fallen, is fallen happen in Los Angeles in one of those years then in the end is again fallen totally just as Revelation 6:12-17 predicts on a lunar eclipse in January of 2019 to make two times Babylon (U.S.) is fallen? Is one of those two fallen the great tidal wave of July-August of 2015, then add three and a half years later it falls again totally in a supernova in January 21, 2019 on a full moon? The moon is given the number 2 as the second angel and the two fallen that Revelation 14:8 predicts for the wine harvest of July-August-September or on two lunar eclipses. The second angel of Revelation chapter 14 when Babylon is fallen for the second time could mean the two great earthquakes that hit the U.S. (=Babylon) on August 10, 2013 and August 10, 2014, plus or minus three days. The year 2014 could mean the chapter number of Revelation chapter 14 as the year when the second great earthquake happens. Those two earthquakes would make Babylon (=U.S.) fall twice in two years from 2013-2014. Verse 8 of Revelation chapter 14 where Babylon (=U.S.) falls twice might mean our eighth month when it falls twice or August of 2013 and August of 2014. The smoke that rises up from her for ever as predicted in the book of Revelation would be the sun's smoke from its supernova at that time of January of 2019 six angels and a half hour, or half a year, from the first earthquake in Babylon (=U.S.) in 2013? Three angels from July-August of 2013-2015 and three angels from 2016-2018 and a half to January 21, 2019, when the seventh angel sounds its trumpet, which is the last of the three angels or three woes Revelation chapters 8, 10, 11 predicts as the last woe and last trumpet to sound at the very end.

Note: The exact hour and/or minutes of solar and lunar eclipses and full and new moons in this book and my other books may be off by several minutes or hours plus or minus because different books give different times. Why this is I don't know.

In the book *Unusual prophecies being fulfilled* Prophetic Series/Book Three pages 66-70 by Perry Stone predicts a old preacher who predicted seven great prophecies which seem to have come true except the last two. The last two were that a woman would rise to power in the U.S.and during her term the U.S. would be destroyed.

Another similar prophecy was that of a story told of how when George Washington was about to go into the great battle for the U.S. that a woman angel visited him and told him great things for the future and some bad things as well. See the book *The Book of angels* by Ruth Thompson, L.A. Williams, and Renae Taylor pages 116-121. Those pages tell of a dark angel blows a trumpets three times as three perils for America's future. The third war was the worst where cities and towns sprung up were destroyed by invading armies by the seas on America. It also predicts invading Europe, Asia and Africa taking water from the ocean and she sprinkles it upon those three places and from each of those three places a thick dark cloud joined into and sprinkled waters from. Could this have meant nuclear war between the U.S., Europe, Asia and Africa? Most of Europe is U.S. allies now (May 19, 2012), but are quickly becoming Muslims and hating the U.S. Does the sprinkle of the water from the ocean at the blowings of this trumpet and the dark thick cloud be the volcano smoke off the West Coast of Africa in the Canary Islands, which is near Europe that rush with a tidal wave towards the

East Coast of U.S. with dark thick clouds of ash, smoke and vapour? Or is the dark thick cloud that of nuclear missiles hitting the U.S. and a nuclear winter? Asia could also be the attackers of the U.S. and these three dark thick clouds from those three nations and trumpets blowing. It also could be a volcano in Asia that tidal waves and smoke, ash and vapor reaches the U.S. covering U.S. towns and cities from the Pacific Ocean. This has already happened years ago to England farer East then the U.S. An Asia volcano erupted with such forces it was felt thousands of miles away. A king at the time describe strange blackness or rains and clouds over England. For many years they just thougth he was a kook. But after further study the found this Asian volcano eruption happened near the time that the king of England describe the strange black rain and clouds. If this happens again it could destroy America just as the three soundings of the dark angel and the trumpet. It would turn great cities, towns and villages into desolation and very great ghost towns uninhabitable.

The three nations of Europe, Asia and Africa could be the ones the dark angel refers to as surviving these events that destroys the U.S. and they turn to Islam and hate and persecute and kill the Christians, Jews and Americans. Also Africa and Asia has two volcanos that could do this to the U.S. and world, but also Sicily, Italy and maybe other places in Italy have volcanos that could do this as well and Italy is apart of Europe. Thus, the three great places that sends darkness on the U.S. destroying it. The sprinkle of water that gets rid of the darkness and the invading armies could be tidal waves after the volcano eruptions that destroy the ships and armies in them coming against the U.S. at this time as Habakkuk 3:8 predicts along with verses 9-16 of that same chapter. It also could be Nor'Easters or great hurricanes that destroy the ships and armies. The sun and moon in those verses that stand still and go at the sight of thy arrows and glittering spear could be the earth's rotation stopping causing night time over the U.S. for three days and nights. Then when the nuclear missiles (=arrows and glittering spears) start flying they (=the sun and moon) start rotating again by the earth starting rotation and the U.S. is destroyed by them. The angel predicts the U.S. (=Union) to be victorious at the end, but it may not be if Jesus Christ doesn't return and the Americans repent of their sins, humble themselves and follow Christ.

Washington noted at the end of his story that the angel blows the trumpet again and a light of 1000 suns shown down. Is this (=Jesus Christ return or a sun supernova of our sun?) He says the event breaks up the dark cloud (volcano eruption or nuclear bombs, or storms), which envelope America? The angel tells him America will win the battle and the villages, towns and cities springing up where they were seen before. Is this the Second Coming of Christ and not a supernova of our sun. Will Christ restore peace and rebuild Amercia and restores the villages, cities and towns. He is as the Bible claims the restorer of the breaches and places to live. And as Jeremiah predicts God may not leave the U.S. destroyed or loose the battle but win it. He will punish her, but will not leave her totally undone or destroyed. He may intervine for both Israel and the U.S. and world if many repent, turn from their sins, humble themsleves and turn to God and live for God. It's never to late. Isaiah also predicts this that if we repent and turn to God and heed the harbingers God will save us like Ezekiel chapters 38-39 predicts when Iran and Russia attacks Israel God will intervine. But right now with Jews at 82-92 per cent secular (=non-religious) and the U.S. that way too and the world worshipping other gods it looks more likely these bad events may happened.

The woman angel Washington saw could be predicting a woman U.S. President at the time of these events. And the Ocean sprinkling could be tidal waves or storms hitting the U.S. that the armies of Europe, Asia and Africa have to sail through to attack the U.S. as we just saw Habbakkuk and other Bible prophecies predicted. Nostradamus also predicted this as an army sailing through a storm at sea towards palm trees of Florida. See my books *The Divine Code 2* and *Prophecies that have, will, or didn't happen* and Quatrain C1:Q30.

Amos 1:1 predicts two years before a great earthquake and/or volcano eruption and tidal wave. In chapter/year codes Amos chapter 1 is our year 1995. Add 12 years to that and it equals 2007. Add six years polar opposite that and it equals 2013. Then add three or four years to that as the book Amos 1:3 predicts as three or four transgressions and it equals 2016-2017-2018-2019.

Luke 21:9 predicts wars and rumors of wars which may be happening now (2012) and in 2011 and may continue in 2012-2013 then wars and attacks with commotion's, but the end is not by and by. The "by and by" could be two years from these events and a terrible disaster happens and many may think it's the end, but it's not. That year would be 2015 when a tidal wave, or an earthquake and volcano eruptions and cause trouble in the U.S. Another way to interpret this is that the Greek word for the Second Coming of Christ in the Greek dictionary of the *Strong's Concordance of the Bible* is numbered 2015. Could that have meant our year 2015 as the end and Second Coming? My book, *The boy who could predict earthquakes* gives this same date in November 11, 2015. See chapter 7. It also told of red waters and wild life dieing that Revelation predicted in March- April of 2010-2011-2012. I almost and was told by the Holy Ghost to put the date April 20 and didn't for one agent told me I give to many possibilities. The oilrig fire happened April 20, 2010 and turns the waters to blood or red and poison the waters and killed the wild life. See xviii of that book which predicts trouble with wormwood that Revelation predicts poisons the waters or sea and turns them to blood by the oil and by chemicals dropped on the oil by planes as a star falling from heaven and poisoning the sea, which the word "wormwood" means "bitter or poison."

That same book of just mentioned predicted a earthquake on Friday 11 (I had December, but also gave March-April) at 2:43 p.m. that would cause nuclear power plants melt down. The Japan earthquake and tidal wave happened on March 11, 2011 on a Friday at 2:46 p.m. (three minutes off). See pages viii,xi- xii,xix of my book *The boy who could predict earthquakes*. That same introduction predicted a man made inventions (-nuclear power plants) to have trouble caused by an earthquake in March- April of 2010-2011-2012. See xi-xii and xix in the introduction to my book *The boy who could predict earthquakes*. The Psalms chapter 99 that predicts these inventions to fail by man says God sitteth between the Cherubs. The Cherubs are symbols of the sun, which nuclear power plants are based on and are the symbol of the Pisces sign, which March 11, 2011 is and in Japan that date is March 12 (=Pisces 12th sign). And nuclear power plants are sun based (nuclear), which makes them symbols to Pisces where God sits between them just as Psalms 99 chapter predicts man's invention fails and causes trouble. Add 12 years to 1999 and it equals 2011 on March 12, the 12 month to the Holy Bible's calendar when this very event happened.

On May 6-13, 2012 first Vice President Biden spoke on national TV saying he approves of same sex marriage. Then later that week President Obama said he is in favor of same sex marriage. That same week JP Morgan Chase bank lost two billion dollars. Another "harbinger?" Will seven months, counting each month or not, from those dates will another harbinger occur when God takes away his protection and a war, attack, tidal wave, volcano eruption, earthqauke or storms hit the U.S. and Israel. The book *The Harbinger* claims seven years to the week of 9-11-01 when the attacks occurred on the U.S. and the Americans didn't repent, humble themselves and turn and follow God, the great economic crash happened in September of 2008 (=2001+7=2008). Will seven months from this last disobeidence of May 6-13, 2012 in Novemeber 6-13, 2012 or December 6-13, 2012 have another great harbinger and trouble if President Obama is re-elected. If he's not we may avoid or delay the trouble. The trouble if he is re-elected may come in November- December of 2012 or 2013. May 6-7, 2012 by the way is the exact polar opposites of the dates when the U.S. Presidential elections takes place on November 6 into November 7, 2012.

Could Zechariah 11:8 "three shepherds killed in one month" be these events at these times when Iran, Syria and Russian leaders are killed when they attack Israel. They are shepherds as that term means leaders and are greatly hated by God because of their hatred of Israel. Remember those who bless Israel will be bless and those who curse Israel will be cursed.

Nostradamus' quatrains C1:Q50, C6:Q66 aand C2:Q5 might predict some of these events of this book happening in three waters signs on a Thursday. February 14, 2013 is Saint Valentine's Day and is in the Aqurius the "water-bearer" and that is the end of the Chinese Year of the Dragon and the beginning the Chinse Year of the Snake on February 10, 2013. Both the Dragon and Snake are water signs which makes two, plus one as Aquarius, equal three on a Thursday February 14, 2013 or another Thursday in that month and year.

The earthquake in quatrain C6:Q66 may happen in April in Rome sometime in our futrue. C2:Q5 might predict a sub launch nuclaer missile at Rome, Italy in March-April in our future. Is that when the king or kings (=EU or Russia if still around) of the North destroys the great whore (=Catholic Church) on the seven hills of Rome, Italy with fire as Daniel chapter 11 and Revelation chapter 17 predicts?

Will the earth turn upside down as Isaiah 24:1 predicted in our future? Many have predicted this event for decades. The Mayans may have even predicted it. The one documentary on this called *Watchers 2* by L.A. Marzulli claims the magnetic poles our shifting according to compasses.

After reading through the book of Isaiah in the Bible several times I found that not only in our near future the U.S. and Israel will be destroyed and left desolate, but the whole world will be destroyed then or over a period of time. Isaiah 6:11-13 predicts these things and also may hint at what causes it. Isaiah 6:11-12 predicts a forshaking of the midst of the land will cause the cities to be left inhabitated. The great Yellowstone Park volcano is in the midst of America's land and if it erupts it would destroy all the U.S. with smoke, ash and vapor in which may also effect the rest of the whole world too. And with no food coming from America the the rest of the world will soon die and their houses and cities left desolate. Is this the silence of an half hour that Rvelation 8:1 predicts to happen in our future for 30 minutes or 30 years from 2026- 2030+30=2056-2060. A comet of asteroid impact in the middle (midst) of America could also cause these events to happen. They would be followed by extreme faminies, economic failure, pestilence's, collapses of goverments, law and court collapse and complete violence and lawless and chaos till all are dead from these things or weather, earthqaukes, volcanos, tidal waves, freezes, heat, droughts, hail, pestilence's and any other natural or man made disasters. There may remain a few pockets of nations or people who survive but they will turn on Americans, Christians and Jews as everyone else after the wars and attacks of Isreal, U.S. and Iran happen earlier before these events. This time would be the end of the world, but not by a suprenova at least not to the very end in 2060-2070 A.D. If no supernova happens then it's possible Christ will return and resurrect the Saints and return the earth to paradise and reign a thousand years. The "how long" of Isaiah chapter 6 and Revelataion chapter 6 may be connected to this time when the Saints have been persecuted after the wars of 2012-2019 and then these other events just mentioned in 2025-2030 till 2060- 2070. That is when Americans, Jews and Christians are most hated and the dead ones in heaven under the alter ask "how long" and told till all are dead and killed by the muslims and other people and religions. Revelation 6:11; Haggai 2:6; and Isaiah 29:17 predicts a "little season" or "little while" as three months/years or 30 years as the length of time these events happen till the end of the Saints suffering and all Saints are killed. Three months added to November-December of 2012 equals February-March and April of 2013. Three years added to November-December of 2012 equals 2015 when we return to fight with Iran (=Persia) as Daniel chapter 10 opredicts and/or a great tdial wave, earthquake or storm hits the U.S. The 30 years would be from 2030 to 2060 when the end comes. Isaiah 43:27-28 predicts because the princes of the sanctuary profane it that God will give Jacob (=U.S.) to the curse and Israel to the reproaches. Could this mean Presidents allowing and supporting gay marriages from their office (=sanctuary) and other very disturbing things against what God wants? Vice President Biden and Presidnet Obama both came out in May 6-13, 2012 in support of gay marriage. It occurred to me that Perry Stone once quoted a book that is mentioned in the Bible but not in it. And someone had found it and he had a copy of it and told how judges or leaders of Sodom and Gorromah allowed and supported beds to be in the streets so gays could have sex in public. Was that the final straw to God that caused him to utterly destroy those cities with nuclear fire? Are the first fathers and teachers of the Bible of old that now preach and has always taught money for gospel preaching, for healing, for casting out demons, for prophesying are in error? See Malachi 1:8, 2:1, 8-13 and 3:8-10, Micah 3:11 and Matthew 7:22-23 in the Bible.

Isaiah chapter 6:13 predicts a tenth and when leaves fall from the trees as to when these events happen on. Our tenth month is October and Solomon the holy seed was born October 15. Is this when these events happen in 2012-2013-2019 or 2026- 2030? The Cuban Missiles Crsis started on October 15 and almost ended in nuclear war. Jeremiah also predicts the birth of Solomon as the date when cities are ovrethrown. See Jeremiah 20:14-18.

Isiah 50:2-3 predicts drought and the heavens turned black. Are these events from wars and attacks and volcano eruptions or comet or asteroid impacts in 2012-2013-2019 and beyond?

Jeremiah 4:28 also predicts the earth to mourn and the heavens above be black. Is the earth mourning the mourns or groans from hell at the baseball game and at a earthquake as the DVD's series *The Watchers* told of. One Bible verse claims the earth moans or groans or travaileth in pain since creation. See Romans 8:22. I also once read that demons under ground from hell up set off nuclear devises or nuclear bombs that cause earthquakes. *The Watcher* series also mentioned this.

Isaiah 24:18 predicts the pit and earth to shake and moan. Over the past years from 2003-2012 there have been strange sinks holes perfectly around like a pit going down into the earth. There also been reports of strange noises like moanings and horrors from hell heard at one TV broadcastinbg game and other places as mentioned earlier. See *Watchers 1-3*.

Isaiah 26:17 predicts a woman in pangs of birth. Was this the trouble we seen on 9-11-01, which is the Virgo sign of the Virgin who gives birth in pangs or great pain. *The Harbinger* book quotes Isaiah 9:10, but Isaiah 9:11 or 9-11 is our date 9- 11 predicts the enemies to come together against someone. On 9-11-01 our enemies gathered together and attacked us on the very date of Isaiah 9:11-12. In Isaiah 9:11-12 it predicts Syria and its allies to go against Israel and its allies together. Syria's allies are Iran, Russia, China and North Korea. And Israel's allies are the U.S. Was the woman that is in birth pangs that of Virgo the virgin sign? In Chinese astrology Virgo rules the Chinese Rooster Year, which is 2017, 2029 into 2030 ending in January or February of 2030. The Rooster being Virgo polar opposite is March-April. Is this when these events happen?

The Belfour agreement was sign November 2, 1917 which aloud Jews to live in Israel. The year 1917 is the Chinese Year of the Snake the same as the year 2013. Will something happen then to Israel? November 2 is known as the Day of the Dead.

Isaiah 40:2 predicts double trouble for the sins of Israel and the U.S. The U.S. invaded Europe in June of 1917 and in June of 1944. Is that the double trouble? Israel had a war in June of 1967. Will it again have war or attacks in June of 2012-2013-2019 and beyond?

Isaiah chapter 21 predicts whirlwinds (=hurricanes) to past through the south when Media (=Iran) and Elam (=Iran) are about to attack. It predicts in that chapter a "lion" and the "corn of my floor". In August and September the full moons are called green corn moon and corn moon. The lion is our Leo sign. Leo the lion sign and stars time run from July 21-September 23. The polar opposites of these dates are January-February-March and they are opposite July-August-September. Are these months the final fulfillments of the prophecies of Isaiah chapter 21 when Iran faces trouble in 2012-2013 or 2015-2019?

Isaiah 34:4,12 predicts the sky to roll back as a scroll. Was this predicting nuclear wars with mushroom clouds seen at these times with Iran and Israel and possibly the U.S. and other nations that leave then desolate for ever as verse 12 predicts. This same chapter predicts figs fallen to cause the sky to roll back as a scroll in a mushroom cloud of nulcear bombs falling from the sky as missiles just as Revelation 6:12- 17 predicted on a solar or lunar eclipse or makes the sun, moon and stars to be drakened?

Isaiah 24:22-23 predicted the Saints in prison many days when the moon is confounded and the sun ashame. Does this mean when there's a solar eclipse with a new moon blocking the sun? Or does it mean as L.A. Marzulli suggests the sun and moon acting strangely. Another interpretation is that when Christians and Jews are persecuted and put in prison before, during or after those times the sun and moon will be covered with smoke, ash and vapors from the volcano eruptions. See also Isaiah 13:10 that predicts the sun, moon and stars to not give their light when God punishes the world for their great wickedness and being proud. That chapter goes on to predicts Babylon, a term used for the United States, to be destroyed like Sodom and Gomorrah with nuclear fires and not dwelt in for generation to generation and there is just left ghost towns and cities where weird animals and birds live.

Matthew 12:39-45 predict Nineveh to rise up against this generation. In both Iraq wars Saddam Hussein arose up against America and other nations. Saddam Hussein was born in Northern Iraq where Niveneh and Assyria are which the Bible tells of a leader who will try to destroy other nations. It could of just said Babylon (Iraq), but it said Nineveh where Saddam was born or near where he was born in the Northern Iraq.

Isaiah 13:17-18 predicts the Medes (=Iran) not to regard children. During the eight year war between Iran and Iraq in 1980-1988 Iran sent children to the front to be killed.

Every time the book of Isaiah in the Bible mentions a nation far off, or far off, Isles, Islands, beyond the rivers of Ethiopia, a terrible people, a strange speech and people and Jacob and Israel it can always be translated the United States that became Israel and Jacob 1706 years after the Jews final rejection of Christ. After that rejection they were killed and scattered all over the earth and their temple destroyed each stone thrown down just as Jesus predicted. He also predicted it would occur in a generation of 40 years after He predicted it in 30 A.D. (30+40=70 A.D.) Add 2000 years to that date and it equals 2070 when the end may come just as Psalms 90:10 claiming 80 years added to 1990 equals 2070 A.D.

The front cover of this book shows the ancient Egyptian Sphinx, which is a body of a lion, or Leo, and the head of a woman or Virgo in symbolism. The head of the Sphinx may have a male headdress on symbolizing a she-male joined together with a lion a male sign and Virgo is a female sign. Those two signs run from July 21 to September 23. Are those days when some of the events of this book happens? Or is Orion the time of these events. As the book called *The Orion Mystery* claims the great Egyptian pyramids at Giza, Egypt are the belt of Orion and other great monuments around Egypt line up with the Orion constellation with the great pyramids at Giza as the belt with one pyramid set off slightly just as Orion's belt is. The great Orion constellation is seen over head behind the sun at noon on June 24-25. It is seen overhead in the night sky on December 24-25. Were these things and dates predicting the end at one of these times with good and evil (Leo-Virgo) joined together in the sun (=Leo) causing a great supernova of our sun at one of those times in the future? The Sphinx may just of been symbolizing the great joining of good and evil as Alpha (=creation=good=male) and Omega (=destruction=evil and female) at the wedding of God or the marriage supper of the Lamb and the Bride of Christ in the end. The Sphinx and pyramids at Giza, Egypt are on or near the Virgo-Libra zones and the Sphinx is a body of a lion and head of a woman showing when the end comes. It is joined together as a circle when you start at Virgo in September when the Jewish Civil calendar starts a new year and goes around in a circle to when you come to Leo as the end. The circle represents outer space and eternity as a complete circle and the beginning and end from the big bang to the sun supernova. Thus, as Isaiah 48:3, 16 and 46:10 predicts God declares the end from the beginning and the beginning from the end.

The Leo, Virgo, Libra signs are from July 21 to September 23. A Wednesday-Thursday is also what could be meant by these monuments because Virgo is ruled by Mercury in which we get the name our Wednesday from in Latin. Thursday is Latin for Jupiter in which Libra is. And Libra goes fgrom September 23 to October 22. Revelation's seven churches were just above the Sphinx and pyramids making them too a Wednesday-Thursday or Virgo-Libra and Leo-Virgo. The book of Revelation written down June 12, 96 A.D. by the Old Julian Calendar is to us by the new Gregorian calendar June 24-25 when the end may come. The polar opposite of December 24-25, 2060 is June 24-25, 2061 as the time of the end. See chapter 31 for more details of these dates. June 24- 25, 2061 is the Chinese Year of the Snake the same year and day Christ was born. The date of December 24-25, 2060 may be widely known by many for 2060 and when nothing happens then people go on to mock and scoff at dates and Bible prophecies during the Christmas Holidays and New Year's Eve and Day with over eating, over drinking amnd partying and the cares of this life and then in June of the next year in 2061 the end comes quickly on the polar opposite of Christmas day, which equals June 25, 2061. See Luke 21:34-36, II Peter 3:2-7 and Matthew 24:45-51. Polar opposites mean the same date and time of the event. Jesus was born June 24-25, 4 B.C. which is the Chinese Year of the Snake the same as 2061. See my book *The Nativity* for all the documentation.

Zephaniah 1:16 predicts trouble for the "high towers." In year/chapter codes Zephaniah chapter one is our year 2001 when on 9-11 the Twin Towers fell. They were two of the most highest towers in New York City. Luke 21:9-11 predicts this time as when wars and commtion's happens with great signs and fearful sights in the heavens. Luke chapter 21 with two zero's in between equals 2001 and verses 9-11 equals the exact date of 9- 11-2001. Add 12 years to that date and you have September 11, 2013. Will something happen then?

Zephaniah 1:18 predicts the whole land of the U.S. and/or Israel to be speedily destroyed by fire. The 9-11-2001 attacks came in the Virgo sign which rules the Chinese Rooster sign of 2017 and 2029-2030 when high towers, alarms and trumpets (air raid sirens or new moon) blast for incoming nuclear missiles and/or storms or tidal waves and volcano eruptions like in Yellowstone Park or the Canary Islands. Thus, making a speedily destruction of the U.S. at one of those times. Zephaniah 1:14- 18 predicts that day as a day of darkness, gloominess and thick clouds. This could refer to a volcano eruptions that causes smoke, ash and vapors to cover and darken the sun, moon and stars like so many Bible prophecies predict for the end time signs. Nuclear bombs going off could also cause mushroon clouds and nuclear winter with great darkeness. Also a great Nor'easter or hurricanes or comet or asteroid impact could all cause this great darkness at one of these times in 2012-2013, 2015-2017 and 2029-2030. Virgo as the beginnning of sorrows that Matthew and Mark predict start the great downward fall of the U.S. with upcoming persecution of Christians, Americans and Jews is the Rooster sign in Chinese astrology. The Year 2017 is the Chinese Year of the Rooster and the year 2029 into 2030 is the Chinese Year of the Rooster or Virgo. Are the latter times when there is a great silence in heaven for an half hour (=30 minutes=30 years) for prayers of the dead Saints and those who will go through 30 years of persecution from 2030-2060? The sons and daughters will be betrayed by mother and fathers and the mothers and fathers will be betrayed by sons and daughters at this time because they are not Muslim. A daughter already had this happen to her here in the U.S. when she coneverted to Christinaty from Islam. See Matthew 24:8-14. And Mark 13:8-13 for more detials.

The "fenced cities" of Zechariah 1:14-18 might mean NORAD, SAC, ICBM silos, and Navy and Army bases around the U.S. that are destroyed by these man made or natural disasters in the Virgo sign of the Rooster in Chinese astrology which 2029-2030 is an earth sign as Virgo is always an earth sign. The Year 2017 in Chinese astrology being the Rooster too is a sign that year of fire. Could that be volcano fire or nuclear fire? The book *The Harbinger* predicts a 20 year span from warning to when God withdraws His hand of protection from the U.S. If you begin those 20 years from 2008-2012 it equals 2028-2032 when these events may happen. See page 220 of that book. The year 2030 is the Chinese Year of the Dog or jackal in which the polar opposite is the Dragon, both of which are signs of the end as we will read later in this book.

The book *The Harbinger* gives two dates for the destruction of Israel by Assyria. Why this is I don't know. The second date is 722 B.C. preceded by three years on page 218 of the book *The Harbinger*. *The Ryrie Study Bible* page 2026, *Smith's Bible Dictionary* page 62 also gives the dates of 722 or 721 B.C. with three years before it, which equals 725 B.C. The Year 725 B.C. is the Year of the Dragon the same as 2012 A.D. The Year 722 B.C. is the Chinese Year of the Sheep, which rules our Cancer and July and polar opposite of January and Capricorn. If the 722 B.C. was by Israel's calendar in the fall then it would have been 723 B.C. the Chinese Year of the Horse. The polar opposite of the Horse is the Rat that rules our Sagitttarius sign from November 21 to December 21 and star time from December 21 to January 19, 2013. Will the harbinger happen then in the Chinese Year of the Dragon in 2012? Or will it be those other dates and years of 2013, 2017 and 2029-2030? Three years added to 2012-2013 are 2015-2016 when these events could happen from the time of the harbinger in 2012-2013 when certain events happen to when the others happen in 2015-2016.

In 2005 on August 25 hurricane Kantrina hit Louisiana which was not only the Vigro sign (=Rooster) but was the Year of the Rooster. Just like in 2003 the second Iraq war started on March 20-21, the Aries sign of the ram or sheep just as that year rules the Chinese Sheep.

The "days of Noah" predicted in the Bible could mean end time signs of a flood by heavy rain, Nor'Easter, hurrcianes and tidal waves. It also could mean times like Noah when evil angels in UFOs appear openingly to people of earth and cause great apostasy as II Thessalonians chapter 2 and Revelation chapter 13 predicts.

I studied very closely Matthew chapter 24, Mark chapter 13 and Luke chapter 21. Luke and Mark note synagoges and councils. These predictions could have been for the Christians after Jesus left up till 70 A.D. when the religious Jews persecuted the new Christians in their synagoges and to their leaders. But Matthew chapter 24 and Mark 13 predicts councils and kings and leaders and doesn't mention synagoges. Were they predicting the time of the end when Christians would be brought to Muslim leaders and kings and be persecuted? Why I say this is because it is very unlikely the Christians would be brought into Jewish synagoges at that time, which are the Jews religious temples. Luke chapter 21 goes on to predict in detail the 70 A.D. times of trouble for the Jews who done this persecuting of the early church and Christians.

In Revelation chapter 12 it predicts a dragon. In the Northern constellations there's a figure of a dragon called Draco. Its head according to Perry Stone is pointing at the woman virgin named Virgo the woman with 12 stars and clothed with the sun and moon under her feet as Revelation chapter 12 predicts. The woman, or Virgo sign, runs from August 23 to September 22. The "serpent" also mentioned in Revelation chapter 12 is the Chinese Year of the Snake, which year is our year 2013. Revelation chapter 12 predicts the dragon to pull down a third of the stars from heaven upon the earth. Is the third of the stars three nuclear bombs Russia or Iran or Syria send down on Israel in the Years of the Dragon or Snake, which are 2012-2013. The President of Russia now (May 27, 2012) is Putin born October 7, 1952, which is the Chinese Dragon Year. Or does the dragon represents Wormwood that was satan's planet the dragon and serpent was orginally between Mars and Jupiter that is now the asteriod belt that causes these events that destroys Israel and/or the U.S.? A comet, asteroid or nuclear missiles that fall from the sky on Israel and the U.S. in 2012- 2013, 2017, 2026-2030 might just be what Revelation chapter 12 was predicting of stars falling from heaven. A third could also mean 2000-3000 missiles with chemical and biological warheads on them. The serpnet or snake could be our sign of Taurus that rules the Chinese Snake Year and sign from April 20 to May 20, 2013 when these events may happen in.

These events as the days of Noah as Perry Stone also notes is after Genesis 7:11 that "the fountains of the great deep are broken up" might just mean earthquakes under the seas causing great tidal waves along with heavy rains, Nor' Easters and hurricanes causes great floods at these times in the Virgo sign of Augusts-September-October or some other months in the years 2012-2013, 2026-2030. The child tried to be killed in October 15, 1954 may have satan wrath again in these months and years in our future. The woman was born September 27. Her husband September 19 and her youngest son October 15. All possible dates of these events and others in this book as happening then in the years to come and beyond.

The NLT translation of the Bible Perry Stone also cliams translates Luke 21:25 as "roaring seas and strange tides." During the Japan earthquake and tidal wave of March 11, 2011 people claimed they heard a roaring from the sea. In the great tidal waves that hit Asia on December 26, 2004 people notice the tides to go way out off of the shore line right before it hit. Is this the roaring of the seas and strange tides the Bible predicted? And is a Nor'Easter or great hurricane the roaring of the seas and strange tides they call "storm surge?" And these events could be seas and waves roaring and strange tides as end time signs now and in our future.

Perry Stone on his DVD about the stars claims the blood moon or lunar eclipse is a bad omen for Israel. On November 28-29, 2012 is a lunar eclipse and blood moon. Will it be a bad omen for Israel at that time? If war breaks out then if Israel and the U.S. attack Iran the world will blame Israel and the U.S. for all that trouble it will cause and persecute the Christians, Americans and Jews all over the world to the end just as Matthew 24:6 13 predicted. These things and the latter in 2026-2030 will be the beginnning of sorrows or birth pangs of a woman that Matthew 24:8 and Mark 13:8 predict coming after those events but before the day of the Lord or return of the Lord and end of the world. Virgo is a woman who the "birth pangs" means in these predictions of the beginnning of sorrows when they begin to happen then many turn on many Christians, Americans and the Jews. The woman's "birth pangs or sorrows" might not just mean these events but in August-September when the Virgo sign runs and in the year of the Chinese Rooster, which rules the Virgo sign in 2017 and 2029-2030. The Year 2017 is fire when some type of fire affects the earth and the Year 2029 is earth when some type of earth affects the world in the form of volcano eruptions, earthquakes, and tidal waves caused by earthquakes and volcano eruptions.

The years 26 A.D. and 30 A.D. were important dates for Christ when He and John the Baptist came preaching the kingdom of God is at hand in 26 A.D. the Chinese Year of the Dog. In 30 A.D. Jesus was crucified and resurrected and ascended into heaven. That year was the Chinese Year of the Tiger, which its polar opposite is the Monkey or our Year 2016. The polar opposite of the Dog is the Dragon or our year 2012 into 2013. Add 2000 years to both 26 A.D. and 30 A.D. and it equals 2026- 2030 A.D. when these events could happen in.

Chapter Two
End Time Signs II

The Bible predicted trouble for Israel, the U.S. and Iran at times known as the "days of Noah" and of "Pentecost", when there is a blood moon, a darkened sun, smoke and vapor, seas and waves roaring (tidal waves? Nor'Easters? hurricanes?), great volcano eruptions, earthquakes, famines and pestilence's are happening. These events are predicted in these verses:

"And I will shew wonders in the heavens and in the earth, blood, and fire, and pillars of smoke.
The sun shall be turned into darkness, and the moon into blood, before the great and the terrible day of the Lord come." Joel 2:30-31 (Old King James Version).

"And when the day of Pentecost was fully come,...
And I will shew wonders in heaven above, and signs in the earth beneath; blood, and fire, and vapour of smoke:
The sun shall be turned into darkness, and the moon into blood, before that great and notable day of the Lord come." Acts 2:1,19-20. (Old King James Version).
"And I Beheld when he had opened the sixth seal, and, lo, there was a great earthquake; and the sun became black as sackcloth of hair, and the moon became as blood.
And the stars of heaven fell unto the earth, even as a fig tree casteth her untimely figs, when she is shaken of a mighty wind." Revelation 6:12-13 (Old King James Version).
"And ye shall hear of wars and rumours of wars: see that ye be not troubled: for all these things must come to past, but the end is not yet.
For nation shall rise against nation, and kingdom against kingdom: and there shall be famines, and pestilence's, and earthquakes, in divers places.
All these are the beginning of sorrows.
"But as the days of Noe were, so shall also the coming of the Son of man be." Matthew 24:6-8, 37 (Old King James Version)

"And there shall be signs in the sun, and in the moon, and in the stars; and upon the earth distress of nations, with perpexity; the sea and the waves roaring;" Luke 21:25 (Old King James Version).

My book The Experiment in Philadelphia puts Noah's (=Noe) flood in May or November 2341 B.C., which was the Chinese Year of the Monkey (=Tiger=30 A.D. and Leo, August). See Genesis 7:11. The day of Pentecost came 50 days after the resurrection of Christ April 9, 30 A.D. Pentecost that year would have been on May 28-29 of 30 A.D. See Acts 1:3 in the Bible. "Pentecost" in Greek means "50" or 50 days, which would be from the day of the resurrection of Christ on April 9, 30 A.D. till May 28-29 of 30 A.D. The polar opposite of May is November. Revelation chapter 12 predicts a great red dragon in heaven pulling down stars from heaven when a woman is clothed with the sun and the moon under her feet with 12 stars. The other prophecies quoted above predict a lunar eclipse with a great earthquake, pillars of smoke and vapour (=vapor) of smoke with the seas roaring in tidal waves and/or storms followed by famines and pestilence's. The red dragon that Revelation chapter 12 predicts might be the Chinese Year of the Dragon in 2012 A.D. The "days of Noah" when the flood came might also mean a tidal wave (=flood) preceded by an earthquake and volcano eruption in the Canary Islands off the African West Coast that hits Florida from Miami to Boston with 100-300 or 2500 feet high tidal waves that goes 20-50 miles in land and kills 10 million Americans. This could happen on May 28-29 or November 28-29, 2012, plus or minus 30 days, or at that time is when the Israel and Iran (=Persia) war and/or attacks (Daniel 10) happens and later the tidal wave and/or another attack and wars hits Israel and/or the U.S. in months or years (=three years later=2015-2016=Daniel 10:4,13) to come from then (=2012-2013+3=2015-2016).

There is a lunar eclipse (=blood moon) on November 28, 2012 which is a Wednesday at 9:34 a.m. EST near the time when the 9- 11 attacks happened in 2001 on a Tuesday, which May 29, 2012 is a Tuesday. Is this "The Harbinger?" The Harbinger is a book written by Jonathan Cahn that uses Isaiah chapter 9 to predict 9-11 and other events after it because America didn't repent and humble themselves after 9-11, but became proud and claim we will rebuild and go on without God like Israel did long ago and disasters happened to them at certain time periods afterwards. The word "harbinger" means "a person who goes before and makes known the approach of another" and "anything that foreshadows a future event." In this case it maybe this book and my others, all written by April 17, 2012, and the future events they predict will happen if the Americans don't repent and turn to God. The lunar eclipse of November 28, 2012, which maybe one of these times of future events, is seen in Alaska, Hawaii, and Asia.

Wednesday (=November 28, 2012) is a Latin word for Mercury that rules Virgo (=Wednesday) the woman clothed with the sun (=polar opposite Virgo is Pisces the sun) in Revelation chapter 12. The moon (=lunar eclipse November 28, 2012) under her feet in that same chapter 12 of Revelation equals a full moon and lunar eclipse. The number 12 as the chapter number and 12 stars might mean the 12 tribes of Israel and the Eastern U.S. ruled by the Pisces zone (=12=sun=Pisces) where these events happen. The great red dragon in Revelation chapter 12 is the Chinese Year of the Dragon, or red dragon, which is a lunar eclipse in the Bible and is called a "blood moon" or red. See the cover of this book. That same chapter of Revelation chapter 12 predicts a flood (tidal wave?) that comes inland after a woman born May 19, but the earth swallows up the flood before it can reach her. The darkened sun could be from the earthquake and volcano eruption with pillars of smoke and vapor that darkens the sun, moon and stars and starts these great tidal waves with the seas and waves roaring when there are signs in the sun, moon and stars. See Luke 21:25-26. More on that in later chapters. See also Revelation 8:8. In Latin the name Tuesday means Mars the great red planet of the Dragon in 2012 on May 28-29 and is known as the "god of war."

In the book The Harbinger it claims prophets warned Israel of their sins and the coming trouble it would face if it didn't turn from their sins and repent. And according to that book the trouble came sometime in 732 B.C., which is no other than the Chinese Year of the Rooster the same as 2017 A.D. is the Chinese Year of the Rooster. Will America and Israel face trouble then? Or is the time in September of 2012-2013, which is the sign of Virgo, which rules the Chinese Rooster? More on this later.

The many stars falling from heaven might mean missiles or bombs falling on Iran and/or Israel and the U.S. at this time causing the heavens and earth to shake. There maybe a double or triple fulfillment of these prophecies when they happen on May 28-29 or November 28-29, 2012, plus or minus 30 days, and sometime in 2015-2016-2017 and January 20-21, 2019 in which two of those exact dates are lunar eclipses. The latter is on a Sunday-Monday. In Revelation chapter 12 it predicts these days as the woman clothed with the sun (=Sunday) and the moon (=Monday) under her feet in which January 20-21, 2019 is a Sunday-Monday and the woman is the female sign not only of Virgo when 9-11 happened, but of Capricorn star time or cusp (=January) when these events happen in 2019. In Isaiah 40:2 predicts a double trouble for Israel and/or the U.S. at one or two of these times. Are the two times both in June, one in June 1967 and one in June of 2012? Or will May-June 9-12, 19- 21, 27-29 and 20-25,29, 2012-2013, plus or minus 21 days, be the dates when both events happen? Those dates could be when these great events could happen according to Bible, Egyptian, Mayan and Nostradamus C9:Q83 prophecies. Other dates like the ninth of Av (=July 27-29, 2012 and July 16, 2013) and May 27- 28, 2012 (=the dates of Pentecost in 2012 and May 16, 2013), August 6, 9-13, 28-29, 2012, September 7-8,11, 19, 26-27, 2012- 2013, March 1, 9-12, 20-21, 24-25-26, 29, 31, April 1, 6-10, 12-17, 19-21, 24-25, 29-30, 2012-2013, December 9-16, 24-25, 29, 31, January 1, 3-4, 16-19, 24-25 or February 1-2, 9-14, 24, 2012- 2013, 2015-2017-2019 and beyond, plus or minus 3 days could be possible dates of these events. Other dates in 2012- 2013 are on new or full moons, solar or lunar eclipses, Chinese New Year (February 10, 2013 or any Chinese New Year from 2013-2019) and beyond, first month 24th day (=Daniel 10:4), ninth month 24th days (Haggai 2:18-23) on the Jewish Civil or Bible calendars or our Gregorian of Old style Julian calendars for 2012-2019 and beyond. Get books or computer software on astronomy moon phases and eclipses and calendars up to 2100 A.D. if you can. Still another date is during the summer Olympic games as Nostradamus quatrain C10:Q74 predicts in the great seventh number which can mean seventh month (July) seventh Day (=Sabbath=Friday evening, Saturday and Sunday or July 27-29, 2012). Those games last from July 27 to August 12, 2012. These events could also be on or during other summer or winter Olympic games in the future or Good Friday, Easter, Passover, Pentecost, ninth of Av, Rosh Hashanah, Yom Kippur, Feast of Tabernacles, Halloween, All Saints Day and Day of the Dead (=November 1-2), England's Old Halloween (=November 11), Thanksgiving, Hanukah, Christmas Eve and Day, New Year's Eve and Day, and Purim from 2012-2013-2019 and beyond. Nostradamus also predicted in these quatrains C10:Q67 and C6:Q66 April and May earthquakes. Nostradamus' quatrain C6:Q24 predicts a great war in Cancer or by Cancer on a Thursday (=sceptre=Jupiter). That quatrain predicts when Mars and Jupiter (=sceptre) are in Cancer (=June-July) a great war will start and end by a Cancer born man Jesus Christ who brings peace to the earth for a long time. It also could mean this war starts on a Tuesday or in the Scorpio-Aries signs after Mars and/or on a Thursday or in the Libra sign.

Nostradamus' quatrain C1:Q50 predicts the three water signs and a Thursday maybe sometime in February near the Chinese New Year when the Dragon Year ends and the Snake Year begins, which are both water signs and Aquarius is a Water sign making three water signs and a Thursday. See Amos 5:8, Daniel 10:4 and other documentation given in this book. All these dates are anniversaries of past events and important times. More on these dates later.

May 28-29, 30 A.D. was when Pentecost first happen. These prophecies were suppose to happen then, as Acts and Joel chapters 2 predicts, but not all did. The polar opposite of them is November 28-29, 2012. At that time is a lunar eclipse and as Revelation 6:12-13 predicts as blood moon (=lunar eclipse) when stars fall as "untimely figs." The "untimely figs" means when the figs are not in harvest. November 28-29, 2012 is not the time of harvest (untimely) of figs.

The date of when "untimely figs" fall as stars from heaven as missiles, bombs or planes on November 28-29, 2012 on a lunar eclipse (=blood moon) that Revelation 6:12-13 predicts maybe just one of the dates of these events. Others maybe November 13, 2012 and/or May 19-20, 2012 when there are two solar eclipses (=darkened sun=Revelation 6:12) when one or some of these events happen and the others on the lunar eclipse on November 28-29, 2012 or in December of 2012 just as Revelation 6:12-17 predicted. Those same verses of Revelation chapter 6 predicts a great earthquake to hit causing every island and mountain to be moved out of its place. Was this predicting just one island in the Canary Islands off of Africa's West Coast that has a earthquake and volcano eruption (=mountain) that causes a tidal to hit Florida and the East Coast of the U.S. on these dates or three weeks or years later (=Daniel 10:4) and/or five years (=Virgo=5=Rooster in the dream in the second chapter) later in December of 2012, or 2015 or 2017. See the next chapter for more details on these set time periods.

The "days of Noah" and the time of "Pentecost" as times or dates of these events might not mean the dates or months when those events happened long ago, but "as" the people were doing on those first events of the flood and Pentecost long ago they will be doing today. They were going about their daily business and then sudden destruction came upon them possibly on the other dates given in this book other than May-November. See Luke chapter 17 and chapter 21:24-26, 34-36. It also could mean that both the days of Noah and Pentecost of May and polar opposite November is when people are going about their daily business then sudden destruction comes like in the days of Noah with the flood and the days of when Pentecost happened when the Holy Ghost came and revealed much truth about end times and the future. See Daniel 12:4 and John chapter 16.

Chapter Three

The Dream

I had a dream on Sunday March 11, 2012 of me showing the woods behind my grandparent's home to many people and seeing several wild fruit trees, then a monkey chewing on a wooden pigeon and then seeing Shania Twain with one or two other people then coming to the cove in the woods with a metal bridge flooded over leading into it.

Shania Twain was born August 28, 1965, which is the Chinese Snake Year. Her and the one or two people with her makes three the same as the wooden pigeon equals Gemini (=bird sign of the air) that is the third sign of our astrology. Add or subtract three months to August 28, Shania Twain birthday, and it equals May 28-29, 2012 or November 28-29, 2012, plus or minus 21 days, or July 28-29, August 9-13 and 28-29, 2012 when these events happen described in this chapter and chapter one of this book and then in 2013 (=Snake Year as 1965) blessings come or more trouble. July 28-29, 2012 are the dates of the ninth of Av to the Holy Bible's calendar. Zechariah chapters 7-8 predicts when a fast happens in the fifth month for those 70 years as Daniel chapters 9-10 predict is when Persia and Israel see trouble. Those 70 years ended in 516-515 B.C., the Chinese Dog Year (=2018-2019) and Chinese Rooster Year (2017), which began in 586-585 B.C. with the destruction of the Jewish temple, which happen twice on the same date in 586-585 B.C. and 70 A.D. on the ninth of Av. Will the end come then also in the Dog Year of 2018 on the ninth of Av, the wine and grape harvest of Revelation chapters 14 and 19 as we have or will read is predicted? Or will some of these events happen then on the ninth of Av or July-August of 2012 (=Dragon), which polar opposite is the Dog Year (=515 B.C.) and the Rooster Year (=2017) on the ninth of Av? Seven years of Daniel 9:27 prediction added to July-August of 2012 equals June-July of 2019 as the end. If you add three years plus two years to 2012-2013, as Shania Twain (=two), Daniel 10:4,13,19 and the wooden pigeon represent, and it equals 2015-2016-2017-2018, which the Years 2016 and 2017 are the Chinese Years of the Monkey and Rooster (=pigeon), which the monkey was chewing on the wooden pigeon in the dream. Two or three years added to those years of 2015-2016-2017 equals 2018-2019 when the end comes. Will at one of these times Israel will be destroyed by Iran, Syria, Turkey and Russia and only thorns and briers grow up there for generations to come because it is uninhabitable. See Isaiah chapters 7 and 13. Then many people, after Israel is destroyed in November-December-January of 2012-2013 or 2015- 2017, and/or the Mayan date expires on December 21, 2012, will they begin to mock and scoff at the date setters, and Bible teachers, preachers and writers proclaiming: "where is the promise of his coming for since the fathers fell asleep things continue as they were since the beginning of creation." See II Peter 3:2-8. See my entitled book *2012* or see that book in later chapters. The "fathers" who fell asleep are the dead Jews in this war in which many claim the Bible predicted God would save them out of but didn't. These prophecies of II Peter 3:2-8 could mean that the war in 2012-2013 or 2016-2017 with Israel and Iran, Syria, Russia, Turkey and others may destroy Israel as the Bible's Ezekiel chapters 38-39 predicts, but without God protecting them as those same chapters also predicts He would and the land lay desolate for years to come as Isaiah chapters 7 and 13 predict. Then people mock, laugh and scoff at the TV preachers and writers of Bible prophecy who may die of old age by then, or later, and after the date of December 21, 2012 that the Mayans predicted for the end. Thus, they say "where is the promise of his coming for since the fathers fell asleep things continue on as they were since creation." Peter also predicts in his books about Noah, creation and the end as all being the same time in which happens on the dates of May 19-20 and November 11 when the flood happened, along with creation and the beginning and possibly the end. But this time in 2016-2017 the flood comes as tidal waves and/or Nor'Easters or hurricanes on the U.S., if it still exists since the war in 2012-2013, or it sees Israel destroy then, but the U.S. and Jews around the world don't repent. This happens in the years 2016-2017 because no one heeded the warnings of the harbinger in the U.S. from the wars of 2012-2013 and 9-11 and turn not to God who brought them up as a great Christian nation and bless and prosper them yet their people turn their backs on God. And Israel's harbinger happens because they would not repent and turn to God after the holocaust, and God brining them back and starting Israel again and saving them through five wars with very great miracles, especially the Yom Kippur War, and made them prosper. The estimate of secular Jews living in Israel at this time (2012) is approximately 82-92 per cent meaning that many aren't religious. The United States is quickly taking God out of everything connected to Him and the young, middle age and old hate God, Christians, Church and the Bible. There was once an estimate of 100 million Americans as born again Christians out of a population of about 250 million. But right now (2012) the estimate is approximately 40-60 million out of a population of 300 million. There's been a great falling away (apostasy) just as II Thessalonians chapter 2 predicts a apostasy or the great falling away from Christian faith, beliefs and morals would come before the end, even to the elect (Christians). This falling away happened even after 9-11 and all of what God did for the U.S. from its beginning in 1776 till now in 2012 there still was a falling away. So God will then remove His hand of protection from it just as He will with Israel and the great destruction will come. And these events of tidal waves and wars in 2012-2013 and 2015-2017 are as Joel and Acts chapter 2 before the great and terrible and notable day of the Lord. This means these events are not the end, but happen before the end when the Lord returns. They will scoff and mock at this that the preachers and writer's of Bible prophecy who claimed since 1949 the end is near and the Lord soon will return but didn't. But neither the end came or the Rapture or the Second Coming or 1000 year period in 2012-2013 or 2016-2019 or 2026- 2030. But the many Jews (=fathers) died (=fell asleep) in that war and events and the TV preachers and Bible prophecy writers die (=father fell asleep) of old age by then (=2016-2019), or in the war, or by the other events of 2012-2013 or 2016-2017 or 2026-2030 yet there's still no end and things continue as they were since the beginning just as Peter wrote and predicted in the Bible.

If these wars happen on May 28-29 or November 28-29, 2012 or June or December 12 or 24-25, 29, 2012 and/or it's reported in newspapers or on TV at those times and the sales of this book and my others happen at that time then in September and December of 2012 the royalties will come in. The book of Revelation was written down on June 12, 96 A.D. to the seven churches in Western Turkey, which is the end of the Virgo zone, which sign is in early September. And the opposite of June 12, 24-25, 29 is December 12, 24-25, 29 of 2012 when more royalties come in from the sales of this book and my others or these events happen then. But if these events happen on November 28- 29, 2012 or in December of 2012 and this book is in newspapers and/or on TV in December or January then in March and May-June of 2013 the royalties will come in as the dream shows as I will show to you later on in this chapter. November 28, 2012 is a Wednesday, which is Latin for Mercury that rules Virgo (=seven churches of Revelation). And June polar opposite is December and June is when Revelation was written in the Year of the Chinese Monkey that rules Leo and our month of August and the year 2016 A.D.

The "*The Dreamer's dictionary*" claims wild fruit trees in a dream mean a comfortable lifestyle, but not luxury. See Proverbs 30:7-9. Will in 2013 I receive royalties from the sales of this book and my others that last to 2016 then two years to be strong till the end when during those two years I run out of money or it continues to come in from 2013-2019. If a book excerpt of this book is put in a newspaper or reported on TV in June or December of 2012 then people might respond by buying it and my other books. There maybe no angels appearing to them at these times as this book and my others predict. But an angel or person seen on the rooftops at one of these times or all of them might be a warnings to run or flee out from Florida or to its West Coast and from the Eastern U.S. Coast so the floods or tidal waves or storms or attacks don't kill you. Do I die at the age of 70 as Psalms 90:10 predicts, which would be for me in 2024 shortly before the great destruction of the U.S. happens and a 30 years silence in heaven for that time as we read earlier.

The flooded bridge near the cove in the dream could mean floods or tidal waves or storms in May 28-29, 2012, or November 28-29, 2012 and/or in 2015-2016-2017 and January 2019. See my other books entitled *Predicton (Predictions) for 2015, 2012, Predictions for 2011-2019, The Experiment at Philadelphia, The Nativity, The Antichrist, The Life of Kurt B. Bakley, The boy who could predict earthquakes, Prophecies that have, will, or didn't happen, The Balanced Life* and the rest of this book for more documented details of all these events.

The day I had this dream was March 11, 2012 the one year anniversary of the great Japan earthquake and tidal wave. Will another great earthquake and/or volcano eruption happen on May 28-29 or November 28-29, 2012 causing a great tidal wave? Or will the Israeli attack on Iran happen then and no tidal wave, but two or three years later from 2012-2013 one tidal or flood or storm happens in 2015-2016 on May 19-20,28-29, June 24-25, November 11, August 28-29 (=Shania Twain's birthday and day after) or some other date in those years and a second flood, tidal wave or storm in January of 2019? January 2019 is three years after 2016 (=Monkey Year in the dream) as the pigeon represented in the dream as two wings of a bird (=Gemini), two twins (=Twain=two=Shania) of Gemini and three as Gemini is the third sign. Thus, it would make two or three fulfillment's of these ancient prophecies. A flood or tidal wave or storm or war in 2012-2013 another in 2015-2018 and another in January- February of 2019 making three floods and/or wars. Or are there three fulfillment's in 2012? One on May 19-20, 2012, which has a solar eclipse (=dark sun) as Revelation 6:12-13 predicts when Israel attacks Iran and/or a tidal wave, or great storm-flood happens. Then on July 28-29, August 9-12, 28-29, 2012 a great hurricane comes upon the U.S. and/or Israel attacks Iran. And the final third fulfillment happens on November 28-29, 2012 when there is a lunar eclipse (=blood moon) as Revelation 6:12- 13 also predicts as a flood or tidal wave and/or Israel attacks Iran. Is the half hour of silence in heaven that of Holy Ghost prayer on or near Pentecost on May 27-29, or May 19-20, 2012, plus six months as a half a year (=the half an hour) till when all of these events are fulfilled on November 28-29, 2012 just as Revelation 6:12-13 and 8:1 predicted. The trumpet sounding can sometimes mean in the Bible the day of a new moon, which May 20, 2012 is. And Revelation chapter 8 not only predicts a half hour but a fire and mountain thrown into the sea (volcano eruption, but earthquakes, attacks, wars and tidal wave=flood) on the sounds of trumpets (new moons?) and/or followed by three woes or troubles at the sounds of the next three trumpets. Those three trumpets could be in 2012 and/or 2012-2013, 2016- 2017 and 2018-2019 or 2026-2030. In January of 2019 there is a solar on January 6 and lunar eclipse ending on a Sunday-Monday on January 20-21, 2019. Revelation chapter 12 predicts a woman (=Capricorn=female=January of 2019) clothed with the great sun (=Sunday) and the moon (=Monday) under her feet (=Pisces=12=21= January 21, 2019 and the sun) when there is war in heaven (=sun supernova). At that time is when a woman born May 19 gives birth and is to run into the wilderness on the solar eclipse (=January 6, 2019) or near the lunar eclipse of January 20-21, 2019. January 3-4, 2019 maybe the time to run away after my experience on those same dates in 1983 when I saw a man on the rooftop and I hid myself in Silver Springs. The Bible's book of Proverbs in the predicts a wise man foresees the trouble and hides himself. This maybe true of many in the end both men and women as Luke chapter 17 predicts. Pray that your flight be not in winter nor on the Sabbath Day (=Sunday) just as Matthew 24:19-20 predicted.

The Chinese Monkey seen in the dream rules our Leo sign the fifth sign. Add five years (=fifth sign) to March 11-12, 2012 and it equals March 11-12, 2017 when a tidal wave or great war, Nor'Easter or hurricane strikes the U.S. Add five months to that date and it equals August 10-11-12, 2017. Another date for this event is August 28-29, 2017 (Shania Twain's birthday). There also could be other dates this event happens on in 2017 along with wars or attacks and other man made or natural disasters on those dates in 2017. The Japan earthquake and tidal wave happen in 2011. The polar opposite of that year in Chinese astrology is 2017 when these events could happen. The three and a half years that Revelation chapter 12 predicts as this time for a woman to run into the wilderness or south and this case west maybe three and a half decades (=35 years) from 1981 when my mom, father and me moved down from the north to the south (=wilderness) to Florida. Add 35 years to that and it equals 2016 when a woman is to flee inland from Florida's East Coast or the U.S. East Coast from a flood (=tidal wave, Nor'Easter, hurricane) from reaching her. The Monkey eating the wooden pigeon in the dream would be the Chinese Monkey Year of 2016 when the earth (=Virgo=earth sign=Rooster) swallows up the flood inland so the woman born May 19 survived just as the book of Revelation chapter 12 predicted. Then in January of 2019 she flees again after she gives birth and there is war in heaven as our sun goes into a supernova and possibly war around Florida's Coast and the U.S. East Coast and/or a tidal wave again and/or a Nor'Easter or hurricane. The woman born May 19 may die in these events of later at the age of 70 or 80 or 84 before she gives birth in heaven at the end in 2060-2061.

If these events happen before these dates and on May 28-29, 2012 or November 28-29, 2012 it is early in prophecy because my other books put them at these later dates. Is this what Psalms 90:14-17 meant by "early" and the "works of thy hands being made known?" If December 2012-2013, 2015-2016-2017 and 2018- 2019 is when these events happen, and some could, it wouldn't make them early. But if they, or some of them, happen May 28- 29, 2012 or November 28-29, 2012 it would make them early.

The monkey chewing on a wooden pigeon could mean August which rules the Chinese Monkey. It also rules Leo the lion which is our fifth sign. Was this dream predicting that on the fifth anniversary from March 11, 2012 (=the dream) that another great tidal wave and earthquake will strike somewhere in the world on March 11-12, May 28-29, August 28-29, September 26-27, November 11, 2017? The Year 2017 is the Chinese Year of the Rooster or bird seen as the pigeon in the dream and the monkey and Shania Twain (=birthday) equals August 28-29, 2017, which is the 12th anniversary of hurricane Katrina that flooded New Orleans in the year 2005 (=2005+12=2017) on August 25-29. This interpretation could also mean five years from the date of the dream on March 11-12, 2012 a tidal wave, Nor'Easter, a great hurricane, earthquake, wars or attacks could strike the U.S. on the exact anniversary of the Japan's earthquake and tidal wave in 2011 on March 11-12, 2017. These events could happen on other dates in that year (2017), such as five months from March 11-12, 2017 equals August 9-12, 2017 when these events happen. These interpretation fulfills all the meanings and prophecies of the dream and Bible. You also could add two years to 2017 (=Rooster) and come to 2019 when a tidal wave, Nor'Easter or hurricane strikes the U.S. counting the pigeon as two wings or Gemini as the twins as two years added to the Rooster Year (2017+2=2019). The Monkey rules our Leo sign which is ruled by the sun that is fire where volcano eruptions come from at the center of our earth. And the pigeon rules our Virgo sign that is an earth sign that swallows up the flood from the great tidal wave that the volcano fire and earthquake causes just as Revelation chapter 12 in the Bible predicted in the Chinese Year of the Rooster (=pigeon) in 2017. November 28-29, 2012 is a Wednesday-Thursday in which are Latin for Mercury and Jupiter or Virgo and Libra zones that are near the seven churches the book of Revelation was written to and when these events happen. The Monkey in the dream being Leo our fifth sign could also mean five years added to March 11, 2011, when the Japan earthquake and tidal wave happened, to March 11-12, 2016, or the other dates given when another great earthquake, volcano eruption and tidal wave happens.

My mother was in this dream and near the end of the dream and looked back for her and she wasn't there. My mother died in July 29-30 (=Saturday-Sunday) of 2006 which was the Chinese Year of the Dog the same as 2018 and January-February of 2019 when we all die at the end as the pigeon was wood and dead, which equals two years from 2017 (=Rooster=pigeon) when all die (=wooden pigeon). In July, when my mother died, is the polar opposite of January. And July of 2019 maybe when the end comes. July 28-29, 2012 is a Saturday-Sunday the same as July 29-30, 2006 when my mom died. Will something happen then?

My grandmother was born August 4, 1896 and died June 21, 1981 the first day of summer. The year 1896 when my grandmother was born is the same Chinese Year as 2016, which is the Chinese Year of the Monkey seen in the dream. Will in that year, on the dates given in this book or my other books, we see a great tidal wave, storm, earthquake, attack, war or volcano eruption happen then? The year she died in 1981 is the same Chinese Year as 2017 (=Rooster) when these events of a flood (tidal wave, Nor'Easters or storms?) may happen as predicted in this dream as a flooded bridge, which is about 40-50 miles inland from the Atlantic Ocean. My grandfather was born February 11, 1893 and died March 21, 1976 the first day of Spring. The year 1893 is the same Chinese Year of the Snake as is 2013 when I become not poor nor rich. February 11 polar opposite is August 10-11-12, in 2012-2013 or 2016-2017 or 2018-2019? The year that my grandfather died was 1976 the same Chinese Year of the Dragon in 2012 on August 10-11-12 or 28-29 in May-November (?) when my books sell then in the next year (=2013) I receive the royalties from them. Three months added to the date of birth of my grandfather is May 11, 2012 and the polar opposite of it is November 11, 2012 when these events may happen on. The day he was born (=February 11) plus or minus three days may also be the time of these events on February 11, 2013-2019 or beyond. These events described in the first chapter of this book may happen after my grandfather death year of 1976, the Chinese Year of the Dragon, on August 9-13, 28-29, May 28-29 and November 28-29, 2012 after Shania Twain birthday with a plus or minus three months to it. Why their birthdays are important are because I was showing the land to many people (=20,000=Psalms 68:17?) behind their house with wild fruit trees that means a comfortable living but not luxury starting in Spring and Summer of 2013 (=Grandfather born 1893 and Shania Twain 1965=Snake= 2013) when both Shania Twain and my Grandfather were born. And both my grandmother and grandfather died on the days of the start of each of those seasons and one in the Chinese Year of the Dragon (=2012) and the other in the Chinese Year of the Rooster (=2017). Royalties for my books might come in Spring and Summer in early March (=Spring) or late May or early June (=Summer) and/or September (=Fall) and December (Winter) of 2013. My grandmother being born August 4 (is August 4 the date of these events?) plus five for the monkey seen in the dream as Leo the number five sign and adding five days to it equals August 9-10, in the years of 2012-2013, 2014, 2016-2017. In August of 2013 might have prophecies from my book entitled *Predictions for 2013-2014* come true in August of 2013 and sells many more of my books making royalties come in December of 2013 and other sales in May-June making royalties come in in early September 2013 or late December 2013. Five months and years added March 11, 2012 (=the dream) equals August 11, 2017 when some of these events may happen on. February 11, 2012 is my grandfather's birthday and his year of death by the Chinese calendar. Add five years (=monkey=Leo=fifth sign seen in the dream) to that year and go to the polar opposite and it equals August 11, 2017, plus or minus three days, when some of these events may happen. My grandfather's year of death was 1976 the Chinese Dragon Year, which polar opposite is the Chinese Year of the Dog (2018-2019). The 12 month of the Chinese calendar is January-February of 2019. The exact date of January 20-21, 2019 is on a Sunday-Monday (=January 20-21, 2019). That is just as the book of Revelation chapter 12 predicted. It predicts a the woman clothed with the sun (=Sunday) and moon (=Monday) under feet with 12 stars (=12th month in Chinese calendar) in the polar opposite of the great red dragon (=Dog) equals exactly January 20-21, 2019.

Add the one person seen in the dream next to Shania Twain as one month, plus or minus, to Shania Twain's birthday (August 28) and it equals September 26-27 or July 27-28, 2012 when some of these events may happen on. Pentecost was originally on a Sunday-Monday, which January 20-21, 2019 are just like Joel and Acts chapter 2 predicts of these events on those days after a darkened sun (=solar eclipse on January 6, 2019) and a blood moon (lunar eclipse) on January 20-21, 2019. Add one month to my grandfather's birthday of February 11 and it equals March 11-12, 2013 or 2017 when certain events happen as told in this book and my book *Predictions for 2011-2019*. April 20, or May 20, 2012 or 2013, plus or minus three days may also be the dates of these events as 20 degrees equals the 20th day of the month when Taurus rules in April and May.

The Nostradamus prediction of twenty degrees into Taurus (=seven stars=Amos 5:8 and Revelation 1-5) in his quatrain C9:Q83 might be May 9-10 or June 9-12, 2012 or 2013-2017 when these events happen on. There's a 30 degree or day difference because of the precession of the equinoxes. The Taurus sign (=seven stars) starts April 20 and ends May 20. And Taurus star time begins May 21 and end June 21 making 20 degrees to mean May 9-10 or June 9-12 when these events or some of them happen. There is a solar eclipse on May 20, 2012, which maybe the time of a great earthquake and/or attack. The "theater" in that quatrain of Nostradamus might mean Hollywood in the city of Los Angeles where movies are made for the theater and where this great earthquake and/or attack happens. Los Angeles is in the end of the Taurus zone making the date of May 20, 2012- 2013, plus or minus three days even more important. Psalms 68:8,17 prediction of chariots of God an a earthquake on Mount Sinai might just mean the constellation Auriga The Charioteer that is near or behind the sun during May-June of 2012-2013. Mount Sinai (=May-June when the law was given there) could be the volcano eruption off the West Coast of Africa with and earthquake and part of the island falls into the sea causing a great tidal to rush towards Florida and the East Coast of the U.S. at one of these times in 2012 or 2013 or 2015-2017 and January of 2019, 2026-2030 and beyond. Auriga has one star as part of it that is also part of Taurus know as the seven stars in the book of Amos 5:8 and in the book of Revelation as a little book (=this book?) in the hand of the Lamb. The book of Revelation was written down on Sunday June 12, 96 A.D. OS calendar, which to us would be June 24-25, 2012 or 2013-2019 or 2026-2030 or beyond by the NS calendar. As for June 29 of those years is when a special event happen on in 1992 on a Monday and on a new moon, which was predicted in Isaiah chapter 57. And June 20-23, 2012-2019 is the birthday of John the Disciple on June 20th and June 21-23, 2012-2019 are the first days of summer as Jesus predicted to look for and June 24-25, 2012-2019, 2026-2030, 2060-2061 is Jesus' real birthday.

April 19-21, 25, and 29-30, 2012 or 2013-2019 are important dates for future events because they are special days of past events. April 19, 1993 and April 19, 1995 was when the cult disasters in Texas happened and in April 19, 1995 was when the Oklahoma City bombing happened. April 20 is Hitler's birthday and April 25 is a day of trouble also, along with April 29-30, 2012-2019 which are the anniversaries of when World War II was ending in Europe and the Holocaust ended then and Hitler killed himself. April 21, 2012 is a new moon and is when predicted events are favored to happened with attacks or wars as is every new moon in every month from April 21, 2012-2019, 2026-2030 and 2060-2061.

My grandfather being born February 11, 1893 along with one person seen by Shania Twain in the dream could mean plus or minus one month from his birthday in 2013 the Chinese Year of the Snake the same as 1893, is when these events happen. The exact date could be January-February-March 9-12, 2013-2015- 2017-2019 or the polar opposite of them in the months of July- August-September 9-12, 2012-2013-2015-2017-2019. Shania Twain's birthday we saw was also the Chinese Year of the Snake. In Jeremiah 23:19-20 and 30:23-24 it predicts these prophecies will become perfectly clear with the intents or thoughts of God's heart at a time when a whirlwind comes. The "heart" is ruled by the Leo sign, which rules July-August-September and its polar opposite is Aquarius that rules in January, February and March when these events happen in 2012-2019. The great "whirlwind" in those verses may not only mean a hurricane, but can be a tidal wave and/or a Nor'Easter or attacks and wars that shake the heaven and earth at these times. Will a great storm hit the U.S. when this book is published in 2012? Or the anniversary of when it was published?

My mother's death on July 29-30, 2006 might have been a warning for these events to happen six years later on those dates plus or minus three days. Those dates would be July 29- 30, 2012 when it's the ninth of Av and a day after it. Psalms 90:10,14-17 might predict 70 years from the Year in chapter codes of Psalms being Psalms 90 as 1990+70=2060 when the end comes. It also may have predicted my mother's death at age 84, which equals fourscore=80, plus four years in strength until she flies away to heaven. My mother born 1922 plus 84 equals 2006 in July 29-30 when she died. Add six months as the polar opposite of that date and 30 days plus or minus and it equals June 29-30 and August 28-30, 2012 when these events happen. Psalms chapter 90 may also predict the beginning of the works of my hands on these books starting exactly August 28-29, 1976 which was the Chinese Year of the Dragon the same as August 28- 29, 2012 is when these events and the last of my fourteen books are written by. I first thought February 14 or April 17, 2012 was the end of my writing these books, but now I believe in this prophecy of June 24-25, or August 28-29, or September 7-8, 11, 26-27, 2012 as when they are finished the exact dates of when I started them and other events and is the same Chinese Year of the Dragon six years and a month after my mother died as shown in the dream as not seen by me any more. The Monkey and pigeon might be Leo-Virgo signs or times in 2012, which July-September equals or it could mean these events and/or some of them happen at that time of in the future in 2016 (=Monkey) and 2017 (pigeon Rooster). Psalms chapter 90 may also mean 80- 84 years or more added to 1990 equals 2070-2074 or beyond as when we all fly away in the Rapture to heaven at the end.

Revelation chapter 12 predicts a great red dragon, a serpent (=snake) and a woman in the wilderness (=south) fleeing from a flood (=tidal wave, Nor'Easter, hurricane) that the earth swallows up saving her. The "serpent" is known as the snake and is the Chinese Year of the Snake in 2013. The "Dragon" is the Chinese Year of the Dragon in 2012. The mouth of the dragon or serpent spits out the flood. Another name for satan the dragon and serpent is lion which mouth spews out the flood at this time of Leo the lion sign (=fire sign that are volcanoes erupting). The Virgo sign is a earth sign that swallows up at this time in 2012-2013 or 3.5 years (=1260 days) later in 2015-2016 in the Leo or Virgo signs from July 21 to September 23. With one month added to both signs and star times intermingle in August-September making a lion (=Leo) spews out the flood and the earth (=Virgo) swallows it up.

The pigeon in the dream could mean Chinese Rooster, which in Chinese astrology rules our Virgo sign of August and September and is the sign of Shania Twain when she was born. The year she was born we seen equals 2013. Virgo we also seen equals the Chinese Rooster, which Year is 2017 and 2029-2030 when these events may happen in or beyond in 2060-2061.

Chapter Four

𝕿𝖍𝖊 𝖈𝖆𝖗𝖛𝖎𝖓𝖌 𝕴

Does the ancient Egyptian carving from the temple Hathor at Dendera, Egypt dated 100-300 B.C., in which part of it seen in my book, *The Experiment at Philadelphia,* see drawing 47 page 464, show interesting prophecies for our times? On that drawing you see a lion below and in the middle of Libra the scales with the lion's two front paws on a box with two or three wavy lines in it. On the top of Libra is a circle with a man in it with a jackal on top of it. To the side of the lion is a ox or bull horns on a man.

The meaning of this ancient carving and those figures might be that Leo the lion sign in the middle of Libra is when three earthquakes and/or volcano eruptions, attacks, wars, storms or comet or asteroid impacts happen on in three years and/or three and half years from 2013 to 2019. Libra in numerology is given the number six and is the seventh sign. The lion in the middle below Libra means half of six, or three years, or half of seven years, or three and half years from when the first earthquake, tidal waves and other events happen near each other as the wavy lines in the box (=coffin-death-trouble) on August 10-11, 2013, plus or minus three days, which is the Leo sign. This equals three years from then August 10, 2013+3=August 10, 2015, counting each year, plus three and a half years from August 10, 2015 equals January 21, 2019.

This would make the first earthquake happen on August 10, 2013, and other events one year later on August 10, 2014, plus or minus three days of each date. That date is a full moon as the circle in the middle and on top of Libra. Then the third (=three wavy lines in the box) earthquakes and/or volcano eruptions happens the next year on August 10, 2015 in the Leo sign. This would make three earthquakes (or volcano eruptions or comet or asteroid impacts) on the same dates as my other books shown as three woes or three troubles predicted in the Bible.

Then three and a half years from then comes the end of the world, Second Coming and the kingdom of God exactly 1260 days that equals three and a half years by God's 360 day years. Add 1260 days to August 10, 2015 and it equals January 21, 2019. That date is a full moon and in the Capricorn cusp or star time. In Chinese astrology the polar opposite of the Sheep or Goat equals the Ox or Bull that has horns we seen on a man in the carving standing near the lion. And January 21, 2019 is the Chinese Year of the Dog or jackal seen on top of the circle on top of the middle of Libra. The circle represents a full moon, which on January 21, 2019 there is a full moon exactly three and a half years from August 10, 2015 the middle of Libra or seven divide by two equals three and a half years from the Leo sign (=lion below Libra) on August 10, 2015. That date plus three and a half years after it comes the end on January 21, 2019. The three years from August 10, 2013+3=August 10, 2015 August 10+3 and a half years to January 21, 2019. Three and a half years before August 10, 2015 equals February 2013. Is that when these events happen on?

This same ancient Egyptian carving shows another box with three wavy lines in it that equals earthquakes on the Richter scale, stormy seas or waves and volcano eruptions and wars or attacks or comet or asteroid impacts that shake the air and ground. Those events are what the wavy lines mean in a box or coffin causing death by them. This other box with three wavy lines in it is near

Pisces the two fishes with a circle near it with a woman inside the circle holding a jackal with her left hand. Above those figures are a jackal back to back with a monkey or baboon with a bird on top of the head of the monkey. Th baboon with the jackal back to back to it has it's tail going down to the beginning of Aries the Ram.

The Aries sign rules the head and Aries is given the number nine and begins on March 21. Subtract (left hand of the woman in the circle on the carving holds a jackal in her left hand) nine days and one year (Aries=first sign=one) from March 21, 2018 (Dog year and the beginning of Aries) equals March 12, 2017, which is a full moon as the circle with the woman in it who is holding the jackal (=dog) near Pisces on March 12, 2017 represents. See the front cover of this book for that picture of part of the ancient Egyptian carving referred to here. That date is the Pisces sign (two fishes), full moon (circle) and a Sunday as Pisces rules the Sun in which get the name Sunday from and the circle also represent the sun as well as the moon. Pisces is the 12th sign making the date of March 12. The mark or symbol of the sun is a circle with a dot in the middle. Pisces also is a female sign that represents the woman in the circle near Pisces and the box with three wavy lines in it. Does on March 12, 2017 a great earthquake happen and/or volcano eruptions, tidal waves, storms, wars or attacks or comet or asteroid impacts happen?

The bird on top of the baboon or monkey (Chinese Monkey Years is 2016) could be one year (Aries=head and one=first sign) from the Monkey Year to the date of March 12, 2017, which is the Chinese Year of the Rooster (=bird). In Proverbs 30:30- 31 it predicts these same signs describe in this chapter when these events happen. It predicts a "lion". It also predicts a "greyhound" or Dog or Jackal. The "greyhound" is translated "rooster" in some Bibles. It also predicts a "he goat" or ram or the Aries sign. All these figures fit in with the carving and the events and dates to happen in 2013-2019.

Will a great earthquake and/or storms, wars, attacks, comet or asteroid impacts and volcano eruptions happen on March 12, 2017 as one of the three wavy lines in the box as the Richter scale's wavy lines, stormy seas wavy lines and bombs shaking the earth and/or sky as a wavy line? And will as August 10, 2013 to August 10, 2015 we saw the same three dates in three years we see again great earthquakes, storms, wars, tidal waves, attacks, comet or asteroid impacts and volcano eruptions, but this time on March 12, 2016, March 12, 2017 and March 12, 2018, which are the Monkey Year, the Rooster Year, and the Dog Year (jackal) as seen on the carving? Will the middle date be a full moon like before on August 10, 2014 and a earthquake a year before and after then on August 10, 2013 and August 10, 2015, plus or minus three days, just as the three same dates of March 12, 2016-2018 has troubles on? This would make an earthquake or some event happen on March 12, 2016 then on the anniversary a year later on March 12, 2017 another earthquake or some event on a full moon and Sunday just as my book *Predictions for 2013-2014* predicted in chapter one for those years (2013-2014).

These are the three woes and three angels or six angels of woes Revelation 8:13 and chapter 14 predicted. Three of them are from August 10, 2013 to August 10, 2015, and three from March 12, 2016 to March 12, 2018, making six angels of woes or trouble for people of earth. This is just as the carving showed two boxes with three wavy lines (=times of troubles) in them to make six times of trouble three in the wine harvest of August the Leo sign and three in March 12, which is the Pisces sign of two fishes and the polar opposite of Leo is Aquarius, which star time is on March 12, 2016-2018. Or is it six times of trouble in the wine harvest of July-August from 2013-2018?

The middle of Libra, the lion's two front paws on the box, the box in the middle of Pisces and Revelation chapter 14 as the second angel all equals the middle date of two sixes? Those dates are on a full moon, which is the circle on top of Libra, the woman in a circle holding a jackal in Pisces, and ends on a full moon six years later. This equals six years added to the year 2013+6=2019 on January 21, 2019, which is a full moon. The reverse of the Pisces sign number is 12, or 21, in the 12 month of the Chinese calendar equals that exact date. See my book titled *The Experiment at Philadelphia* drawings 45-46-47, pages 462-464, to see part of this ancient Egyptian drawing for reference to these figures and events predicted by it and the Bible.

Half of Pisces the number 12th sign is six, which equals those six times of trouble three in August and three in March from 2013-2018. See my other books entitled *Predictions for 2013-2014*, *Predictions for 2015* and *The Divine Code 3* for more details and documentation of these codes for these six events.

Pisces is ruled by Jupiter that is given the number three. Minus three months, counting each month from Aries March 21, 2019, and it equals January 21, 2019. That time is the Chinese Year of the Dog or jackal and a full moon as the time of the end as the ancient carving predicted the exact date of the end. It may even give the time of 12:12 a.m. (=two fishes or two times 12=12:12). When you add plus six (2 times three wavy lines in the two boxes on the carving and half of Pisces=12 divided by two equal six) minutes to it it equals 12:12+6=12:18 a.m. January 21, 2019. That is when the end of the world, Second Coming and the kingdom of God or Rapture happens.

The dates of March 12, 2016-2018 could be April 12, 2016- 2018 going by star time or sun time when the sun is in Pisces not on March 12, but April 12, plus or minus three days. Every time you see March 12, 2016-2018 in this book it could mean April 12, 2016-2018, plus or minus three days. March 12 is the Aquarius sign nowadays due to the movement of the equinoxes. The polar opposite of Aquarius is the Leo sign that runs from July-September when these events may happen in this book and my other books. The other dates might be July-August of 2016-2017- 2018-2019 in the grape harvest (July-August) as Revelation chapter 14 and 19 predicts these events happening as recorded in this book and my other books. The eagles and birds that eat the dead bodies as Revelation chapter 19 predicts could be vultures that eat the human bodies killed in the tidal waves on the East Coast of the U.S. and/or by wars or attacks and earthquakes and storms happening at those times and years. August 28-29, September 7-8, 19, 26-27, and October 15, 2013- 2019 may also be the exact dates of these predicted events in this book and my other books.

The lion below Libra with its two front paws on a box with two or three wavy lines in it on the carving could mean two times five or 10 in the Leo sign. Leo is the fifth sign and the two front paws on the box would be two times five or 10 in the Leo sign on a year ending on five. July 10, 2015 is the Cancer sign. September 10, 2015 is the Virgo sign. The only tenth date in the Leo sign would be August 10, 2015 which last digit of the year is a five with the Leo sign as the fifth sign and part of that month as also the number five to the Bible's calendar. Leo is a lion which mostly come from Africa and the wavy lines in the box could represent tidal waves on that date from an earthquake and volcano eruption off the West Coast of Africa (=lion). Leo the lion rules the Chinese Monkey and the month of August. In my book *Predictions for 2013-2014* I show how Zechariah chapters 7-8 relate to November-December of 2013. The year Zechariah 7:1 was written was 518 B.C. three years before 515 B.C. when the Jewish temple was completed in the Chinese Year of the Dog making 518 B.C. the Chinese Year of Sheep, which 2015 A.D. is when these events happen in the Leo sign (=Monkey) on August 10, 2015 plus or minus three days or July-August 2015. The Sheep not only rules 2015, but also the Cancer sign, which star time is on August 10, 2015. Zechariah 7:1 could be December 7, 2013 when blessings come as chapter number 7 is the day and December is the month of Chisleu as predicted in that verse as does the book of Haggai as the ninth month and 24th day. That same chapter of Zechariah 7 in verse 5 predicts the fifth month equals July-August or August 10, 2015. December in Latin means ten. Was these prophecies relating to these two different dates in August 10 (=December=10 and Chisleu) and also December 7-10 (=nine or tenth month) in 2013- 2015? The 10 days of Leo might also mean ten days into Leo starting from July 22-23 or August 1-2, 2015 when these events happen. That's the same date when Saddam Hussein invaded Kuwait in 1990.

Chapter Five

Predictions for 2016

In Chinese Yearly cycles of 12 the year 2016 equals 2004, 1992, 1980, 1968. The events that happened in those years are four storms hitting Central Florida in 2004. Will several storms hit Florida or Central Florida in 2016? In 1992 one great storm hit South Florida named Andrew. Will another great storm or tidal wave hit Florida and/or South Florida in 2016? In 1980 on May 18 Mount St Helens volcano erupted. Will that same volcano erupt in 2016? On April 4, 1968 Martin Luther King, Jr. was assassinated. Then on June 4-5, 1968 RFK was assassinated. Will we see some assassination of someone famous in 2016 in April or June or some other month in the year 2016?

January 6, 1986, April 26, 1986 saw two nuclear accidents in the U.S. and Russia. Will in January or April or some other month in 2016 we see some nuclear accident some where in the world? Those Chinese Years are 12 years apart twice to equal 24 years, plus six years as a polar opposite, making 1986 equals 2016 when these events may happen in.

On June 30, 1908 in Tunguska, Russia there was a tremendous explosion in the sky similar to a nuclear explosion when nuclear bombs didn't exist. Afterwards people at midnight in England inside could read with out candles or lights because of the light in the sky. No one was recorded killed, but reindeer were reported with sores on them and many trees all around the blast site were blown down for many miles. To this day no one knows what exactly it was that caused such damage. The Year 1908 is the Chinese Year of the Monkey the same 2016. Will in 2016 we see some paranormal event like that or by a comet, asteroid or meteorite or UFO in June or some other month?

In the Bible it predicts the end as "the days of Noah." Was this a clue to not only how people will be at that time, but also the date when Noah's flood started to end the world on that same date? Is the flood of Noah that of the great tidal wave of our 2015-2016 when a volcano erupts and part of the island slides into the sea causing a great tidal wave to hit from Miami to Boston killing 10 million or more? Noah's flood started according to the Bible on the 17th day of the second month. Which second month it is may be a mystery because the Jews have two calendars. One in the Bible that starts in March-April and the other in September-October. In my other books I show how Noah's flood started May 19-20, 2341 B.C., which was a Chinese Monkey Year as 2016 is. The polar opposite that date or the second month and 17th day from September equals November 10-11. Will on one of those dates of May 19-20 or November 10-11, 2015-2019 we see a great tidal wave and/or the end of the world or other great events happen?

There was a prophet back in 1100 A.D. that predicted 113 Popes starting from his time unto the end and gave details of each Pope with the last Pope being named or connected to the name Peter. The 112th Pope is today (November 11, 2011) reigning. We are only one Pope away from the last Pope and the end. Nostradamus in quatrain C2:Q41 predicts a great star to burn for seven days. Is this an attack or earthquake or comet impact on Rome, Italy that kills the current Pope 112? Or is it the Holy Bible prophecy of Isaiah and Revelation 16:8-9 that predicts the sun to strengthen for seven days or times and great heat? Nostradamus predicts in that quatrain C2:Q41 a great cloud (mushroom cloud=nuclear bomb attack) and that the sun appears double as nuclear bombs are made of the same thing the sun is. Or is the double sun one or two comets flying by and around the sun and by the earth at one of these dates? This same quatrain predicts the pontiff (=Pope) to change his abode (dies) when the mastiff (Dog=large=Canis Major appears) comes and howl. Is this a reference to star time when Canis Major is seen at night? Or is it the Chinese Year of the Dog in 2018- 2019 when the Pope dies? Is that Pope the 113th name Pope in January of 2019 that dies or the current Pope to die in 2018- 2019 then the last Pope dies shortly after he takes over? Could these events also predict a comet or asteroid to strike Rome or someplace or be near the sun making it look double at these times? These events could happen between 2016-2019. And a earthquake may be what causes the Pope's death making way for the 113th Pope just as Malachy predicted when the end would come. A plane crash of the Pope is another possible prophecy for this current Pope to die between 2016-2019 as Obadiah 1-6, Amos 2:14 and Daniel 11:19-20 predicts. In Daniel 11:19-20 predicts a election when a new leader and/or Pope is elected. The year 2016 just happens to be a U.S. Presidential election year in November. And the one elected then for four years comes to power in January 20-21, 2017 and will be in power until 2019-2020 unless he or she dies in office from 2017-2020.

I couldn't understand these verses in the Bible for a long time now but I think I understand them now and here they are followed by my explanation:

"Behold, a whirlwind of the Lord is gone forth in fury, even a grievous whirlwind: it shall fall grievously upon the head of the wicked.
The anger of the Lord shall not return, until he have executed, and till he have performed the thoughts of his heart: in the latter days ye shall consider it perfectly." Jeremiah 23:19-20 (Old King James Version).

"For thus saith the Lord, Thy bruise is incurable, and thy wound is grievous. There is none to plead thy cause, that thou mayest be bound up: thou hast no healing medicines."

Alas! For that day is great, so that none is like it: it is even the time of Jacob's trouble; but he shall be saved out of it." Jeremiah 30:12-13 and 30:7 (Old King James Version).

"I have declared the former things from the beginning; and they went forth out of my mouth, and I shewed them; I did them suddenly, and they came to pass.
Because I knew that thou art obstinate, and thy neck is an iron sinew, and thy brow brass;
I have even from the beginning declared it to thee; before it came to pass I shewed it thee: lest thou shouldest say, Mine idol hath done them, and my graven image, and my molten image, hath commanded them.
Thou hast heard, see all this; and will not ye declare it? I have shewed thee new things from this time, even hidden things, and thou didst not know them.
They are created now, and not from the beginning; even before the day when thou heardest them not; lest thou shouldest say, Behold, I knew them.
Yea, thou heardest not; yea, thou knewest not; yea, from that time that thine ear was not opened: for I knew that thou wouldest deal very treacherously, and was called a transgressor form the womb.

For my name's sake will I defer mine anger, and for my praise will I refrain for thee, that I cut thee not off.

Go ye forth of Babylon, flee ye from the Chaldeans, with a voice of singing declare ye, tell this, utter it even to the end of the earth; say ye, The Lord hath redeemed his servant Jacob.

And they thirsted not when he led them through the deserts: he caused the waters to flow out of the rock for them: he clave the rock also, and the waters gushed out.

There is no peace, saith the Lord, unto the wicked."
Isaiah 48:3-9,20-22 (Old King James Version).

"And thou wentest to the king with ointment, and didst increase thy perfume, and didst send thy messengers far off, and didst debase thyself even unto hell.

I will declare thy righteousness, and thy works; for they shall not profit thee.

But the wicked are like the troubled sea, when it cannot rest, whose waters cast up mire and dirt.

There is no peace, saith, my God to the wicked." Isaiah 57:9,12 and 20-21 (Old King James Version).

""Behold, I will stir up the Medes against them, which shall not regard silver; and as for gold, they shall not delight in it.

Their bows also shall dash the young men to pieces; and they shall have no pity on the fruit of the womb; their eye shall not spare children.

And Babylon, the glory of the kingdoms, the beauty of the Chaldeans' excellency, shall be as when God overthrew Sodom and Gomorrah.

It shall never be inhabited, neither shall it be dwelt in from generation to generation: neither shall Arabian pitch tent there; neither shall the shepherds make their fold there.

The wild beasts of the desert shall lie there; and their houses shall be full of doleful creatures; and owls shall dwell there, and satyrs shall dance there.

And the wild beasts of the islands shall cry in their desolate houses, and dragons in their pleasant palaces: and her days shall not be prolonged." Isaiah 13:17-22 (Old King James Version).

"And it shall come to pass in that day, that every place shall be, where there were a thousand vines as a thousand silverlings, it shall even be for a briers and thorns.

With arrows and with bows shall man come thither; because all the land shall become briers and thorns." Isaiah 13:23-24 (Old King James Version).

The phrases "intents of His heart" and "thoughts of His heart" in the above verses and Jeremiah 30:23-24 that are made perfectly clear in the latter days by a whirlwind might just mean hurricane Andrew that hit South Florida in August of 1992. And in April to June 29, of 1992 I had terrible kidney (loins or reins) pains. Then on June 29, 1992 at evening on a new moon they instantly were healed. Later that summer hurricane Andrew hit South Florida hard. I had at these times the books on the intents of God's heart and the heart is ruled by Leo when Hurricane Andrew hit in the cusp of Leo or Leo star time on August 24-25, 1992. Leo is given the numbers 1-4 that spell out the short name of Andrew the Zodiac with a upside down "Y" on the end and that he was born on Heart's Day or Saint Valentine's Day. And just as the first beast or antichrist (head of the wicked) was born in the Bahamas off the coast of South Florida so did hurricane Andrew hit there making the prophecy perfectly clear in the latter days from when Jeremiah wrote it. The phrases in the verses above in Isaiah chapter 48 and 57 predicted no rest for the wicked and troubled sea was hurricane Andrew at this time it came ashore on the Bahamas and South Florida kicking up the sea and waves and dirt and mire.

And at this time of August 1992 two month before hurricane Andrew I was healed as Jeremiah 30:7,12-13 and Isaiah 48:9 predicted from the kidney pains in which no medicine or no cure was possible.

The year before these events was January of 1991 when the first Iraq war started. That time in January was the first month. God's wrote through me the end of it before the start of it. Thus, declaring the end (=end of Iraq) from the beginning, or the "former things from the beginning." These prophecies all came true and God did them suddenly just as Isaiah chapter 48 predicted. You can translate "former things from the beginning" as "former things from former times." That means the Bible predicted many events long ago (former) about the first Iraq war. It also predicted it would start in the first month in January, which is our beginning month of 1991 as the former things (=beginning) from the end (=December-1990).

What God wrote through me about that war came true suddenly just as predicted in Isaiah chapter 48. See my book entitle *The Experiment at Philadelphia* Appendix D for details and documentation of how the Bible prophecies of the first Iraq War were predicted.

After that war in 1991 the next year I learned hidden things then, and from before then, that were the intents or thoughts of God's heart. Along with learning those things I also learned that the antichrist and false prophet (messengers= demons) that Isaiah chapter 57 predicted as coming up from hell to a king (President) with perfume. The "perfume" is ruled by Neptune or Capricorn, which polar opposite is the Cancer sign, which June 29, 1992 was the Cancer sign. This is recorded in my book *The Antichrist* that documents exactly how the Bible predicted 30 years after the death of a U.S. President (king) that UFOs would come up from hell and land on the White House front yard and out comes a former U.S. President killed by a fatal head wound. He would be with his wife or the false prophet and they have books that explains the deepest darkest secrets of the Universe that leads many to apostasy and a great falling away into lawlessness, sin and evil. But as Isaiah chapter 48 predicts those events I knew would not come to pass as a time when thou hearest not nor knoweth not, meaning you see not those prophecies come too pass. Isaiah 48:4-9 predicts God's image (=satan) had knowledge of hidden things he would use to deceive the world with at this time, but was with held by someone in a 14 chapter book. That person was me who had a book of 14 chapters that showed the hidden things of God then and was sealed until the antichrist was revealed and then when open would ruin his appearance and ability to deceive the whole world. You can read those 14 chapters in my book entitled *The experiment at Philadelphia* chapters 1-14. See II Thessalonians chapter 2. This is why Isaiah chapter 48 predicts I could not say I knew these events (heard not-see not) because by my with holding them not only stopped the appearance of the antichrist (=image), but stopped those 14 chapters from being used to deceive the world. The "hidden things" are the "intents" or "thoughts" of God's heart that Jeremiah 23:19-20, 30:23-24 predicted.

I would be saved out of those times and God would defer his anger that he cut me not off (kill me) and the antichrist would not appear then because I withheld him by my books that reveal his secrets. See Isaiah chapter 48 and also II Thessalonians chapter 2. And since I didn't die that made way so that the antichrist couldn't appear with his books that I had written by 1989 and for three years to 1992. Then on June 29 they withheld him and the false prophet. If I had died he would of appeared from a UFO on the front yard of the White House. But my books or inheritance of my books left to my family may have helped those left to his deceptions, like Ecclesiastes predicts wisdom (books) are good with an inheritance or portion. The "portion or inheritance" for seven or eight year that Ecclesiastics 11:2 predicts is from then 1992+7-8=2000-2001 when the end would come as told of in my book *The Divine Code*. This time of June 29, 1992 was the time of Jacob's trouble that Jeremiah chapter 30 predicted who would be saved and redeemed out of it. See my books *The Antichrist; The Experiment in Philadelphia; The life of Kurt B. Bakley; Prophecies that have, will, or didn't happen; The Divine Code 3*.

Isaiah chapters 7, 13 and 48 might predict the U.S. and/or Israel being destroyed by nuclear attack or a tidal wave and to flee from it. Babylon could mean Florida where the antichrist was born as to where to flee from in these troubled events in 2015-2019.

As for Isaiah chapters 7 and 13 the predicts of a nuclear attack like that on Sodom and Gomorrah long ago could happen along with a gush of waters from a rock (=Volcano) as Isaiah chapter 48 predicts as a tidal wave that destroys parts of the U.S. and/or Israel. The prophecies of Isaiah chapter 13 predicts the "Medes" which are the modern day Iranians that launch this attack on Israel with one or two or three nuclear bombs or missiles followed by Syria launching 2000-3000 scud missiles at Israel with chemical and biological warheads followed by terrorist groups in South Lebanon and Gaza launching 10,000-50,000 rockets at Israel. If this happens Israel would be annihilated. And all the chemicals, poisons and radiation could cause animals and birds living there or wonder into there afterwards to give birth to strange deformed babies that Isaiah chapter 13 predicts. And it would make the land not inhabitable for generations to come. Only biers and thorns grow there in or near empty houses with weird animals and birds. It's been taught God would protect Israel from this attack if it is the one predicted in Ezekiel chapters 38-39, but He may not as Isaiah chapter 13 predicts. Babylon by the way could mean not only Florida and the U.S., but also Israel in a spiritual sense if it is secular as most of the U.S. and Israel are quickly becoming. This would be the reason God doesn't protect both Godly nations, or at lest were Godly nations. But God may protect Israel and the U.S. in these wars.

The war of Ezekiel chapters 38-39 may have already happened or partly happens in this war with Iran and/or will happen at the very end in 2019 or 2025 or at the end of the thousand year period in 3005-3015.

The year 2016 may be the year when a woman President is elected in the U.S. according to prophecies given in this book of my other books. Will she be born in a water sign as coming up out of the sea as Daniel chapter 7 predicts?

In my last book *Predictions for 2015* I showed how Isaiah chapter 29 predicted earthquakes, storms, wars or attacks and tidal waves for 2015. I also show how that same chapter predicted prohibition in 1919-1920 on January 16, which the year 1919 is the Chinese Year of the Sheep as is 2015. In that same chapter I show how it predicted a book to be delivered to one person learned and one person unlearned and them saying it is sealed or they are not learned. This happen to me in 1985 when I advertised my book and one person answered me and I sent them the book and even though I never heard from them I knew that they were learned, but the book was sealed. Then another answered my ad in 1985 and I could tell by her letter she was unlearned. The Chinese Year of 1985 was the Year of the Ox, the polar opposite of the Sheep. The Ox rules our month and sign of January and Capricorn when in 1985 my dad died. The Chinese Sheep Year is 2015, when as Isaiah chapter 29 predicts, along with what I just said, an earthquake, attacks, storms and troubles happens in that year.

Will a year before that year of 2015 I ride prosperously as Psalms 45:4-5 when the king (President=U.S. and/or Israel) is killed in a attack in 2014 or 2015 by arrows (=missiles-bombs) from the king's heart (=rules Leo August 4 President Obama's birthday)? Is Spring time or Summer time in

2014 when many that read these books should move from Florida and the Eastern Coast of the U.S. far in land and store up food and water and buy a place with a fireplace and store up much fire wood? Does "the ride prosperously" mean double years of prospering for me in 2013 and 2014 as double for my shame in the two years from 2001-2003? Then 2014 I drive a car or ride up north and inland? Deuteronomy 32:13 and Song of Solomon 2:7-17 and 8:14 predicts as roes, hinds and harts as deer leaping upon the mountains is me riding a car upon the hills of the roads skipping upon them like a dear (roe, hind, hart) does skipping upon the mountains. The chapter/year codes for Song of Solomon chapter 2 equals 2002+12=2014 when in the spring or summer, as Song of Solomon 2:11-13 predicts me to ride (=car) right after messengers or angels speaks to people telling them where to buy my 14 books. Song of Solomon 8:13 a verse before 14 where it predicts the voice of the beloved (angel of the Lord) speaks to the women in the garden (Florida) then I ride prosperously up north and in land. In Zechariah 9:11-17 and Isaiah 61:1-7 it predicts double or two years of prospering. At that time I am to drive by car to a new home (inheritance-portion-lot). In that year is when I proclaim the acceptable Year of the Lord like John the Baptist and Jesus did in 26 A.D. That year was the Chinese Year of the Dog the same year as January of 2019. I claim in these books that are available in 2013-2014 that angels speak to certain people telling them of them. Those same books give the dates of January 2019 as the end or Rapture and the flood or tidal wave of July-August of 2015. Are the two or three be strongs and double in Daniel chapter 10 and in the Book of Haggai in the Bible and Zechariah 9:10-14 mean the shame I had in 2001 to 2003 will be rewarded in 2013-2015? Is that when these books sell because of the prophecies coming true and the angels tell people of them? Are they the double trouble and double blessing of August 10, 2013 and December 6-7, 2013 and August 10, 2015 and December 7-8, 2015? Psalms 90:15 predicts God to give his servant good for the years he saw evil or from 2001-2003 and 2013-2015, or 2011+2-3-2013-2014. And Psalms 114 is our year of 2014. That chapter is when it predicts waters or floods or springs gush out of the rock as Isaiah 48:21 also predicts. Are these events the eruption of the volcano off the West Coast of Africa with an earthquake that slides part of it and the island (=rock) into the water causing a great tidal wave (waters) to gush forth towards Florida and the East Coast of the U.S.? Is that the prophecy of the great tidal waves for August 10, 2015 that I predicted that happens early as Psalms 90:14 predicts? Sometimes prophecies documented for one year happen a year before or after. Why this is I don't know. The volcano that erupts in the Canary Islands off the West Coast of Africa causes an earthquake and the island to slide into the sea causing a great tidal to head towards Florida and the U.S. East Coast. Could that happen in August 10, 2014, plus or minus three days or July-August 2014, instead of those dates in 2015. The Israeli and/or U.S. being attacked or at war may also not be in 2015, but in 2014 as noted above on August 10, 2014, plus or minus three days, or July-August of 2014.

Or does the 20,000 chariots of God and thousands of angels and Mount Sinai in Psalms 68:17 mean August 10, 2014-2016 when angels will appear telling people where to buy these 14 books of mine? That time is at or near when a volcano erupts off the West Coast of Africa and sends tidal waves to Florida and the U.S. East Coast. Mount Sinai equals a mountain or volcano even though it may have not been one. It may also represent the latitude degree from Mount Sinai to near the Canary Islands where the volcano erupts and sends a tidal wave to Florida near the Bahamas or Central or Northern Florida Coast and the East Coast of the U.S. As for the 20,000 chariots of God in that verse it may predict 20,000 people have angels sent to them at this time or before it on August 10, 2013. They then tell them where to buy these 14 books of mine. At that time is the summer months when many people travel by cars (=to and fro) on summer vacations. Before that time they should travel by car inland to be saved from the tidal waves and/or storms, hurricanes, attacks and earthquakes. The 20,000 chariots can mean 10,000- 20,000 people angels are sent to on August 10, 2013 and/or August 10, 2014-2015-2016. Is the double of Isaiah 61:1-7 and Zechariah 9:10-14 mean 20,000, or two times 20,000, in two different years as 2013 and 2014 or 2015-2016 are on August 10 or July-August of those years? Psalms 68:8,17 both mention mount Sinai and verse 8 predicts an earthquake there when angels are sent out in verse 17 when cars (=chariots) travel a lot for summer vacations as Daniel 12:4 predicts. Mount Sinai was when Moses went up the mount to get the 10 commandments from God after Passover, which was the Chinese Year of the Ox. The polar opposite of the Ox is the Chinese Year of the Sheep or our year of 2015 when these events could happen. "The heavens dropped at the presence of God" that Psalms chapter 68 predicts could mean incoming missiles or bombs at these times in August 10, 2014-2015-2016, plus or minus three days, or July-August of those years. See Psalms chapter 68.

Chapter Six

Predictions for 2017

The 12 year cycles backwards from 2017 are 2005, 1993, 1981 and 1969. The year 2005 was when Hurricane Katrina hit hard Louisiana, Ms, Al and other states on August 25-29, 2005. Will we see another great hurricane hit those areas or some where else on those dates or other dates in 2017?

The storm of the century hit Florida and the Eastern sea board of the U.S. on March 12-14, 1993. That date is the same as the ancient Egyptian carving shows as a box with wavy lines in it as stormy seas or waves (=wavy lines). Will we see another great storm on those dates or other dates hit the Southern and/or Eastern U.S. Coast in 2017?

Also in 1993 we saw great river flooding of the Midwest in the U.S. in July-August. Then in September of 1993 we saw the Israeli-Palestinians Peace Treaty signed at the White House. Will there be river flooding and peace treaties signed in 2017 in those months or some other months in 2017? Both Jeremiah 6:14 and I Thessalonians 5:3 predicts when people say "peace, peace, and peace and safety" then sudden trouble will come from the north as that chapter predicts in Jeremiah? Does the repeating of peace, peace and peace and safety represent two years after the signing of a peace treaty that great sudden destruction comes from the North. If a peace treaty is signed in 2017 two years of peace, peace and peace and safety would be 2017 and 2018. Then early the next year sudden destruction in January of 2019 comes as the Bible and ancient Egyptians predicted. Is the year 2017 when the U.S. and Israel deploy a great SDI system to protect their nations from incoming nuclear missiles?

In 1981 Japan and the U.S. had nuclear accidents on April 25, 1981 (Japan) and February 11, 1981 (U.S.). Will on those dates or other dates in 2017 we see again nuclear accidents or trouble with nuclear power plants caused by or earthquakes, floods, or attacks?

Chapter Seven

Predictions for 2018

The 12 yearly cycles from 2018 backwards equals 2006, 1994, 1982 and 1970. On June 12, 1994 on a Sunday we saw the gruesome murders of Nicole and Ron Goldman. Then a great car chase and then the trial the next year ending in a not guilty verdict and a storm forming and hitting Florida near or on that verdict all predicted in the Bible. See my books titled *The Experiment in Philadelphia* and *The Divine Code 2* for documentation of these events. Will we see another gruesome murder on the same date or other dates and the same events happen that year of 2018 or 2019? Are the dates August 28-29, September 7-8, 19, 26-27, October 15, November 11, December 24-25, May 19-20 and June 24- 25 important to those events in 2018-2019?

We also saw the comet impact Jupiter on July 16, 1994. Will we see in 2018 another comet or asteroid hit there or some other moon or planet or the earth causing great destruction? Or will it be plane crashes or solar flares at those times?

On March 28, 1982 there was a volcano eruption in Mexico. Will we see another volcano eruption in Mexico or somewhere else in 2018?

The great flu outbreak in 1918-1919 killed millions of people. A hundred year cycle would put that time of trouble again in 2018-2019 when we may again see a great or new flu out break or pestilence (epidemic) that kills millions as Jesus predicted in Matthew 24:7 and Revelation chapter 6.

Chapter Eight

Other predictions

Sometimes people and even scholars studying Bible prophecy, especially the book of Revelation, put certain prophecies as for the future when they already been fulfilled in the past. One example of this is Isaiah 17:4 and Jeremiah 30:7-10 as when the Jews go through the great tribulation period. This could happen that way or in other ways considering Jacob as the servant of the holy One of Jacob as the son of man. But putting those prophecies as in the 1940's when many of the Jews in foreign lands were put in concentration camps and staved to death and making many of them (Jacob as Israel the Jews) wax lean and thin. This was fulfilled exactly at that time and it was a time of great trouble for Jacob (Israel=Jews) as Jeremiah 30:7-10 predicted along with them coming out of those horrible times and returning to Israel and become a great prospering nation again. This too also came true after WWII when Israel became a nation again after 2000 years of being spread around the world into nations that were enemies of them. On May 14- 15, 1948 Israel became a nation and Jews from all over the world started coming back (return) to Israel from the lands God spread them out to and given them over to the hand of their enemies-the antichrist-Hitler. And today Israel is a prospering nation. Those prophecies were fulfilled exactly in WWII and after, so there is no need for those prophecies to be fulfilled today even though they can again happen in the same way or in a different way.

Some scholars do the opposite of this and put prophecies of the book of Revelation and other Bible prophecies as happening in the past when they are prophecies for the future. They put them as past prophecies that have happened hundreds-thousands of years ago. These mistakes many make with the Bible is that they think most, if not all the prophecies in it are for the 70 A.D. events that have already happened when they are for the great seven year tribulation at the very end or right up to the 1000 year reign of Christ. A third mistake and meaning of the prophecies of the book of Revelation and other great Biblical prophecies is that they do cover all these things and have more than one meaning and more than one event, which means they can be fulfilled in the past, present and future events all in one prophecy over the space of thousands of years. Revelation 1:4 predicts its prophecies as was, are and is to come. Some of those prophecies can also partly come true then fail like I Corinthians chapter 13 predicts in the past, present and future. The prophecy and interpretation can be true and some detailed things come to past, but they fail in the end.

In one of my other books I documented how WWII was the seven year tribulation and all the many prophecies that were fulfilled in it. Some thing I didn't mention were the third of the ships destroyed in that war is just as the book of Revelation predicted. The scorched earth that Revelation predicted could also have been fulfilled in WWI and/or the first Iraq war in 1991 when Saddam Hussein burned or scorched the land or earth with oil rigs fires after being pushed out of Kuwait. The third part of the waters that are spoiled and/or turned to blood in that war could also be the fulfillment of Revelation's prediction of the third of the waters to turn to blood (oil) causing death to fishes and the wild life in the sea. During the first Iraq war in 1991 Saddam Hussein had his men turn the oil on in Kuwait into the Persian Gulf covering about a third of Kuwait's shore line. There were actual pictures of the wild life there covered in oil and dying just as Revelation predicted.

Saddam Hussein was the first horse of the apocalypse that went and conquered one nation or crown, which was Kuwait and fulfilled many of Revelation's prophecies and other prophecies in the Bible. He invaded Kuwait on August 2, 1990, which is the Leo sign, the lion, or the first beast or cherub described in Revelation chapters 4-6. This makes him the first horsemen of the apocalypse. Saddam Hussein is actually pictured in a book riding a white horse, which in Revelation 6:1-2 is the first horse of the apocalypse being white.

The second red horse of the apocalypse in Revelation 6:3-4 could be the two atomic bombs dropped on Japan in August of 1945, which was also the Leo sign that is ruled by Mars the red planet or the red horse. The planet Mars is known as the god of war, which perfectly describes Hitler that started WWII and Japan and Italy were his allies. The great sword predicted in Revelation 6:3-4 could be the two (=second horse) atomic bombs dropped on Japan in that war that made the sky roll back like a scroll (mushroom cloud) exactly as Revelation 6:14 predicted.

The third horse of the apocalypse is black and has a pair of balances in his hand and is told not to hurt the oil or wine. The balances or scales represents money or the economy because in ancient times people weighted in scales silver, gold and other metals for their worth. Could this be the economic break down in the U.S. and the world starting near when President Obama was elected and became the U.S. President in 2008-2009 A.D.? He is a black man and possibly the black horseman of the apocalypse. He is slowly taking away all the poor's money and giving it to others that have more and he doesn't hurt the rich that the oil and wine represents. Social Security to the poor, disable and poor retired people haven't seen one January cost of living increase in their checks since President Obama took office until now (January 2012). Not only that but his health care bill takes away parts of Medicare from the poor and the disable and gives to the richer. Right now (September 8, 2011) he says he is going to take more money away from Medicare and Medicaid to help jump start the economy. This will further take away from the poor and disable and those on Social Security retirement and gives it to others who are more richer. Yet he bails out the banks, car makers and AIG and other big and rich people with money borrowed causing a massive U.S. debt making the rich richer and the poor poorer just as Revelation 6:5-6 predicted. The CEO's of the banks after doing acts of fraud with many mortgage foreclosures rewarded themselves. Then when their customers can't pay their mortgages the banks kicks the people out so they are homeless while President Obama pays billions to the banks for the market crash while the foreclosures are homeless and poor. Then to add to this mess the banks and all CEO's give themselves that same year millions in bonuses after they ran their banks into the ground with fraud and are bailed out by President Obama and the rich get richer and the poor poorer. Could the scales in Revelation 6:5-6 prediction of a penny for bread mean a very great depression or famine (=due to volcano smoke and ash eruption and/or another dust bowl and drought?) for exactly seven years (seven=seventh sign Libra=scales) from 2011-2019? Or will that happen for half that time as three and a half years from August 10, 2015 to January 21, 2019? Some of the plains states are already experiencing drought and lack of crops. Will the smoke and ash from a volcano eruption, or comet or asteroid impact, at that time cover the sun and destroy the crops making a loaf of bread cost very high? A penny is said to be a full days wages for one loaf of bread in the ancient past. Or does President Obama's by printing up so much paper money suddenly cause great inflation causing bread and food to cost very much, a full day's wages? Is the oil ways interrupted causing famine because trucks can't get the bread and food to the stores causing bread to cost a lot? Will a bomb explode over the U.S. destroying all electronics and engines stopping all food supply?

The fourth horseman of the apocalypse is pale as Revelation 6:7-8 predicts with death and hell following it over the fourth part of the earth and kills with the sword and with hunger and with death and with the beasts of the earth. The word "pale" means green in the Greek dictionary and is near the word for "gall, green and wormwood." The planet wormwood in the Bible was satan's planet Virgo which zone runs through the center of Africa. Satan being black, as Song of Solomon 1:5 states, could mean AIDS diseases caused by monkeys (=animals) in Africa. The tribal war fare in Africa could be the sword that this pale horseman brings. The hunger could mean famines in Africa that causes other diseases and trouble over the fourth part of the earth or in Africa. These things are coming to past in 2011 and may happen afterwards up to the end just as Revelation 6:7-8 predicted. The fourth part of the earth could mean a quarter of the population dies or the fourth continent meaning Africa or the fourth of Africa's population dies. It also could mean Africa where the fourth beast and the first antichrist was conceived at Giza, Egypt where the Virgo zone ends and the Libra zone begins. The commotion's we seen in Egypt and other African nations in 2011 could be what these prophecies mean. Death and hell that this green horseman brings is satan as the fourth beast that Daniel chapter 7 predicts is far worse. See Revelation 6:7-8. Will those nations that had their leaders overthrown in the Spring and later in 2011-2012 become enemies of Israel, the U.S. and Christians like the overthrow of Iran in 1979? Texas seeing great trouble at this time with wild fires and drought in 2011 could be the trouble for that great and large state like in 1963 when JFK was assassinated in Dallas, Texas. Both times of trouble and both times of the Chinese Rabbit Year. And Texas is known for its oil that Revelation chapter 6 predicts to protect. And that year is when the Zodiac serial killer is identified in 2011-2012 who killed five people (=fifth seal) seen as souls under the alter in Revelation 6:9-11 predicts in heaven.

The four horsemen of the apocalypse are referred to in Revelation chapter 6 after the four beasts in heaven (=sun) that have wings (=flying). Could the constellation Pegasus, the flying horse, be what the four horsemen represents in prophecy? In that constellation it has what is known as the "great square". Is that the four horsemen as four sides of the great square? Pegasus is seen near or behind the sun (=heaven) in March-April. Is Pegasus, seen at those times, the event predicted for March-April 2003 when the second Iraq war with Saddam Hussein started? As mentioned earlier Hussein is seen in one picture riding a white horse just as the first horsemen of Revelation chapter 6 is white? Are the next three horsemen seen to appear on March 12-April 12, or March-April of 2016, March 12-April 12, or March April of 2017 and March 12-April 12, or March-April of 2018 the times of when all four horsemen had or will set off great prophetic events in the world? Or are the four horsemen four seasons of Spring, Summer, Fall and Winter when events prophesied happen? The four beasts are the start of the four seasons known as the equinoxes and solstices.

The flying horse Pegasus might have fire to it at Christ return because January 20-21, 2019 is in the cusp of the Sagittarius sign, which is a fire sign and the ninth sign. Mars is given the number 9 and is known as the "god of war", which Revelation chapter 19 predicts Jesus Christ return on a flying horse with fire and to make war. Nine is the number of God the Father, His Son and the Holy Ghost. In fact, 999 the opposite or upside down of 666 the evil trinity equals the Holy Trinity as Mars (9) Aries or Scorpio (9) and Sagittarius (9). Mars as God the Father. Aries as the Lamb or Son of God Jesus Christ. And Sagittarius or Scorpio as the Holy Ghost. And Revelation chapter 19 might be our year ending in 19 or 2019.

After the four horsemen, which is also the first four seals of a book, comes the fifth seal in Revelation 6:9-11. Is that fifth seal with dead martyrs under the alter in heaven five dead people killed by Muslims from 2012-2060?

One astrology book I once read had Miami, Florida as being ruled by Leo the lion. Leo is the fifth sign or the five pointed star of the pentagram, which spells out the zodiac's first and last name. Leo is also given the numbers 1-4, 5 or 5x5=25. Those numbers spell out Andy the Zodiac that was born on Saint Valentine's Day or heart's day. The heart is ruled by Leo the lion which rules the month of August when hurricane Andrew hit Miami, Florida hard as the place of the head of the wicked as Jeremiah 23:19-20 and 30:23-24 predicted. That place, or the Bahamas near to it, is where hurricane

Andrew also hit hard as a place known as the head of the wicked born there long ago as the very first antichrist. His father, also known as the head of the wicked, fell from heaven in August the same month as when hurricane Andrew hit there (Miami-Bahamas). The head of the wicked could also mean Aries which rules the head and its symbol looks like a "Y" added to Leo's 1-4 or 1, 14, 4, and y to form Andy. Leo being ruled by the sun is a circle and Leo rules the heart equals a cross, or the circle with the cross through it that the Zodiac signed some of his letters with. I never read or heard that the circle with a cross through it mean the Zodiac as many suggested and were wrong. What I just said makes the prophecies perfectly clear.

That same phrase "perfectly clear" that Jeremiah 23:19-20 and 30:23-24 predict for a whirlwind (=hurricane and/or tidal wave or attacks) means to not have God's wrath return until the intents or thoughts of his heart are revealed in this book and my 14 books (=God's heart or thoughts) which are finished by Saint Valentine's Day February 14, 2012. The heart being key to the Zodiac's name might mean not another great hurricane and/or tidal wave or attacks happen upon Miami, Florida until after (will not return) these things of the Zodiac's identity is revealed and these 14 books of God's heart and thoughts are revealed or finished. Then on the exact date of August 10, 2015, which is the Leo sign, a great tidal wave and/or attack or storm happens on Miami, Florida making the prophecies perfectly clear at that time in the latter days exactly as Jeremiah predicted. August, Miami and the Bahamas are the same month of satan's fall from heaven, the place where the very first antichrist was born and hurricane Andrew hit and these events happen in our future after these 14 books and the Zodiac identity are revealed or finished on February 14, 2012. If a storm hits Miami, Florida at this time or in the months of July-August 2015 or 2014-2016 will its name be special as was Andrew's? Will it be another "A" named storm or named after another serial killer at that time or in the past? Will the storm form or hit, along with a tidal wave and attack at the time of the verdict of some famous trial as Jeremiah 30:11,23- 24 predicts? Will it hit Miami, Florida on the exact dates of August 10, August 24-29, or those dates or July-August of 2014- 2016, along with tidal waves and attacks? And just as Jeremiah prophesied these events won't happen (God's wrath won't return) until He has performed the intents and thoughts of His heart, which are revealed in 14 books of mine and the identity of the Zodiac killer revealed through the great hurricane Andrew both in February 14, 2012. All of these events make Jeremiah's ancient prophecies perfectly clear about a very great whirlwind (=hurricane-tidal wave-attacks-volcano eruption-earthquakes) on all those exact dates, places and names in the latter days. The word "measure" in Jeremiah 30:11 means "verdict" guilty or not guilty. And you maybe saying a couple of events may happen on the same date or near it or in the same months of July- August. This maybe what Isaiah 40:2 means as double trouble in one or two dates, places, events and years.

The sixth seal of Revelation 6:12-17 predicts stars falling from heaven and a great earthquake which I document in this book and my other books as happening from 2011-2019. See those other books of mine for all the details.

The seventh seal in Revelation 8:1 is about an half hour or half a year of five (about) to six months from July-August 2018 to January 21, 2019. Or 60 years from 2000?

Chapter Nine
U.S.A.

One preacher on TV told of how Daniel 7:4 was predicting Britain as the lion and the eagle's wings plucked out of it as the birth of the U.S.A. on 7.4.1776 after Daniel 7:4 (7.4=July 4, 1776) when the U.S.A. was born. He claimed when he was in Britain or England he saw many statues of lions around it. And the U.S.A. with its dollar bill on its back cover has an eagle. Thus, having Britain as the lion with wings of an eagle plucked up or flown away from that nation to start a new nation with eagles as its national bird and on the back of dollar bills. See the book entitled *World Almanac and book of facts* under calendars for George Washington birthday and year.

The first United States President was George Washington born February 11, 1731 by the Old Julian calendar. That year is the Chinese Year of the Pig the same as 2019 is the Chinese Year of the Pig. Daniel 7:4 predicts a man's heart is given to it, the first beast, in this case a good beast or cherub, which was George Washington. February 11, 1731 is the Aquarius sign, which polar opposite it is the Leo sign that rules hearts. Was that what Daniel 7:4 mean by a man's heart was given to it? Or does it mean the first U.S. President would be born then and the last U.S. President would be born as a woman in the heart sign or polar opposite that sign in Leo or Aquarius? Or are they born in one of the water signs, which could mean Cancer, Scorpio, Pisces and Aquarius, which is the water-bearer? President Obama was born in the Leo sign of the heart and could be the last President killed in office near the end. George Washington had a vision or angel visitation from a woman showing him the entire U.S. history right before his great battle for freedom from Britain. She shown him at the end a great battle would destroy all the great cities of the U.S.A. Being a woman was it referring to a U.S. woman President at the time of the end of the U.S.A.?

Daniel chapter 7 prediction of three horns plucked up by the roots could be in WWII when the U.S.A. conquered Germany, Italy and Japan, winning the war. The other prophecies of Daniel chapter 7 noted in this book and my other books could also be true and this is not a contradiction because prophecies in the Bible have many different fulfillment's.

Daniel 7:1-4 predicts the winds upon the seas blows over from a lion (Britain) to an eagle (U.S.A.) and starts a new nation and king (President). England is partly in the Cancer zone, which is ruled by the moon that rules tides and seas as the first beast or king come up from. The U.S.A. was formed by British colonies sailing (winds upon the seas) in sail boats from England across the Atlantic Ocean (=seas) to the U.S.A. to start a new nation.

This same man on TV that told of July 4 as Daniel 7:4 also showed and told how a green (=pale) horseman was photograph right in the middle of a protest in the Middle East in 2011. He also said the fourth horseman of the apocalypse maybe Muslims that are over the fourth part of the earth or the fourth part of the population of the earth. He estimated the Muslim population as between 1.3-1.6 billion which is almost approximately a quarter of the earth's population.

Obadiah 1-6 predicts a rumor of war from the Lord when a ambassador (messengers=angels) appear at the name and place of Edom in the grape harvest (July-August). In Jeremiah 51:46 predicts a rumor of war for the U.S. and/or Israel one year and then the next year war happens. In my books

I show how the Bible predicted angels to appear to certain people telling of them of these books in July-August of 2013. That year (2013) is the time of the rumor of wars against Edom (a type of Israel and U.S. and the twin brother of Jacob named Esau, who lived in Edom). Then the next year rumor and then war in 2014 in the grape harvest of July-August of 2014 (Amos 1:6). Edom being Esau and the twin brother of Jacob (=Israel) equals Gemini the twins. In Chinese astrology the Horse rules our Gemini sign and month of June. The year 2014 is the Chinese Year of the Horse. Song of Solomon 6:10,13 predicts "four returns" at the time of "two armies" on a "full (=fair) moon and clear Sun" (=Sunday August 10, 2014.) Those two armies are ones that attacked and destroyed Jerusalem two times once in July-August of 585-586 B.C. and the other in July-August of 70 A.D. both on the exact same date to the Jewish calendar. Does the "four returns" mean the fourth year as 2014 ends in four? And does the "return" mean twins, or Gemini, that the Chinese Year of the Horse rules in 2014 when these wars and rumors happen? Will also the volcano off the West Coast of Africa erupt then causing a great tidal wave to hit Florida and the U.S. East Coast on August 10, 2014? Or is the rumor of war in 2011 at or near December 2011 and then the beginning of the next year rumor and then war in January 1-4, 14, 15-24 of 2012 or later in 2012-2013 on February 11, 14, 26-29, March-April-12, 1, 6, 9, 10, 14-15, 20-21, 24-25, 19-20, May 9-10, 19-20, 26-29, June 9-12, 20-25, 28-29, July-August, August 9-10-11, 9th of Av, September 7-8, 19, 26-27, October 15, 22, 31, November 1-2, 11, 28, Thanksgiving, December 4-16, 20-22, 24-25 (Christmas Eve and Day), 31, or on Hanukah, Purim, Passover, Pentecost, Rosh Hashanah, Yom Kippur, Feast of Tabernacles when after another rumor that year or two in 2012-2013 is when war (on those dates or December 24-25, 2012-2013) happens between Iran and Israel and the U.S.? See my other book *2012* for more details of this. Or does these events of war with Iran and the other events predicted in this book and my other books happen on August 10, 2011-2019, or those other dates that were just mentioned in those years 2011-2019? The "arrows" of Deuteronomy 32:22-23, Zechariah 9:14 and Isaiah 7:14,24 predicts might be missiles or bombs or attacks on Iran and Israel and the U.S. on one of the above dates in the year 2012-2013. Isaiah 7:14 predicts Jesus' conception which would lead to His birth a year later are in the Chinese Years of the Dragon and Snake in 5-4 B.C. In that same chapter it predicts "arrows" or missiles or bombs. Was it predicting a Christmas or Hanukah or December or June 24-25 (=Jesus' real birthday) or the dates above for an attack by Israel and the U.S. on Iran or vice-versa in those same years of a Dragon and Snake, which are 2012 (=Dragon) and 2013 (=Snake)? Is it a time of a great earthquake, great volcano eruptions, tidal waves, famines, pestilence's, fearful and great signs from heaven and darkness at noon or all day? See Deuteronomy 32:22-23, Isaiah 7:14,24, and 16:3, Amos 5:8, Revelation 16:10 and Luke 21:9-11. Will both places be left uninhabitable for years to come as Isaiah chapters 7 and 13 predicted with briers and thorns growing up among the empty or destroyed houses and buildings? If the Canary Islands volcano doesn't erupt and cause a tidal wave then or 2014-2016 then maybe the great Yellowstone or Mount Saint Helens volcano will erupt causing these same events and troubles for the U.S. in 2011-2019. Or does a EMP bomb explode over the United States knocking out all electronics and our electrical power causing great darkness, heat, famines, pestilence's and other problems on one of these dates and years mentioned above?

Amos 1:1 in the Bible predicts "herdmen" and a hill or mount "Tekoa two years before an earthquake" when trouble will come upon the U.S. and/or Israel. The "herdmen" are connected to Sheep in which the Chinese Year of the Sheep is 2015 A.D. With Amos chapter one being our year 1995 and you add 12 years to it that equals 2007 A.D. Add the polar opposite that of six years and it equals 2013 A.D. Then add the two year more to when a hill or mount (Tekoa) falls into the sea and causes a great tidal wave that hits the eastern U.S. destroying much and maybe killing 10 million Americans. Two years added to 2013 equals 2015 when this volcano erupts off the West Coast of Africa and part of the island slides into the sea and causes a great tidal wave (=whirlwind=Amos 1:14) to race across the Atlantic Ocean and destroy the Eastern Sea Coast of the U.S. from the Coast to 20-40 miles or more in land. Add 12 years to 2007 A.D. and it equals 2019 when the Pig (=1995 and 2007) rules. In Bible chapter/year codes for Amos chapter 1 in the month and sign of the polar opposite of the Herdsmen, or Sheep, which is the Ox that rules our month and sign of January and Capricorn. That time is January of 2019 in the Capricorn sign or its star time or cusp. Amos 1:1,14 predicts a day of battle and whirlwind and tempest or wind at this time in 2015. The elevation of Tekoa is 2700 feet according to *Halley's Bible Handbook* page 359. Could 2700 feet be an anagram for the year 2007, which is 12 years from 1995 in Bible chapter/year codes for Amos chapter 1? We seen that the polar opposite of that year (=2007) is the Chinese Year of 2013+2years=2015 when a volcano (Tekoa=mountain or mount) erupts and sends a tidal wave across the Atlantic to Florida and the U.S. East Coast. When that tidal wave hits there maybe war or attacks and/or storms or hurricanes hitting the U.S. at the same time or some other time that year fulfilling the "double" trouble predicted in Isaiah 40:2. It could mean double trouble for two nations in two times and ways in two years. Those two nations would be the U.S. and Israel. Isaiah 40:2 is our year 1940 the Chinese Year of the Dragon, which 2012 is also the Chinese Year of the Dragon. Will in 2011-2012-2013 we see these double trouble for the U.S. and Israel? Is the "double" those two nations and/or two types of troubles for those two nations in attacks, tidal waves, storms and great earthquakes on the dates given above for the years of 2011-2012-2013 or 2014-2016? Are the two troubles (double=Daniel 10:19=two be strongs) and possibly three or four troubles as Haggai (=three be strongs) and Amos (3-4 transgressions) predict in the Bible as the number or years of events of trouble for the U.S. and Israel? Amos chapters 1-2 repeat eight times "for three transgressions and for four." Eight times four is 32 the number of the Song of Moses in Deuteronomy chapter 32 and Revelation chapter 15. And we seen in my book how in 1981 me and my mom and dad came south to Florida 27 years (=2700 feet elevation of Tekoa of Amos 1:1) after my birth (=1954=27=1981) when I was born in a storm (=whirlwind=tidal wave). My first name Kurt has a "K" as the first letter that means hand which has 27 bones in it which equals 27 years from my birth. Add 32 (=4x8=32 transgressions of Amos chapter 1-2) to 1981 and it equals 2013. Add the two years to the earthquake or volcano eruption in the Canary Islands that causes a great tidal wave to hit Florida and you have 2015. That is when the grape or wine harvest of July-August is and these events happen as Amos chapter 1 and Obadiah 1-6 predicts. The name Edom in Amos 1:6,9 is Esau who is Jacob's twin (=2=2 events and 2 years=double) brother born September 19, which is the Virgo sign. The Virgo sign is ruled by the Chinese Rooster, which 1981 was, plus the 32 years and two years added to it equals the great earthquake in 2015 (=herdmen=Sheep=2015=Sheep Year). That year is when a volcano erupts and a earthquake causing a great tidal wave (=whirlwind= tempest=tidal wave=battle and/or hurricane and attacks) as Amos 1:14 predicts. The rumor of war may happen in 2013 or 2014 with messengers sent out in 2013 (=two years before the earthquake and volcano eruption). But no war happens then. But in 2015, two years later, another rumor of war and messengers are sent out to tell of these books. Then war and tidal waves happen near or when this earthquake and volcano erupts just as Obadiah 1-6 predicts, which tells of Edom and the grape harvest of July-August of 2015. Amos 3:12 predicts this time after the 32 times (4x8) of three or four transgressions repeated eight times in Amos chapters 1-2, as a time of the two paws of a lion. This is seen on the ancient carving from the temple Hathor as mentioned in my books and seen in a picture in them. Two paws times five equals 10 in the lion sign of Leo which is the fifth sign (=2x5-10). July 10 is the Cancer sign and September 10 is the Virgo sign, only August 10, 2015 is the Leo the lion sign in the fifth month of the Bible's calendar and the year ending in five (=2015). In year/ chapter codes Amos chapter 3 would be our 1997, which is the Chinese Year of the Ox, which polar opposite is the Chinese Year of the Sheep in 2015 on exactly August 10 (=Leo the lion two front paws as Amos 3:12 and the ancient Egyptian carving shows). See my book *The Experiment at Philadelphia* drawing 47 page 464. That drawing shows the lion with its two front paws on a box (=coffin=death) with three wavy lines in it. Was that carving predicting three events over three years from August 10, 2013, August 10, 2014 and August 10, 2015? The volcano island in the Canary Islands off the West Coast of Africa erupted in 1949 and caused a great crack in the island. If another eruption and earthquake happens the whole side of the volcano or mountain will slide into the ocean causing a great tidal wave to head for Florida and the East Coast of the U.S. People studying this island said the crack has been slowly sliding down toward the ocean ever since the 1949 eruption. The year 1949 in Chinese astrology is the Year of the Ox, which polar opposite is the Chinese Year of the Sheep in 2015 on August 10. Are the double blessings and double troubles for the U.S. and/or Israel on or near Hanukah and/or the grape or wine harvest of July-August of 2013 and 2015? Hanukah in 2012 is from December 9-16 and in 2015 is December 7-8-15-16 and is November 28-December 5, 2013. Are any of those dates when Israel and the U.S. attack Iran or Iran attacks them causing a great response from Israel and the U.S. back? If Rick Santorum is elected in 2012 as the U.S. President he was born May 10, 1958 and has said that he would bomb Iran. May 10 is the Taurus sign and the President of Iran now (January 2012) if still in office then was born October 28, which is the Scorpio sign. The one star chart I show in my book *The Experiment at Philadelphia* drawing 25 page 441 shows the Milky Way going from Scorpio to Taurus not seen. Was that star chart predicting many missiles and bombs being sent out between Israel (=Taurus=born May 14-15) and the United States (Santorum=Taurus) to Iran (President at this time is Scorpio born) on the dates of this book or my others in 2012, 2013, 2014, 2015 or 2016? Or is the Milky Way (missiles) on that star chart Sagittarius the archer of arrows (missiles) shooting at Scorpio (D.C.). Iran is partly in the Sagittarius zone and Washington, D.C. is ruled by Scorpio just like that star chart shows? Will Israel and the U.S. attack Iran and Iran attack back or first on one or two of those dates given in this book for 2012-2013 or later?

In this book I tell how Mount Sinai, the Canary Islands and Florida are all near the same latitude of where these events all happen. Edom is also near that same exact latitude. Revelation chapter 15 that predicts the Song of Moses again is in chapter/year codes is 1995. Adding 12 years to that equals 2007. The polar opposite of that equals 2013+2 years that Amos 1:1 predicts to when this great earthquake and volcano eruption and tidal is to hit Florida in 2015. See also Jeremiah 51:46. Revelation being the 27th book of the New Testament may also relate to that number added to my birth in 1954 to the first chapter of Revelation in chapter/year codes as 1981. Then adding 32 years plus two years to 1981 equals 2015 when these events happen on a Sunday-Monday on August 9-10, 2015. That is when Revelation chapter 12 predicts a baby born in a storm (=flood=whirlwind=hurricane) for satan to try again to kill that person in Florida by a tidal wave that the land (=earth) swallows up as it moves inland just as predicted. The "sun" and "moon" mentioned in Revelation chapter 12 might mean a Sunday-Monday, which August 9-10, 2015 is. The "red dragon" of Revelation chapter 12 could mean the Aries sign that the Chinese Dragon rules, which is a ram connected to Sheep or the Chinese Year of the Sheep in 2015. The "red" part of this prophecies would be the red planet Mars that is Leo the lion, which sign rules on August 10, 2015, plus or minus three days, and is a Sunday-Monday August 9-10, 2015 when a storm or tidal wave hits Florida and the East Coast of the U.S.

In 2011 I became aware of the serial killer's name who murdered in San Francisco in 1968-1969 by a storm's name in 1992. At that time in 2011 the prophecy of a whirlwind (=hurricane or tidal wave) hitting the wicked (Bahamas-South Florida) became perfectly clear to me at that time. These prophecies tell of these things exactly:

> "Behold, a whirlwind of the Lord is gone forth in fury, even a grievous whirlwind: it shall fall grievously upon the head of the wicked.
> The anger of the Lord shall not return, until he have executed, and till he

have performed the thoughts of his heart: in the latter days ye shall consider it perfectly."
Jeremiah 23:19-20 (Old King James Version).

"Behold, the whirlwind of the Lord goeth forth with fury, a continuing whirlwind: it shall fall with pain upon the head of the wicked.
The fierce anger of the Lord shall not return until he have done it, and until he have performed the intents of his heart: in the latter days ye shall consider it."
Jeremiah 30:23-24 (Old King James Version).

"And woe unto them that are with child, and to them that give suck in those days!
But pray ye that your flight be not in the winter, neither on the sabbath day."
Matthew 24:19-20 (Old King James Version).

"And take heed to yourselves, lest at any time your hearts be overcharged with surfeiting, and drunkenness, and cares of this life, and so that day come upon you unaware.
For as a snare shall it come on all them that dwell on the face of the whole earth."
Luke 21:34-35 (Old King James Version).

"Let no man therefore judge you in eat, or in drink, or in respect of an holyday, or of the new moon, or of the sabbath day:
Which are a shadow of things to come; but the body is of Christ."
Colossians 2:16-17 (Old King James Version)

"In the day of prosperity be joyful, but in the day of adversity consider: God also hath set the one over against the other, to the end that man should find nothing after him." Ecclesiastes 7:14 (Old King James Version).

"And from the days of John the Baptist until now the kingdom of heaven suffereth violence and the violent take it by force."
Matthew 11:12 (Old King James Version).

"And they that dwell upon the earth shall rejoice over them, and, make merry, and shall send gifts one to another;…"
Revelation 11:10 (Old King James Version).

"And when he had taken the book, the four beasts and four and twenty elders…" Revelation 5:8 (Old King James Version).

Nostradamus in quatrain C6:Q35 predicted the Zodiac's name and also predicts the plains, cities and woods burning. The summer of 2011 saw Texas and Oklahoma, both plain states, have great drought, heat and wild fires in their woods and houses. This too became perfectly clear at this time when I was working on finishing my 14 books by February 14, 2013 on the intents and thoughts of God's heart as we read in the book of Jeremiah. Is the "heart" in those verses Saint Valentine's Day and/or the Leo sign that rules the heart and is in July-August when Texas saw such great heat, drought and wild fires as Nostradamus also predicted?

Several of those 14 books of mine showed predicted events for 2013-2019 and beyond. But Psalms 90:14 predicted to satisfy early God's servant by an earlier fulfillment of the predicted events of several of his books for 2013-2019 and beyond before another great hurricane (whirlwind or tidal wave) hits South Florida and the U.S. East Coast. The "return not until" that Jeremiah predicted from one whirlwind to another as Psalms 90:14 predicts shall not come until these wars and attacks happen in Israel, Iran and the U.S. Then another great hurricane and/or tidal wave (whirlwinds) can hit Florida and the Eastern U.S. Coast line as my book *Predictions for 2015* predicted for that year or 2014-2016 caused by an earthquake, volcano eruption and tidal waves. Psalms 90:14 to "satisfy early" may mean that the tidal wave doesn't strike in 2015, but in 2014 making this book and my others sell well and have great success. Psalms chapter 90 is the Chinese Year of the Horse the same as 2014 when that tidal wave strikes and this book and others sell very well earlier than 2015. If that tidal wave strikes August 10, 2014, plus or minus three days, or July- August of 2014, the world wide popularity of this book and the others would be known and many would want to be read them. That would be satisfying God's servant early. It would make his days of evil and shame for two years in 2001+2=2003 come good (glad) days in two years from 2013-2014 with great rewards of the works of his hands (=books) just as Psalms 90:14-15-16- 17 predicted. On December 25, 2000 I saw what I believe were two angels on Christmas Day. If Psalms 90:14-17 predicts an early success on that Day of Christmas in 2011+2 years of being glad and again another success on December 7, 2013, as we read or will read in my books, it would fulfill these prophecies perfectly. Could two sets of angels one set coming on December 24-25, 2011. And then again on August 10, 2013 to tell people of where to buy my books making the servant of God to be satisfied early and for two years more from December 2011+2= 2013? I had a dream December 21-22, 2011 of me putting on pink pants. *The Dreamer's Dictionary* under colors says the color pink means "predicts unusual great success." My books up to this point showed no interest or success, but maybe these things will come true. Song of Solomon 8:11-14 predicts 1000 people to bring a 1000 pieces of silver as Isaiah chapter 7 and Deuteronomy 32:30 predicts. A 1000 pieces of silver is approximately 610-620 dollars. The books I have published at this time times ten the royalty rate equals almost exactly 610- 620 dollar. If each of the 1000 people bought ten copies of each of my books at this time in December of 2011 it would equals 610-620 dollars each. Then on August 10, 2013 angels the second time, the two angels seen on Christmas Day in 2000, will tell 10,000 or 20,000 people where to buy a copy of each of my 14 books just as Psalms 68:17 predicted. These ancient prophecies could also mean two or three times publicity is shown my books for their predictions of several earthquakes, attacks, storms, volcano eruption and tidal waves in 2013-2015- 2016 just as the ancient prophecies predicted. The angel (spirit) you see at this time if chosen will be a bluish-white light that sparkles and makes you smile ear to ear and will speak to you. Do what ever he tells you to. See Revelation 2:29.

Or does Psalms 90:14-17 "satisfy us early" mean the events of Iran and Israel and the U.S. attacking each other happens in 2012 or 2013 as my book *2012* predicted a war between those nations in those years earlier then 2014-2016 as this book and some of my other books predict. And one or two years after that (=2012-2013) comes the great tidal wave, volcano eruption, earthquakes, and storms in 2014-2016 on the exact date of August 10 making the prophecy perfectly clear of a whirlwind (=tidal wave and/or hurricane) happening then. See Jeremiah 23:19-20 and 30:23-24. The word "early" in Psalms 90:14-17 are the wars that come early, but the other events come on the times predicted in these books. The wars could come in 2012- 2013 and the volcano eruption, earthquake, tidal waves and storms could come in 2014-2015-2016. If the wars come in December of 2012 on the 24-25ᵗʰ day it would fulfill many prophecies. One is that of Revelation chapter 12 (=2012) where it predicts a woman clothed with the sun and the moon under her feet and a great red dragon that pulls down a third of the stars (=missiles-bombs). December 24-25, 2012 is a Monday (=moon) Tuesday, which Tuesday is Latin for Mars. The planet Mars is called the red planet and rules Leo and the sun. Thus, the woman clothed in the sun (=Tuesday) and the moon under her feet might mean the day of Monday is ending and going into the day of Tuesday. The red dragon is the Chinese Year of the Dragon in 2012. Revelation chapter 12's red dragon is not only the Chinese Year of the Dragon in 2012, but chapter number 12 equals the year ending in 12 (=2012) and in the 12 month of December and on the date 21, which is reverse of 12, thus the exact date of December 21, 2012. The Mayan prophecies, along with II Peter 3:1-7 and Luke 21:34-36, may predict December 21, 2012 is when the Mayan calendar ends on and many people think something will happen then, but nothing does. So they mock God, Christians and the Bible for those prophecies and go about celebrating Christmas Eve and Day by partying with much food, drinks and giving of gifts then sudden destruction comes. See Luke 21:34-36 and Revelation 11:10 for these times of giving gifts one to another all over the world, which we do exactly on Christmas Eve and Day and all the partying (=drunkenness) we do in celebrating that day. Mars (=Tuesday=Leo) also is known as the "god of war," which may happen on Christmas Eve and Day of December 24-25, 2012. This maybe what Ecclesiastes 7:14 in the Bible predicts as the day of prosperity (=Christmas Day) is the same day as adversity (war). II Peter 3:2-7 prediction may mean that Israel is destroyed in this war as their fathers fell asleep (died) and Jesus did not come back to save them and many will say and mock "where is the promise of his coming for since the fathers fell asleep things continue as they were since the beginning." See II Peter 3:2-7 and my book *2012* included with this book.

Another interpretation of these ancient prophecies could be fulfilled in August 10, 2013 by angels (spirits) are sent to 20,000 people telling them to buy a copy each of my 14 books at that time. Then two years (double) later on August 10, 2015 angels are sent out to 20,000 other people (double) telling them where to buy a copy each of my 14 books. See Isaiah 61:1- 7 and Zechariah 9:1-14. The latter date is when the tidal wave strikes after an earthquake and volcano eruption as predicted in Psalms 68:8, 17. At that time is when many people travel (to and fro) by cars (chariots) on summer vacations. See Daniel 12:4 and Psalms 68:17. Mount Sinai in Psalms 68:8,17 is connected to a volcano off the West Coast of Africa. That volcano eruption and earthquake causes a great tidal wave that hits Florida and the East Coast of the U.S. Mount Sinai is also connected to Passover in the year 1484 B.C. That year is the Chinese Year of the Ox, which polar opposite equals the Sheep Year or our 2015 A.D. on August 10, plus or minus three days. We seen these dates to be connected to Revelation chapter 12 as a time in the Leo sign and on a Sunday-Monday.

Still another possible interpretation is 20,000 people (=Psalms 68:17) are told of these books on August 10, 2013 and then 100 million more are told of them on August 10, 2015, plus or minus three days or July-August of 2013 and 2015. See Revelation 5:11 and Daniel 7:10. The "thousands of thousands" and "ten thousand times ten thousands" in those verses means 20,000 and 100 million. The thousands of thousands is also mentioned in Psalms 68:17 which we seen connects to these dates and places and events in 2013 and 2014 when double blessings and double trouble happens in those two years and two troubles in August 10, 2015 when a tidal wave and a attack happens. Revelation chapter 5 tells of a book unsealed in God's hand taken by the Lamb who is from the tribe of Juda the lion (=9=Leo). The "Lamb" is Aries the Ram or Sheep year of 2015 when in August 10, plus or minus three days these events happen in which is the Leo sign of the lion (=tribe of Juda-the lion). Aries is given the number 9 as is Mars that rules Leo the lion on August 10, 2015. Revelation chapter 5 could be the fifth sign of Leo (=chapter 5) when these events happen in the year ending in

5 (=chapter 5), or August 10, 2015. In year/chapter codes Revelation chapter 5 equals the year 1985, which is the Chinese year of the Ox, which we seen is the polar opposite of the Sheep Year of 2015 when on August 10 these events happen. Two years of sadness and shame for me in 2001-2003 and two years or double blessings in 2013-2015 with the sales of these books just as Psalms 90:14-17 and Haggai predicted. Two in the summer vacations of 2013 and 2015 and the two blessing from those events at that time equals Hanukah or Christmas in December of 2013-2015 just as predicted. The latter trouble in 2015 could be a double trouble and double blessing (=10,000 double equals 10,000 x 10,000=100 million) when on August 10, 2015 two trouble occurs in the forms of great tidal waves and attacks and/or storms or earthquakes. See Isaiah 40:2, 61:1-7 and Zechariah 9:10-14. Revelation chapter 5 also predicts that book in the right hand of the Lamb to have seven seals that are seven eyes and seven horns that go around the world. Are they these 14 books, which equals 7+7=14, that go around the world in sales on the world wide web or WWW.Authorhouse.Com or Amazon.Com or Barnes&Noble.Com?

In August 10, 2014 after a second earthquake on that same date a year earlier will a rumor come of an attack on the U.S. and/or Israel, then a year later a rumor and then war, king against king, just as Jeremiah 51:16, Isaiah 40:2 and Obadiah 1-6 predicted. "Edom" in Obadiah 1-6 equals Gemini. The Gemini sign is the Chinese Year of the Horse or our year 2014. Is that when the first rumor comes as Luke 21:9 predicts as "by and by" or two years from when these events predicted start happening in 2013-2014 till the great tidal wave and attack in 2015 happens two years later, but that is not the end? The Cancer sign mentioned above as Passover, Sinai, Lamb and book has its star time from July 21-23 to August 21-23, which puts Cancer star time right in August 10, 2015, plus or minus three days, or July-August of that year. The Ox Year is the polar opposite of the Sheep Year of 2015 and rules Cancer, which star time is that time just mentioned putting the exact date of August 10, 2015 or the dates of the two atomic bombs dropped on Japan on August 6 and 9th 1945 in 2012-2019 or beyond.

These prophecies of God's wrath shall not return until he performs or tells the thoughts or intents of his heart might mean that another great hurricane and a tidal wave will not hit Florida until after February 14, 2012 when my 14 books are finished and the Zodiac killer is identified. Those same prophecies could also mean that the great hurricane that revealed the Zodiac killer that hit south Florida in 1992 won't return and a tidal won't hit there until or before two completed Chinese Yearly cycles are finished from 1992. The year 1992 plus 12+12=2016. Between now (February 14, 2012= heart's day), when I have completed the 14 books of God's heart, and the Zodiac killer identified, will there be another great hurricane and tidal wave that returns to hit Florida with God's wrath between those years of 2011 to 2016 exactly as this book and my other books predicted? See Jeremiah 23:19-20 and 30:23-24.

Will Israel attack Iran's nuclear factories on December 23- 24-25, 2011? December 24, 2011 is a new moon, a Sabbath Day (=Saturday=Jewish Sabbath) and a holyday or holiday. That date is Christmas Eve and Day. It is also winter time when people all over the whole world give gifts to one another. This is just as all those verses above predicted for a time of great prosperity (Christmas Eve and Day=Sabbath Days=Saturday-Sunday) and is the same time as the time of great adversity (=trouble= attacks). People will be partying and celebrating hard the Christmas Holidays (=holyday) and over eating and drinking with the cares of this life just as Luke 21:34-35, Matthew 24:19-20, Colossians 2:16-17, Revelation 5:8, 11:10 and Ecclesiastes 7:14 predicted when these attacks happen. Or does the attack happen on Hanukah or near it and/or on Christmas in December of 2012, 2013, 2014, 2015 and 2016 or in that month or the other dates given in these years just given?

The "four beasts and twenty four elders" of Revelation 5:8 are dates of the fourth month (=four beasts) and 24th day (=24 elders). When they are calculated to the Jewish Civil calendar translated to ours equals December 24, 2011-2013, or December 23-24-25, 2011-2013. At that time is when these events of attacks and wars happen between Israel, Iran and the U.S. The Jewish Sabbath starts Friday evening and ends Saturday evening, which are December 23-24, 2011. And Sunday December 25, 2011 is the Christian Sabbath, which is Christmas Day the time of giving of gifts or prosperity and a holyday. The song Silent Night proclaims this day as a holynight or holyday Christmas Eve and Day. See the quotes above for documentation for these events in Colossian 2:16-17, Matthew 24:19-20, Revelation 11:10 and Ecclesiastes 7:14.

Matthew 11:12 tells of John the Baptist's birthday and how on that day the kingdom of heaven is greatly shaken or taken by violence and by the violent. Was this referring to a bomb over Iran that causes all the electronics to fail? Or is it missiles and bombs from the heavens that shake the ground and skies (=heavens) over Iran and Israel in 2011 and 2012-2013? John the Baptist was born on December 24 in the Chinese Year of the Dragon, which 2012 is. See my other book *The Experiment at Philadelphia* for details.

These events happen earlier then expected as Psalms 90:14 predicts and before the return of the fierce anger of the Lord by another whirlwind (=hurricane) and/or tidal wave hits from Florida to Boston in 2013-2014 as this book and my other books *Predictions for 2013-2014, Predictions for 2015, and The Divine Code 3* predicted for 2013-2019. The intents or thoughts of Gods heart are finished and revealed at this time in 2011-2012. His thoughts or heart reveal the great hurricane Andrew (as the identifying factor for the exact name for the Zodiac killer). That hurricane hit South Florida in 1992. After these times is when the return of God's wrath falls again there at the place where the wicked antichrist was born in the Bahamas or South Florida with another whirlwind (=hurricane) or tidal wave. This other great hurricane and tidal wave would be after the years 2011-2012-2013. This is when these attacks or wars with Iran, Israel and the U.S. happen in December 23-24-25, 2011- 2013. That is earlier then what those books predicted for 2013-2019 for those wars making the prophecies perfectly clear as the Nostradamus and the Bible predicted. See Psalms 90:14; C6:Q35.

Did Daniel chapter 10 in the Bible predict Israel's attack on Iran (Persia) then 21 days or three weeks later Iran attacks Israel and Israel returns to attack Iran again? Is this what Obadiah 1-6 and Jeremiah 51:46 meant by rumor in one year then the next year rumor and war? The rumor of war for December 23- 25, 2011 is the one year, then 21 days later is the next year, starting in January 2012 and then another rumor and then king against king as Jeremiah 51:46 predicted. Or is it one rumor of 2013 then in 2014 rumor and war and king against king in the grape harvest of July-August (August 10?) as Obadiah 1-6 and Jeremiah 51:46 predicted? Will a great earthquake, volcano eruption and tidal wave also hit then in 2014 instead of 2015- 2016? Is that the time to flee Florida and the East Coast of the U.S.? Revelation chapter 11 predicts trouble for Israel or Jerusalem in a three and a half day period. Will Israel attack Iran on December 23-25, 2011-2013 then three and a half days later on December 27-29, 2011-2013 Israel is attack and/or an earthquake happens in Jerusalem? Or are the dates of December 31, 2012-2013 and January 1, 2012-2013 important for these events when people are celebrating New Year's Eve and Day all over the world? Do we flee then from the tidal wave to come upon Florida and the East Coast of the U.S. in January of 2012, or the other dates that year or those dates in the years 2011- 2019? The latest report out of Israel is a leader said that Israel will not attack Iran at this time (=December of 2011). But Hal Lindsey on his TV show said attacks may be weeks away. He said that on December 9, 2011. What will happen is not known right now.

If the tidal waves hit Florida and the U.S. East Coast on August 10, 2014-2016 then those on the East Coast of the U.S. and Florida are to flee inland to about 50 miles. This, as Revelation chapter 12 predicts, will save you from the flood (=tidal wave) if it doesn't go inland farther. The land will eventually swallow up the water and tidal wave as it moves inland exactly as Revelation 12:16 saving the woman (May 19) and other women and men (=10,000 women and 10,000 men=Song of Solomon

5:10) in Florida and/or the East Coast of the U.S. It may be wise to move inland before these dates so you can save all your belongings. An angel may warn you of this event. He or someone maybe on the rooftop one day near August 10, 2014- 2016 which is a symbol to flee inland. He maybe an angel or the angel appears at night as a bluish-white light that sparkles and makes you smile ear to ear. He may warn you to flee inland or wherever. Do as he says and don't say this author was in error or insane. It may not be smart to move or travel inland from the East Coast of Florida at these times because after the tidal wave, even if it doesn't reach you 50 miles inland, 20-40 miles inland from Florida East Coast will be destroyed followed by famines, pestilence's and power outages. And if the volcano ash blows over into Florida you may not be safe even 50 miles inland and it too could cause famines and other problems. Flee inland and up I-75 into Georgia and then Road 24 and 65 into Indiana might be the best thing to do.

Hanukah this year of 2011 begins on December 20-21, which is the ninth month and 24-25th days as the book of Haggai predicts a great blessing on and a time to be strong. Is that date when Israel attacks Iran and then three and a half days later Iran attacks Israel on December 23-25, 2011? See Revelation 11. December 8-16, 2012 is Hanukah in 2012. Will we see these events then or on December 20-21-22, 2012 as the ancient Mayans believed or in December or the other dates given in this chapter in 2012-2013?

The "by and by" "wars and rumors of wars then earthquakes, famines and pestilence's" of Matthew 24:6-8 and Luke 21:9-11 might just mean these rumors of wars (2011-2012) and wars with Iran by 2012-2013, along with the two wars with Iraq (1991 and 2003) that have already happened years ago and the one in Afghanistan that is still happening now (2012). Then the "by and by" or two years later a great earthquake and volcano eruption that causes a great tidal wave, famines and great pestilence's (2015) that causes many deaths and many to think the end has come, but the end is not yet at that time two years from 2013 (=2013+2=2015). Then years (2016-2018-2019 or later) after that people will begin to think and mock and scoff God, Christians and the Bible of all those things that happened and no Rapture, Second Coming, the end, or the Kingdom of God has come after all those people died (fathers fell asleep) in the wars and by the tidal waves. See II Peter 3:2-7.

Proverbs 30:30-31 predicts a lion that no one can stand up against and a greyhound (=dog) and he-goat in the Old King James Version as Years and times of predicted end time events. In the NIV version it translated "greyhound" as "rooster." Was this a prediction of a lion a Leo born President of the U.S. kills Bin Laden who was reported to be born in 1957, which is the Chinese Year of the Rooster? President Obama was born August 4 making him a Leo sign born the sign of the lion. As for the "greyhound and he-goat" in those verses it could of given important years for the U.S. and President Obama or someone else. Those years would be 2018-2019 the Chinese Year of the Dog (=greyhound) and its polar opposite the Dragon in 2012 and the he-goat as the Chinese Year of the Sheep in 2015 on August 10 (=Leo the lion sign). President Obama born in the lion sign in 1961 is the Chinese Year of the Ox which is a bull or Taurus the bull sign in which sign Bin Laden (=Rooster=1957= Rabbit=2011 polar opposite) was killed on May 1-2, 2011 the Chinese Rabbit and Taurus the bull sign (=May 1-2).

Matthew 24:37-39 predicts the end times to be as "the days of Noah" when people went about the cares of life and suddenly the flood (=tidal wave and/or hurricane) came and took them all away. On August 10, 2015 people will be on summer vacations enjoying the beach and the cares of this life when the tidal wave strikes the Eastern U.S. sea board and Florida from Miami to Boston and takes them all away. I don't know if we have tidal wave warnings in the eastern U.S., but even if we do they still would be caught in massive traffic jams trying to get away. If the tidal wave strikes at night or early morning then all might be swept away by it suddenly and unaware as they sleep just as predicted a thief in the night.

In January of 2012 there were solar storms and flares on the sun that caused great Northern lights seen on NBC evening news for several nights. Will seven years later (2012+7=2019) in January we see again these same events and the sun becoming seven times brighter along with the moon and stars as the books of Isaiah and Revelation predicted? Will there also be other strange events in the skies as Luke 21:25 predicted and a solar and lunar eclipses then (=January of 2019) as Revelation 6:12- 13 predicted? And/or will strange darkness come in the heavens and/or by volcano eruptions off the west coast of Africa and/or the U.S. in Yellowstone or Mount Saint Helens right after the tidal waves and/or storms (seas and waves roaring) in 2015 or January of 2019 as Revelation and Isaiah also predicted?

Luke 21:25-26 predictions of signs in the sun, moon and stars and seas and waves roaring and men's hearts failing them for fear maybe because of these events mentioned above. And nations in distress could mean tidal waves, Nor'Easters, storms and hurricanes hitting the Northeast U.S. and/or the United States Southeast or out in the Atlantic Ocean in January of 2019 when the above events are happening and then the sun goes into a supernova shaking the powers of the heavens as Luke 21:26 predicted. It could also mean these events of storms and tidal waves (=seas and waves roaring) in 2012-2015 along with these signs in the sun, moon and stars with wars and attacks happening. Or they all happen in January of 2019. Here are these predictions:

> "And there shall be signs in the sun, and in the moon, and in the stars; and upon the earth distress of nations, with perplexity; the sea and the waves roaring;
> Men's hearts failing them for fear, and for looking after those things, which are coming on the earth; for the powers of heaven shall be shaken." Luke 21:25-26 (Old King James Version).

I once watch a network two hour documentary in the 1990's about ancient prophecies. They had a American Indian on it who made predictions. She predicted in the end that the seasons would be all mixed up. Hal Lindsey in one of his books in the 1970's said there would be strange weather conditions in the end times. In June of 2010 or 2011 the people in the Northeast U.S. called it June-u-ary after June and January because June of that year was so cold like January, but it was June the beginning of summer. In January of 2012 NBC evening news mentioned again June-u-ary because most of the whole country was warm like summer in June when it was winter in January. Over 2800 records were broken. The seasons were all mixed up exactly as the American Indian predicted.

On another show recently they discovered that an American Indian prophecy of a "web" happening in the end times. They claim this could be WWW as the world wide web that connects the whole world to the internet. Ecclesiastes 10:20 also predicts a bird's voice in the bed camber to be heard by many. Was this predicting the World Wide Web or WWW as the internet that many have in their bedrooms predicted here in the Bible about 1000 B.C.? The bird's voice is that of what the ancient Egyptian's believed ruled Gemini the air sign where the satellites voice or information flies through the air to all the world in our bedchamber or where ever bringing messages just as Gemini ruled by Mercury represents in astrology.

Chapter Ten

Iran

Will Israel (and the U.S.?) attack Iran in April (6?) or December (24-25?) of 2012 or 2013? Or will they attack on other dates shown in this book in the second, third, fourth, fifth (August 10? Or ninth of Av?), seventh (Rosh Hashanah), ninth (May 9-10, 19-20) or tenth (June 9-12, 20-25, 29) months as to the Holy Bible's calendar or the Jewish Civil calendar in the years 2012 or 2013 as Genesis 7:11, Matthew 24:37, the Nostradamus quatrain C9:Q83, Revelation 1:4,10,11, Isaiah chapters 48 and 57, Zechariah 7:1,3 and 8:19, Amos 5:8, Psalms 68:17, February 26-29 (=1260-2520) and Haggai 2:1,5,6,18 predicted?

In Jeremiah 51:46 it predicts a rumor of war to happen in one year then the next year or year after that there is another rumor and then ruler against ruler and war. In this book and on TV in December of 2011 I documented how a attack on Iran could happen on Christmas Eve or Day and Hal Lindsey on TV predicted in December there could be attacks on Iran in that same month of December of 2011. Are they the rumors of war in one year then the next year or two another rumor of war and then ruler against ruler and war? Or is the second rumor on February 2, 2012 when NBC and CNN announced that the U.S. Sectary of defense predicted Israel would attack Iran in the spring (April-May-June) in 2012? Is that the second rumor then ruler against ruler and war at that time? Is the ruler against ruler an attack on the White House in Washington, D.C. where the leader (=ruler) stays, Jerusalem where the Israeli leader (ruler) stays and on the Iranian capital where the Iranian leaders (=rulers) stays? Are they the "temples" that Haggai 2:18 and Jeremiah 51:11 predicts would be destroyed? Already on the TV news in January 2012 (the next year) there is rumors of war coming with Iran. This things seems to fit these ancient prophecies perfectly. Jeremiah 51:11, 27-28, Zechariah 7:1,5, 8:19 and Haggai 2:18-23 predict Iran (the Medes) to be attacked, or attack Babylon, a spiritual name for the U.S. and Israel. The bright arrows (=missiles) of those predictions maybe on or near a new moon in the fourth or fifth or seventh or ninth or tenth month of the Bible's calendar and/or the Jewish Civil calendar. Those months are March-April, May-June- July-August, September-October and November-December-January of 2012-2013. In the books Obadiah 1-6 and Revelation chapter 14 they put end time events in the grape harvest or wine harvest, which in Israel happens in July-August, the fifth month (the ninth of Av when both Jewish temples were destroyed?) Are the "bright arrows" missiles or bombs or rockets with exhaust fire like a bright spear or arrow that explode with nuclear bombs that lights up just like it was predicted? Here are those predictions:

> "And lest your heart faint, and ye fear for the rumour that shall be heard in the land; a rumour shall both come one year, and after that in another year shall come a rumour, and violence in the land, ruler against ruler."
> (Jeremiah 51:46 Old King James Version).

> "Make bright the arrows; gather the shields: the Lord hath raised up in spirit of

the kings of the Medes; for his device is against Babylon, to destroy it; because it is the vengeance of his temple." Jeremiah 51:11 (Old King James Version).

"Set ye up a standard in the land, blow the trumpet among the nations…"
"Prepare against her the nations with the kings of the Medes, the captains thereof, and all the rulers thereof, and all the land of his dominion."
Jeremiah 51:27-28 (Old King James Version).

"And it came to pass in the fourth year of king Darius, that the word of the Lord came unto Zechariah in the fourth day of the ninth month, even in Chisleu;
"…Should I weep in the fifth month, separating myself, as I have done these so many years?" Zechariah 7:1,3 (Old King James Version).

"Speak unto all the people of the land, and to the priests, saying, When ye fasted and mourned in the fifth and seventh month, even those seventy years, did ye at all fast unto me, even to me?" Zechariah 7:5 (Old King James Version).

"Thus saith the Lord of hosts; The fast of the fourth month, and the fast of the fifth, and the fast of the seventh, and the fast of the tenth, shall be to the house of Judah joy and gladness, and cheerful feasts; therefore love the truth and peace." Zechariah 8:19 (old King James Version).

"In the seventh month, in the one and twentieth day of the month..
According to the word that I covenanted with you when ye came out of Egypt, so my spirit remaineth among you: fear ye not.
For this saith the Lord of hosts; Yet once, it is a little while, and I will shake the heavens, and the earth, and the seas, and the dry land." Haggai 2:1,5-6 (Old King James Version).

"Consider now from this day and upward, from the four and twentieth day of the ninth month, even from the day that the foundation of the Lord's temple was laid, consider it.
Is the seed yet in the barn? Yea, as yet the vine, and the fig tree, and the pomegranate, and the olive tree, hath not brought forth: from this day will I bless you.
Speak to Zerubbabel, governor of Judah, saying, I will shake the heavens and the earth;
And I will overthrow the throne of kingdoms, and I will destroy the strength of the kingdoms of the heathen; and I will overthrow the chariots, and those that ride in them, and their riders shall come down, every one by the sword of his brother.
In that day, saith the Lord of hosts, will I take thee, O Zerubbabel, my servant, the son of Shealtiel, saith the Lord, and will make thee as a signet: for I have chosen thee, saith the Lord of hosts." Haggai 2:18-19,21-23. (Old King James Version).

"Now learn a parable of the fig tree; When his branch is yet tender, and putteth forth leaves, ye know that summer is nigh:" Matthew 24:32 (Old King James Version)

"And when ye shall see Jerusalem compassed with armies, then know that the desolation thereof is nigh.
Then let them which are in Judaea flee to the mountains; and let them which are in the midst of it depart out; and let not them that are in the countries enter thereinto.
For these be the days of vengeance, that all things which are written may be fulfilled.
…Behold the fig tree, and all the trees;
When they now shoot forth, ye see and know of your own selves that summer is now nigh at hand." Luke 21:20-22,29-30. (Old King James Version).

These predictions and others could be that of an attack on Iran on or near Hanukah or Christmas Eve or Day. Haggai 2:19 prediction of trouble happening when it's not harvest time, which is winter time when there is no harvest. The month of Chisleu that Zechariah 7:1 predicts is the ninth month on the fourth day, which could be December 4-7 January 4-7, 2012-2013 when these events happen on. See also Colossians 2:16-17, Matthew 24:19-20, Daniel 12:4, Luke 21:9-11, Ecclesiastes 7:14. Those verses are predictions of trouble on a new moon (=trumpet or air raid sirens), Sabbath day (Saturday-Sunday) on a Holiday or solemn day (=Hanukah, Christmas, Passover, true Christmas Eve and Day=June 12=Old Style Calendar and/or 24-25 NS), days of cheerful feasts (=Zechariah 8:19) and in winter, which the word winter can be translated fall or autumn or in the spring or summer by the other prophecies. Will the Mayan calendar ending December 21, 2012 be the time of this war or sometime in December-January or April-June of 2012 or 2013? Revelation 11:10 and Luke 21:34-36 predicts a month or time of partying, overeating and drinking, giving of gifts one to another all over the whole earth as a time of trouble which can mean not only Hanukah and Christmas Day, but also New Year's Eve and Day on December 31-January 1, 2012-2013. Is Revelation chapter 11 three and a half days that of three and a half days from December 20-21, 2012 to December 24-25-26, 2012 when a attack comes or a counter attack comes from the first attack on December 20-21, 2012? The Mayan prophecies, along with II Peter 3:2-7 and Luke 21:34-36, may predict December 21, 2012 is when the Mayan calendar ends on and many think something will happen then, but nothing does. So they mock God, Christians and the Bible for those prophecies and go about celebrating Christmas Eve and Day by partying with much food, drinks and giving of gifts then sudden destruction comes then or have already came in April-June of 2012 and no end or Second Coming or Rapture happened then so they mock the ancient prophecies. See Luke 21:34-36 and Revelation 11:10 for these times of giving gifts one to another all over the world, which we do on Christmas Eve and Day and all the partying (=drunkenness) we do in celebrating that day. The planet Mars (=Tuesday=red dragon) of Revelation chapter 12 (=2012) also is known as the "god of war," which may happen on Christmas Eve and Day of December 24- 25, 2012. December 25, 2012 is a Tuesday. In Ecclesiastes 7:14 it predicts that the day of prosperity (=Christmas Day) is the same day as adversity (war). II Peter 3:2-7 prediction may mean that Israel is destroyed in this war as their fathers fell asleep (died) in and Jesus did not come back to save them that many will say and mock "where is the promise of his coming for since the fathers fell asleep things continue as they were since the beginning." See II Peter 3:2-7 and my book entitled *2012, which is included in this book.*

The wise men of the Bible that came to worship Jesus at His First Coming most likely were from ancient Persia or the Medes, which is Iran. Will Iranian rulers cause Jesus Second Coming or His Coming secretly to save and protect Israel at these times?

April 6, 30 A.D. was a Thursday when Jesus was crucified and it was a full moon and the beginning of Passover. The year 586 B.C. when the Babylonians came and destroyed the Jewish Temple at Jerusalem the full moon was near April 6. In 1555 A.D. on April 6 there was a full moon and according to one author claimed Nostradamus began his writings of the prophecies on a Good Friday the day before on April 5, 1555 A.D. See C1:Q42. April 6, 2012 is a full moon and the beginning of Passover on a Friday evening (Sabbath Day). Matthew 24:32 and Luke 21:20-26, 29-30 predictions of leaves forming on the trees (spring time) and Jerusalem filled with armies could refer to 66-70 A.D. when the Romans came around Passover (spring time) and then killed many Jews, scattered them around the world and destroyed the Jewish Temple at Jerusalem on the same date as the Babylonians did in July-August (ninth of Av) of 586 B.C.

The ancient Egyptian carving from the temple Hathor shows the Dragon's tail (Draco's) goes down to a circle on top of Libra with a man in it and a jackal or dog on top of it. The jackal is a dog and the Chinese polar opposite of the Dog Year is the Dragon's Year of 2012 on a full moon in the Aries sign the polar opposite of Libra. April 6, 2012 is a Good Friday when in the evening is the beginning of Passover and is the Ram sign called Aries as the sign of the Lamb. Is this when Israel attacks Iran? Is this when the Dragon pulls down a third of the stars as the ancient carving predicts as well as Revelation chapter 12 predicts? See drawings of that ancient Egyptian carving in my book entitled *The Experiment at Philadelphia*.

Or will this attack happen on the true Christmas Eve and Day by Old or new style calendars on June 12 or 24-25, 2012- 2013? Are the "days of Noah" a key to when this attack may happen on in the 9-10 or 19-20th day of May or June of 2012- 2013?

In Daniel chapter 10 it predicted Israel would attack Iran (=Persia) on the first month and 24th day, which is April. Then within 21 days or three weeks Iran attacks Israel and Israel returns to attack (=fight) Iran. These prophecies recorded in Daniel chapter 10 were written in the third year of Cyrus in April of 536 B.C. The Chinese Year of the Ox was 536 B.C. when Daniel chapter 10 was written. Add the 21 days or three weeks as three years to the Year of the Ox (2009 A.D.) and it equals April 2012 when these events happen. The delay of three weeks or 21 days in Daniel chapter 10 might mean Israel delays its attack on April 6, 2012 till April 27, 2012 or on April 23-25, 2012 which was the first month and 24th day in 536 B.C. Or does it mean Israel's attacks starts on April 14-17, 2012, which is the Bible's first month and 24th day? The name of "Cyrus" in Daniel 10:1 in Hebrew means the "sun", which is our Pisces sign. And Cyrus in Isaiah 44:28 is called the "shepherd", which rules our Aries sign. April 6, 2012 is the Aries sign (shepherd) and star time of Pisces (sun).

Joel 2:23-32 and Acts 2:17-27 in the Bible predict the Coming of the Holy Ghost right after the first month when the former and latter rains had finished. See Joel 2:28. It predicts those times of a darken sun and moon and blood, smoke and fire in the land in some sort of attacks or wars. John chapter 16 where Jesus said He soon will be gone and a little while to when He would be back was talking about Him leaving the earth on May 19-20 and ten days latter on Pentecost (May 29) He would return as the first time with the Holy Ghost. He said those things in that chapter of John on the night He was capture after the last supper at or near midnight. Those events would have been on April 5-6, 30 A.D., which was a Wednesday into Thursday, a full moon and the beginning of Passover that began the evening of April 6, 30 A.D. Were these events and the ancient prophecies predicting the Holy Ghost to appear again (afterward-Joel 2:28) after Passover and April 6, 2012 in May-June of 2012? The Holy Ghost of John chapter 16 was meant for the latter days and May of 30 A.D. was not the latter days. There could be a two fold fulfillment of these prophecies one in 30

A.D. and another in 2012 in April-May-June when God shows His Spirit of truth to many at that time. That time is when Auriga the Charioteer constellation and Taurus the bull or ox and seven stars appears behind the sun, which Psalms 68:17 predicts as 20,000 chariots (people and/or angels) appear and the knowledge of the end times increases just as Daniel 12:4 predicted. These prophecies could also mean that these events of attacks on Iran and Israel happen in May-June of 2012 on the dates mentioned in this book. Or they happen in April the first month then afterwards the prophecies are made known in May-June of 2012 when the law was given on Mount Sinai long ago in the Year of the Ox (=Taurus=May-June) just as Psalms 68:17 predicts when chariots and angels appear to tell them of this new knowledge. See Malachi chapters 3-4.

Daniel 9:27 predicts a "one week" time period from when the end time war comes to the end. The week is that of seven years as Ezekiel 4:6 tells us to change day for a year. If these events happen in December 2012 or 2013 then the end comes in 2019-2020. Are those seven years the 70 weeks of Daniel 9:24 minus the zero (70-0=7) and the 70 years (70-0=7) Daniel 9:2 and Zechariah 7:5 predicts? Are they seven years added to these times in 2012-2013? The "abomination of desolation" in Daniel 9:27 could mean the antichrist and/or satan stands not in the Holy place in a new rebuilt Jewish temple, but inside the sun's core at the end of these seven years. By doing that at that time would cause our sun to go into a supernova which destroys the earth and the whole solar system. It would cause great earthquakes, hail, heat, fire and noise as Revelation chapters 6:12-17, 11:19, 16:18 and II Peter 3:1-18 predicted. In Daniel 9:27 the word "overspreading" maybe what starts this seven year count down, which word means the overspreading of the 1967 borders of Israel in the six day war, which angered so many for so long. One preacher calculated that a generation was 51.4 years long. When you add that generation of 51.4 years to 1967 it equals 2018, which runs over into January-February 2019 by the Chinese calendar as when the end happens. Another preacher put a time table starting in December of 2012 plus seven years to the end in 2019.

Adding seven years to February 27, 2012, plus or minus three days, equals January 20-21, 2019. Will we see Israel attack Iran on February 27, 2012 or some other great event happen then? Or is it the time when this book is sent to the publisher or the publisher receives it between then (Saint Valentine's Day) and February 27, 2012? February is known as the heart month not only because of Saint Valentine's Day, but because of medical reasons was picked for heart health. This is the intent or thoughts of God's heart as Jeremiah predicted.

Chapter Eleven

Predictions for 2015

Does Revelation 8:1-13, 9:1-5 and chapters 11-12 predict three woes (troubles) to happen in August 10, 2013, August 10, 2014 and August 10, 2015, plus or minus three days? The one woe could cause smoke to come upon the earth covering a third of the stars, along with a very great earthquake and volcano eruption. Those events would cause a great mountain to be thrown into the sea causing a 100 or 2500-3000 feet high or more tidal waves to hit the Eastern Coast of Florida and the U.S. Read what the Bible predicts:

> "And the second angel sounded, and as it were a great mountain burning with fire was cast into the sea: and the third part of the sea became blood;" Revelation 8:8. (Old King James Version).

> "And the fifth angel sounded, and I saw a star fall from heaven unto the earth: and to him was given the key of the bottomless pit.
> And he opened the bottomless pit; and there arose a smoke out of the pit, as the smoke of a great furnace; and the sun and the air were darkened by reason of the smoke of the pit."
> Revelation 9:1-2 (Old King James Version).

> "And the fourth angel sounded, and the third part of the sun was smitten, and the third part of the moon, and the third part of the stars; so as the third part of them was darkened, and the day shone not for the third part of it, and the night likewise.
> And I beheld, and heard an angel flying through the midst of heaven, saying with a loud voice, Woe, woe, woe, to the inhabiters of the earth by reason of the other voices of the trumpet of the three angels, which are yet to sound!"
> Revelation 8:12-13 (Old King James Version).

Is this describing a volcano eruption that smoke and ash covers over the third part of the U.S.? Is the fifth angel to sound that releases this smoke the fifth sign of our Zodiac, which is Leo the lion sign on August 10-11, 2015? Leo is ruled by the sun and fire where lava comes up from hell and causes volcanoes to erupt with smoke and ash. The smoke and ash then destroys trees, grass and crops causing a great famine, which locust are known to eat the crops causing crop failure from them and the smoke from the bottomless pit, which is where fire and brimstone from hell comes up out of volcanoes. See in the Bible Deuteronomy 32:22-23. Also Revelation 16:10 predicts the beast's kingdom will be full of darkness. The beast is the son of satan the dragon and as I will show was born in Florida or off its coast in the Bahamas. Does the whole U.S. become dark from this volcano eruption or a third of the south where the beast was born?

One cable station called *The History Channel* aired in 2011 a program called *Countdown to Armageddon* that told of a great crack that was open on a island with a volcano off the West Coast of Africa in the Canary Islands. They said if the volcano erupted with an earthquake half the island where the crack is will slide into the Atlantic Ocean and cause 2,500-3000 feet high or more tidal waves to race across the Atlantic Ocean right towards Florida and the Eastern U.S. Coast and totally or partially destroy it for at least 20 miles inland. Is this what the book of Revelation chapters 8-9 and 12 meant? Is that what Revelation 8:8 mountain with fire falling into the sea meant as this event of a volcano in the Canary Islands erupting and sending part of the island into the sea causing this great tidal wave and destruction? Is chapter 8 verse 8 of Revelation a clue to the eighth month of August in 2015-2016 when this drastic event happens? Is Revelation verse 8 of chapter 8, along with the second (number two) angel to sound, that of August the eighth month (=chapter 8) and the eighth day (=verse 8), plus two (angel=8+2=10) equal August 10, 2015 when this event happens? Will the earth on the Eastern sea board of the U.S. and in Florida swallowed up the flood so it doesn't go inland more than 20 miles saving the one woman born May 19 and other women and men just as the book of Revelation 12:15-17 predicted? It also predicted that when that event happens and the serpent or satan sees he didn't kill the one woman or women and men and the one child of the woman, now a grown man, by this flood (tidal wave) he will set out to make war with her seed the Jews and Christians and God's two witnesses living in North Carolina and Virginia Beach by this tidal wave or some other means. Is that war the serpent makes with her seed a attack or war in Israel and war with Christians as the tidal wave that hits the Eastern Coast of Florida and the U.S., or by other means over a space of three and a half years later? The book of Revelation 12:15-17 predicts this:

> "And the serpent cast out of his mouth water as a flood after the woman, that he might cause her to be carried away of the flood.
> And the earth helped the woman, and the earth opened her mouth, and swallowed up the flood which the dragon cast out of his mouth.
> And the dragon was wroth with the woman, and went to make war with the remnant of her seed which keep the commandments of God, and have the testimony of Jesus Christ." Revelation 12:15-17 (Old King James Version).

Does Revelation 12:14 predict this one woman born May 19 to flee into the wilderness (South) and stay there for three and a half years protected from the serpent's wrath. Naples, Florida is South West of Central Florida and may protect her from these tidal waves and hurricanes because of all the land in between it and the Eastern Coast of Florida. How it will protect from other storms, attacks and ash and smoke from the volcano is not clear. There's to the East of Naples, Florida a place called The Great Cypress Swamp and the Everglades towards the South as great places that the Bible calls "wilderness" as Revelation 12:14 predicted. Whether the one woman is to flee there or North and inland is not clear at this time.

Chapter 12 of Revelation tells of time, times and a half or 1260 days when satan is cast out heaven and comes down to the earth. At this time he knows he has a short time (three and a half years) and goes to destroy God's people the Jews (Israel) and Christians (U.S.=God's two witnesses?) with a flood (tidal wave) caused by an volcano eruption cause by the dragon in hell at the time of the old serpent called the devil or satan when he first fell. In my book *The experiment at Philadelphia* I tell how satan first fell from heaven in August and was born in Florida or the Bahamas off the coast of Florida known as the city of Atlantis. Was Revelation chapter 12 predicting trouble for Florida in August of 2015 or 2016 by this great tidal wave (flood=Revelation 12:16)? Then three and a half years later (time, times and a half or 1260 days) will come the end? Counting backwards from the end in January 21, 2019, the exact 1260 days, equals August 10, 2015, plus or minus three days. The end is when satan or the dragon brings a third of the stars from heaven down on earth to completely destroy it. Was this referring to a sun supernova that II Peter in chapter 3 predicts for the end of the world? Are the third of the stars and the great hail the weight of a talent (88-100 pounds each) be parts of the outer sun exploding and coming down upon the earth to cause a great earthquake and destroy every island, mountain and the whole earth just as Revelation 6:12-17 and 16:21 predicts? Or do these events happen three and a half years, or three years from July-August of 2015, which equals July-August or January-February of 2018-2019? At that time there will be a great the roaring of the seas (=waves=tidal waves) and the sun, moon and stars darkened by an earthquake and volcano eruption and/or a solar and lunar eclipses. The solar and lunar eclipses happens in January of 2019 right before and when the sun supernovas and shakes the heavens (planets and moons)? Luke 21:25-27 predicts this:

> "And there shall be signs in the sun, and in the moon and in the stars; and upon the earth distress of nations, with perplexity; the sea and the waves roaring;
> Men's hearts failing them for fear, and for looking after those things which are coming on the earth: for the powers of heaven shall be shaken.
> And then shall they see the Son of man coming in a cloud with power and great glory." Luke 21:25-27 (Old King James Version)

That prophecy could mean both volcano eruptions, tidal waves, attacks, wars and/or storms at these times given that cause the sun, moon and stars to be darkened by those events and/or by solar and lunar eclipses. Will there be at these times strange lights by the sun and the sun giving more light as the light of seven days and/or for about seven days before it goes into a supernova scaring men with heart attacks and greatly disturbs the nations with great perplexity? A sun supernova would shake not only the earth, but all the planets and moons in our whole solar system along with shaking the sun very violently. The son (Jesus) coming with great glory is the strange light by the sun and is the sun giving off great light (glory) at that time in a supernova when Jesus comes back right before to take all people to heaven. See II Peter chapter 3 and Mark 13:13. The glory of His Coming could literally mean the great light coming from the sun when it supernovas. The "cloud" could be smoke and ash from the volcano, a storm, angels, mushroom clouds from a nuclear war or attacks and/or smoke from the sun supernova that ascends up forever as Babylon is fallen for the last time and as her smoke arises up forever just as Revelation predicted. The great heat of Revelation 16:8-9 and Isaiah 30:26, 24:23 might be shortly before these times when the sun goes into a great supernova. At that time the sun becomes much stronger in light and causes the moons and planets to increase in light as the sign of His coming in great glory. Then immediately after tribulation in those days the stars from heaven fall and the heavens shake after these signs in the sun, moon and stars and the seas and waves roaring in tidal waves or storms.

> "For then shall be great tribulation, such as was not since the beginning of the world to this time, no, nor ever shall be." Matthew 24:21 (Old King James Version)

> "Immediately after the tribulation of those days shall the sun be darkened, and the moon shall not give her light, and the stars shall fall from heaven, and the powers of the heavens shall be shaken:

And then shall appear the sign of the Son of man in heaven: and then shall all the tribes of the earth mourn, and they shall see the Son of man coming in the clouds of heaven with power and great glory." Matthew 24:29-30 (Old King James Version)

"Immediately after tribulation in those days" could mean immediately after the earthquakes, volcano eruption with tidal waves and smoke to darkened the sun, moon and stars, war or attacks by nuclear bombs, then will the stars fall and then another great tribulation happens when the sun goes into a supernova. I looked up meteor showers for August and January and there are two sets that appear shortly after or before the dates given on August 10, 2013-2018 and January 21, 2019. They are the Perseids meteor shower of August 11-13, 2013-2018 and the Quadrantids January 3, 2019, plus or minus three days each. Is this what the above verses meant by stars falling from the sky (heaven) immediately after tribulation? It all makes sense this way because you have the smoke, heat, light and the great troubles on earth at this time due to those events. Then a day or two or seven days later the stars fall from the sky in these meteor showers. After that pieces of the sun as stars start hitting the whole earth destroying all islands and mountains and the earth and solar system shaking the heavens with great violence.

During these times a strange light may be seen near the sun, which is the Son of man coming with great glory to take all people off the earth before it's destroyed and taking them to heaven. Comets, asteroid impacts on earth or other moons or planets, and also strange lights and darkness, with solar and lunar eclipses may also occur at this time along with other supernovas and strange lights in other stars way out in space seen at night and day. Revelation 16:8-9 and verse 10 predicts great heat possibly from volcanoes and/or the sun followed by great darkness in the kingdom of the beast (U.S.). It fits perfectly with these old prophecies of tribulation from a volcano with its lava having great fire and heat followed by smoke and ash from it causing darkness in the U.S. and making the sun, moon and stars grow dark.

Will the sun flaring up to seven times mean solar flares and possible disruption or stopping of our TV's, radios, E- mails, internet, phones and electricity? It's no wonder Luke 21:25-26 predicts men's hearts failing them for fear of the things coming upon the earth after these signs from heaven, storms, volcanoes and tidal waves.

These events of volcano eruptions, tidal waves, hurricanes, attacks or wars and earthquakes for July-August of 2014-2015- 2016-2017-2017-2018-2019 are all recorded in these scriptures:

"The burden of the desert of the sea. As whirlwinds in the south pass through; so it cometh from the desert, from a terrible land.
A grievous vision is declared unto me; the treacherous dealer dealeth treacherously, and the spoiler spoileth. Go up, O Elam: besiege, O Media; all the sighing thereof have I made to cease." Isaiah 21:1-2 (Old King James Version).

"Behold, a whirlwind of the Lord is gone forth in fury, even a grievous whirlwind: it shall fall grievously upon the head of the wicked.
The anger of the Lord shall not return, until he has executed, and till he have performed the thoughts of his heart: in the latter days ye shall consider it perfectly."
Jeremiah 23:19-20. (Old King James Version).

"And the Lord shall be seen over them, and his arrow shall go forth as the lightning: and the Lord God shall blow the trumpet, and shall go with whirlwinds of the south."
Zechariah 9:14 (Old King James Version).

In these prophecies Isaiah 21:1-2 predicts "whirlwinds" would happen, which is the plural of that word the same as Zechariah 9:14. Isaiah 21:1-2 also predicts the "desert" twice and a "terrible land" the same as Isaiah chapter 18 does, which describes the United States. Are the "deserts" that of Africa where those terrible whirlwinds come from? The Canary Islands are off the Coast of West Africa and Africa has one on the greatest deserts of the world. Also the desert mentioned twice and the south mentioned twice in Isaiah 21:1-2 and Zechariah 9:14 all mean wilderness and the south where Florida is. And Jeremiah 23:19-20 predicts that these whirlwinds fall upon the head of the wicked. The wicked is satan's son born long ago in Florida or off its coast near the Bahamas. It also says we will know this prophecy perfectly in the latter days when the thoughts of His (God's) heart is known. The thoughts of His (God's) heart may mean these books I written and the heart sign of Leo ruled by the sun and fire that causes volcano eruptions and tidal waves from Africa to this terrible land (=great land) of the U.S. in the south (Florida, which is the home of the first wicked and first antichrist). If the prophecies of this book come true on August 10, 2015, plus or minus three days, then we will know perfectly what that prophecy meant. The places of Elam and Media Isaiah 21:1-2 predicts are modern day Iran and the "arrow" of Zechariah 9:14 could be Israel and Iran attack each other at the time of these great tidal waves and/or hurricanes. They may all happen around the same time or in July-August 2013-2014-2015-2016-2017-2018 or January of 2019.

The words "whirlwinds" or "whirlwind" in those Bible verses above are after the Hebrew words of 5492, 5486 and 5488 in the Hebrew dictionary of the *Strong's Concordance of the Bible*. The Hebrew word 5492 means this: "hurricane, storm, Red Sea, tempest." The word 5486 means this: "to snatch away…i.e. terminate: consume, have an end, perish, x be utterly." The Hebrew word 5488 means this: "a reed, the papyrus:- flag, Red {sea}, weed." The Red Sea is where Moses and the Israelites cross over where Mount Sinai is near on the other side which Moses got the law from in May-June. In May-June of 2014 is when we seen in my books that the sun is near Auriga, The Charioteer, when 20,000 people read this book and my others because of angel visitations just as Psalms 68:17 predicts. Then the next year after that in July-August we see the earthquakes, volcano eruptions and tidal waves (whirlwind). The papyrus and Mount Sinai predicted in Psalms 68:8, 17, along with Jeremiah 23:19-20's "whirlwind" might mean in the Hebrew dictionary these books of mine. The ancients made books from the papyrus weed. The books (papyrus=books) could be this book and my others that 20,000 read by these months of May-June 2014 when an earthquakes and volcano eruption (Mount Sinai) causes great tidal waves (=whirlwinds) then in July-August of 2014 or 2015-2016. Psalms 68:8 predicts God shakes the earth, brings down the heavens (comet impact?; hurricane?; missiles?; smoke and ash?) and mentions mount Sinai, which could represent a volcano off the African West Coast in the Canary Islands. The flag mentioned in one of those words for whirlwinds is what we read in my book *Predictions for 2013-2014* as "banners" of Song of Solomon 6:10. That word "banners" is connected to the word "anniversary," which is that of a great earthquake or events a year earlier on August 10, 2014, plus or minus three days, which is the Leo sign that rules the heart (thoughts of His heart=Jeremiah 23:19-20) and is ruled by the sun (=volcanoes). The flag and trumpet is that of wars, coming disasters and new moons which comes in July-August of 2014-2015-2016 possibly in the Leo sign of those months, which rules the heart and God's heart when he shows his wisdom through these books of mine and you know without a doubt he is right.

Other Hebrew words for whirlwinds are the Hebrew words 5591 that is connected to 5590, which means: "to rush upon" meaning very fast as tidal waves travel very fast where as hurricanes don't travel very fast. We could of along have been misreading and miss-interpreting the word "whirlwinds". The Bible may have meant, at least in some places, tidal waves for the word "whirlwind" and for the word "flood." The Hebrew word for whirlwind being Hebrew 5590 means: "be sore troubled, come out as a (drive with the, scatter with a) whirlwind." The English Dictionary definition for whirlwind means this: "any circling rush or violent onward course." The circling rush (=fast) could be what the Bible calls tidal waves that happen at these times when people read about in this book along with the date and exactly what happens making the very prophecy perfectly clear just as Jeremiah 23:19-20 predicted on the head (place evil was born) of the wicked in the south (Florida) and/or the White House.

Will a volcano eruption cause these tidal waves and the third of the stars to be darkened as Revelation chapters 8-9 predicts? Or will a comet or asteroid impact in the Atlantic Ocean and/or Africa? Will it be like a fiery mountain falling into the sea and causes smoke and dust if it hits on land or if it impacts in the Ocean and causes great tidal waves? If it hits on land than it will kick up dust that covers and darkens a third of the stars just as Revelation chapters 8:10-11 predicts.

> "And the third angel sounded, and there fell a great star from heaven, burning as it were a lamp, and it fell upon the third part of the rivers, and upon the fountains of waters;
> And the name of the star is called Wormwood: and the third part of the waters became wormwood; and many men died of the waters, because they were made bitter." Revelation 8:10-11 (Old King James Version).

The darkened sun, either by volcano ash and smoke or dust by a comet or asteroid, would cause the crops to fail causing a great famine as the book of Revelation in the Bible predicts for August 10, 2015, plus or minus three days, or July-August of 2014-2015-2016. If you see someone on the rooftop in the summer of 2015 and you live in Florida or the East Coast of the United States than drive away from Florida and the East Coast and go inland as far as you can. In Florida get on I-75 and go north through Georgia then pick up Road 24 and then Road 65 into Indiana and stay there till the trouble is over. Read my book *The Divine Code 3* for more details of these events. If these events happen in the summer (July-August) of 2014-2016 and you see a person on the rooftop then do the same thing just mentioned. If an angel appears to you at one of these times and tells you to flee the area then listen to him and not say the author is insane or in error as Ecclesiastes 5:6 predicts. This angel will be bluish-white and sparkling that makes you smile ear to ear.

The "head of the wicked" that the "whirlwind" falls upon grievously as Jeremiah 23:19-20 predicts could be the comet or asteroid from the planet Wormwood that satan was the head of long ago. That planet was between Mars and Jupiter and the asteroid belt there now along with comets are the remains of that planet. Satan blew that planet up when he fell from heaven to the earth to have his son (fourth beast-antichrist) born in Florida or off the Coast of Florida long ago. See Revelation chapters 8-9 and Amos 5:7-8. If a comet or asteroid hits the earth or ocean it would be from Wormwood and be as a fiery mountain falling into the sea that causes a whirlwind (tidal wave or hurricane or nuclear bomb?) to fall grievously upon the head of the wicked (antichrist or President Obama-Cain White House?) in Florida or the East Coast of the U.S. just as Revelation chapters 8:10-11 and Amos 5:7-8 predicted. And as Revelation chapters 8:10-11 predicts that star would cause the waters to become bitter and people and the wild life die because of the bitter waters (=red tide? Or gases or poison form the comet, asteroid or volcano?).

Update: On September 18, 2011 *The Discovery Channel* ran a documentary called *How will the world end?* In that show it told of a volcano off the West Coast of Africa that has a great crack in it. If the volcano should erupt with an earthquake then part of the island it is on would fall into the sea causing a great tidal wave to head towards Florida and the East Coast of the U.S. It would travel 550 miles an hour and be 100 feet tall and destroy everything inland for 40 miles from Miami to New York according to that show. This volcano and island maybe the same one mentioned above seen on *The History Channel* in the Canary Islands off the West Coast of Africa with a crack in it. Why the differing heights of the tidal wave and miles in land it destroys is different is not known at this time.

These events of earthquakes, volcano eruptions, hurricanes, tidal waves, attacks, wars and comet or asteroid impacts could be for July-August or March-April of 2014-2018, or August 28-29 or September 26-27 of those years, but also in January of 2019 and are times when to flee Florida and the East Coast of the U.S. and to flee from Jerusalem, Israel to the mountains in the East or Petra, Jordan. These ancient prophecies may mean massive destruction for the U.S. by tidal waves (=rivers, streams and waters) and massive destruction of Israel by nuclear fire from Iran (=Elam-Media). See Isaiah 30:25-26. The "towers" in Isaiah 30:25 could mean skyscrapers in New York and other East Coast cities of the U.S. destroyed by these great tidal waves at a time of nuclear fire in Israel and/or the U.S. with nuclear power plants melt down because of an earthquake and/or tidal waves. Isaiah 30:25-26 predicts:

> "And there shall be upon every high mountain, and upon every high hill, rivers
> and streams of waters in the day of the great slaughter, when the towers fall.
> Moreover the light of the moon shall be as the light of the sun, and the light of
> the sun shall be sevenfold, as the light of seven days, in the day that the Lord
> bindeth up the breach of his people, and healeth the stroke of their wound."
> Isaiah 30:25-26 (Old King James Version)

Revelation 8:1-7 predicted the half hour in heaven and a golden censer filled much incense (spices) for the prayers of the saints (Billy Graham and Pat Robertson?) when hail falls from the heavens and sets on fire the trees and grass.

> "And when he had opened the seventh seal, there was silence in heaven about
> the space of half an hour.
> And I saw the seven angels which stood before God; and to them were given
> seven trumpets.
> And another angel came and stood at the altar, having a golden censer: and
> there was given unto him much incense, that he should offer it with the prayers
> of all saints upon the golden altar which was before the throne.
> And the smoke of the incense, which come with the prayers of the saints,
> ascended up before God out of the angel's hand.
> And the angel took the censer, and filled it with fire of the altar, and cast it into
> the earth: and there were, voices, and thunderings, and an earthquake.
> And the seven angels which had the seven trumpets prepared themselves to
> sound.
> The first angel sounded, and there followed hail and fire mingled with blood,
> and they were cast upon the earth: and the third part of trees was burnt up, and
> all green grass was burnt up." Revelation 8:1-7 (Old King James Version).

Were these prediction predicting the volcano eruption and earthquake in August of 2015? The "incense" of the prayers of the saints could be myrrh and frankincense, which are ruled by Aquarius and the Sun that rules Leo. August 10, 2015 is the Leo sign, which polar opposite is the Aquarius sign. And the saints killed at this time or by this time would be praying and their prayers in heaven reaches down to earth along with a meteor shower we see or will see happens shortly after August 10, 2015. This time though they reach the earth in fire and blood (death of people hit by them or burned up by them) and burn up trees and grass. Those verses tell of two or three angels, but are not the last two or three angels or the three angels of Revelation chapter 14. Add two or three days and years to verse 7 of Revelation chapter 8 and it equals 8:7+2- 3=8:10, or our August 9-10, 2015, which is the Leo sign, plus or minus two or three years from 2015 equals 2013-2014 and 2016-2017-2018-2019 when these events may happen. Add three years and a half an hour or year of six months to that date and it equals January 20-21, 2019, which is a lunar eclipse or blood moon when pieces of the sun fall to earth as stars mingled with fire and blood in a sun supernova that burns up trees and all, read closely "all" grass is destroyed. To have that happen that would have to mean a sun supernova causing it. The voices, thunderings and earthquakes, along with the hail are meteor shower or missiles. The hail could mean missiles raining down fire from their tails and once on ground nuclear explosions destroying the trees and grass with fire on Israel and Iran on one of those dates. The one date above is August 9, which in 1945 the U.S. dropped the second atomic bomb on Japan. Will on August 9-10, 2015, plus or minus three days or one year Iran attacks Israel with two or three nuclear missiles launched with fire (=blood) from their tails and landing and exploding with fire burning up the trees and grass. This is the fire mingled with the hail (missiles) that Revelation 8:1-7 predicts. And near this same time a earthquake off the West Coast of Africa from a volcano causing a tidal to hit Florida and the U.S. East coast. The "voices" of Revelation 8:1-7 might mean the sun supernova as II Peter chapter 3 predicts when the sun supernova's it makes a great noise and will shake the earth very violently with hail (missiles) or pieces of the sun destroying the trees and grass. The "lightnings" might mean a storm or hurricane hitting the U.S. at one of these dates.

Isaiah 48:1 predicts Jacob (U.S.) to come out of the waters of Judah. Juda or Judah Revelation chapter 5 states is a lion or our Leo sign (Judah) when August 10, 2015, plus or minus three days equals when a tidal wave (waters) hit the East Coast of the U.S.

> "Hear ye this: O house of Jacob, which are called by the name of Israel, and are come forth out of the waters of Judah..." Isaiah 48:1 (Old King James Version).

Isaiah chapter 29 predicts:

> "Woe to Ariel, to Ariel, the city where David dwelt! Add ye year to year; let them kill sacrifices.
> Yet I will distress Ariel, and there shall be heaviness and sorrow; and it shall be unto me as Ariel.
> And I will camp against thee round about, and will lay siege against thee with a mount, and I will raise forts against thee.
> And thou shalt be brought down, and shalt speak out of the ground, and thy speech shall be low out of the dust, and thy voice shall be, as of one that hath a familiar spirit, out of the ground, and thy speech shall whisper out of the dust.
> Moreover the multitudes of thy strangers shall be like small dust, and the

multitudes of the terrible ones shall be as chaff that passeth away; yea, it shall be at an instant suddenly.

Thou shalt be visited of the Lord or hosts with thunder, and with earthquake, and great noise, with storm and tempest, and the flame of devouring fire.

And their multitudes of all the nations that fight against Ariel, even all that fight against her and her muntion, and that distress her, shall be as a dream of a night vision.

It shall even be as when an hungry man dreameth, and, behold, he eateth; but he awaketh, and his soul is empty: or as when a thirsty man dreameth, and behold, he drinketh; but he awaketh, and, behold, he is faint, and his soul hath appetite: so shall the multitude of all the nations be, that fight against mount Zion.

Stay yourselves, and wonder; cry ye out, and cry: they are drunken, but not with wine; they stagger, but not with strong drink.

For the Lord hath poured out upon you the spirit of deep sleep, and hath closed your eyes: the prophets and your rulers, the seers hath he covered.

And the vision of all is become into you as the words of a book that is sealed, which men delivered to one that is learned, saying, Read this, I pray thee: and he saith, I cannot; for it is sealed:

And the book is delivered to him that is not learned, saying, Read thus, I pray thee: and he saith, I am not learned.

Wherefore the Lord said, Forasmuch as this people draw near me with their mouth, and with their lips do honour me, but have removed their heart far from me, and their fear toward me is taught by the precept of men:

Therefore, behold, I will proceed to do a marvelous work among this people, even a marvelous work and a wonder: for the wisdom of their wise men shall perish and the understanding of their prudent men shall be hid." Isaiah 29:1-14 (Old King James Version).

In Bible chapter/year codes Isaiah chapter 29 is our year 1929 when the Stock Market crashed and there was a great depression during prohibition and no food for the dust bowl in those years and no money to buy food. The prohibition act was made on January 16, 1919 and went into effect on January 16, 1920. The five Ariel's of Isaiah chapter 29 added as five days to January 16, 1919 equals January 21, 1919, which was the Chinese Year of the Sheep or Goat. The year 2015 is the Chinese Year of the Sheep or Goat, which marks the time of three and a half years from August 10, 2015 to exactly January 21, 2019 as 360 day years or 1260 days. And in the year 1920, when prohibition went into effect, just as Isaiah chapter 29 predicted, a man staggers, but is not drunk, dreameth of drinking and awakes and is thirsty and dreams of eating, but awakes faint all could mean these times of the great depression and lack of money for food and famine and no alcohol. Will this happen again in 2013 like in 1929, which was the Chinese Year of the Snake the same as 2013 is? The five Ariel's of Isaiah chapter 29 could be five years added to 2013 or 2018- 2019 when these events happen. Or will its polar opposite of 2013 or 2019 be when the stock markets crashes and economic troubles happens in 2019? The years 1919-1920 when prohibition was voted on and put into effect is the Chinese Years of the Sheep or Goat in 1919 and the Chinese Year of the Monkey in 1920, which to us nowadays are the years 2015-2016 when the stock markets may crash literally? Will it be the New York stock market and/or the Pacific stock market, which is in the city of San Francisco when a great earthquake, great tidal waves and/or attack occurs as Isaiah chapter 29 predicts? Do both suffer crashes in 2013 or 2015-2016 or 2019? The lack of alcohol could be from hops and barley in the great plains of the U.S. that have great drought and heat causing the lack of beer and other alcoholic beverages. Is this due to the volcano eruption and darkness?

Isaiah 29:11-12 predicts a book given to someone learned and they say they cannot understand it because it is sealed. Then it is delivered to someone unlearned and they say I am not learned. In 1985 I advertised my book and got two responses for it from one that sounded like a unbeliever and unlearned and from another who sounded they were learned. The year 1985 is the Chinese Year of the Ox, which polar opposite is the Chinese Year of the Sheep or Goat, which is 2015 when the great trouble happens causing death, economic troubles and famines the same Chinese Year as 1985 and 1919. Then three and a half years later the end comes in January 21, 2019 the same month when prohibition was put forth in January 16, 1919 and enforced on January 16, 1920.

There could be wars, earthquakes, volcano eruptions, storms and tidal waves in both August 10, 2015 and January 20-21, 2019 according to these prophecies. Ariel by the way means "lion of God" or the Leo sign of the lion, which August 10, 2015 is. January 20-21, 2019 is the cusp of the Capricorn sign, which is a sea goat. The ancient Jewish people sacrificed one goat for a sin offering. Could the add year to year and kill sacrifices be that of two years (add year to year=1+1=2), plus one year (sacrifice one goat=one year) equals three years from a lion (=Ariel) to a goat (=sacrifice)? That time period being August 10, 2015 the Leo sign of the lion (=Ariel) and the Chinese Year of the Sheep or Goat, plus three and a half years to January 20-21, 2019 as the cusp of the Capricorn sign that is a sea goat (sacrifice). The lion is the fifth sign (=August 10) the fifth year of 2015 and the Goat as Aries the ram family is given the number 9 after the year 2019. Proverbs 30:30-31 predicts this:

> "A lion which is strongest among beasts, and turneth not away for any.
> A greyhound; and he goat also; and as king, against whom there is no rising
> up." Proverbs 30:30-31 (Old King James Version).

The lion is August 10, 2015 in the Leo the lion sign and the he goat is the cusp of the Capricorn sign on January 20- 21, 2019, which is the Chinese year of the Dog (=greyhound). The Lord's prayer states: Our Father that art in heaven hallow be thy name, thy kingdom come…, might have been a clue to these times as well because God's hollowed named spelled backwards equals dog and January 20-21, 2019 is the Chinese Year of the Dog when God's kingdom comes through the doors of heaven.

The "noise" predicted in Isaiah 29:1-14 might be nuclear missiles (devouring flame, noise and earthquake and tempest or great wind) and/or a sun supernova as II Peter chapter 3 predicts for the end. Isaiah 29:1-14 prediction of a great fire, earthquake, noise, storm or whirlwind (tidal wave) could be the war of August 10, 2015 and those same events in the end time in January of 2019. The add year unto year and let them kill sacrifices in Isaiah 29:1 might mean two years added unto the seventh year of 2017 when a peace treaty comes and people say peace, peace and peace and safety then two years later (the add year to year or two years) the end comes in January of 2019 as two added to 2017 equals 2019 in January the month of when prohibition started.

January 20-21, 2019 at midnight has Leo the lion seen over head. On those same dates at noon the polar opposite of midnight has Pegasus the flying horse behind or near the sun. Was this what Revelation chapter 19 predicted in the stars for Jesus Christ return on a white flying horse shining as bright as the sun or more because the sun is in a supernova phase? And Leo has a star named Regulus known as the "prince" or king and Revelation chapter 19 predicts Jesus comes back riding on the white flying horse with the name King or Kings and Lord of Lords. Revelation 22:20 predicts Jesus comes quickly which a supernova of our sun would be a great light and noise with hail or pieces of it flying towards our earth at tremendous speeds (=quickly). Revelation chapters 14 and 19 puts these events at the grape harvest of July-August from 2013-2018 and/or a half year later in January 2019.

The "arrows"-"arrow" of Dueteronomy 32:22-23 and Zechariah 9:14 might mean many missiles or bombs shot at the White House (=Scorpio) and/or Israel (=Taurus=born May 14=Taurus sign) from Iran or Pakistan. In the stars we see at night the Milky Way runs from Scorpio to Sagittarius to Taurus. See drawing 25 in my book *The Experiment at Philadelphia* page 441. Iran is in the Scorpio zone and Israel is Taurus in which the stars of the Milky Way predicts arrows flying at one another in missiles and bombs in a war in July-August-September-October of 2015-2016 or 2013-2014. Pakistan is in the Sagittarius zone and Washington, D.C. is ruled by Scorpio. Sagittarius is an archer of arrows or missiles and bombs shot at each other in a war between the two places and as is shown in the stars and Milky Way.

President Obama and Mitt Romney birthdays are August 4 (Obama) and March 12 (Romney). And as Ecclesiastics 7:14 predicts the day of prosperity or happiness is the same day as trouble (adversity). Will on August 4 or March 12, 2013-2019 we see this happen on one or both of their birthdays? Or will Herman Cain's birthday be the time of these events?

Chapter Twelve

The end 1

Revelation 6:12-13 predicts a solar and lunar eclipse and then many stars falling to the ground. January 5-6, 2019 has a solar eclipse or darkened sun (sackcloth) happen on that day. Then on January 21, 2019 there is a lunar eclipse (blood) moon at exactly 12:12 a.m. eastern standard time give or take a few minutes and its duration. That's very close to 12:18 a.m. when I had the vision of lights in my bed room starting at that exact time and lasting for six hours on August 28-29, 1982, which was the Chinese Year of the Dog the same as January 21, 2019 is. Revelation chapters 9 and 11 predict five-six months of trouble and/or three and a half years of trouble. The lights I saw for six hours in August 28-29, 1982 is six months of trouble when the devil comes down to earth knowing he has but a short time as Revelation 12:12 predicts, as well as three and a half years (See Revelation 12:6). Is that "short time" five or six months starting in August 28-29, 2018 to January of 2019? Or is it three and a half years (42 months; 1260 days; or time, times and half) from the ninth of AV or July 16-17 or August 28-29, 2015 or in July-August, 2015 to January of 2019? Jesus predicted in Matthew 25:1-13 predicts a time of the bridegroom to come is a little after midnight in which I showed in my other books to be 12:18 a.m. the same time I saw the vision of lights in August 28-29, 1982 the Chinese year of the Dog. The stars falling to the ground at that time could be pieces of the sun exploding in a supernova as Revelation 6:12- 13 predicts happens when there is a lunar eclipse (blood moon). That will cause every mountain and island to be moved out of its place exactly as Revelation chapter 6 predicted.

The Billy Graham dream I had of him being insane and then sane and I am playing cards may have the following meaning. The deck of cards is 52. The moon rules insane in which we get the word loony from. The moon is given the numbers two and seven in numerology. Multiply two (=moon) times 52 (=cards) equals 104 minus seven (=moon) equals 97 added to Billy Graham's birth year till the time he dies is 97+1918=2015 in July-August of 2015. That is when he and Pat Robertson die taking away God's two witnesses as Revelation chapter 11 predicted. Thus, leaving satan unchecked and thrown out of heaven at that time to cause great earthquakes, storms, wars, terrorist attacks, volcano eruptions and tidal waves, flooding, hail, red tide or oil spills, strange lights in the sky, plane crashes or meteor or comet impacts on earth or other planets or moons, on the ninth of Av or July 16-17, August 28-29, or July- August or September 26-27 of 2015. At that time floods or storms may strike Florida and/or the U.S. as Revelation chapter 12 predicts when satan is cast out of heaven and causes a flood in the south (Florida) and all kinds of trouble for three and a half years or 1260 days. Is that flood another Hurricane like Andrew that hit in southern Florida in August of 1992? The second Iraq war started in the Chinese Year of the Sheep or Goat in 2003. The Chinese Yearly cycle is 12 years from then when in July-August of 2015 there is war again with the U.S. (=spiritual Babylon) which is the Chinese Year of the Sheep or Goat. From then to January of 2019 is when God withdraws the Holy Spirit from the earth by the deaths of Billy Graham and Pat Robertson (by the tidal waves?) and throws out satan from heaven and he comes down to earth having great wrath for a short time of three and a half years. Israel, the U.S. and/or the world at this same time in July-August of 2015 till January 21, 2019 may also witness great earthquakes, tidal waves, wars, attacks, a great falling away to sins, apostasy with much violence, record river flooding and flooding, red tides, hail, drought, heat, cold, blizzards, wild fires, religious fighting and disagreements, economic disasters and very high inflation, strange darkness, strange lights, twisters, great famines, pestilence's, bugs and insect over populated, great man made invention failures, fearful and great signs from heaven (the sky) and other man made and natural disasters. See the Bible's II Thessalonians chapter 2, Haggai, Revelation chapters 8-9, Isaiah chapters 18 and 42, Matthew 24:7-8, both Joel and Acts chapters 2, Luke 21:19-11,26, Revelation chapter 6 and Psalms 99:8.

Billy Graham and Pat Robertson might die before the tidal wave or the end happens as Isaiah 57:1 predicts the taking away of them from the evil to come. This means both could die between now (August 11, 2011) and August 10-13, 2013-2018 or January 21, 2019 having them taken away from the evil to come as Isaiah 57:1 predicted. Or do they die in the tidal wave or of natural causes or shooting or by the antichrist shortly before (three and a half days) the end on January 21, 2019?

II Thessalonians 2:8 predicts the antichrist is killed by "the brightness of his coming:…. Does this mean when Jesus comes back there's a supernova that shines very bright and destroys the antichrist and the earth with its glory as other Bible prophecies predict? And if that time is a Sunday-Monday then it's like in creation and the creation of Adam and Eve, which equals the one becoming two and the two becomes one. Sunday has the word sun in it, which is given the number one. Monday has the word moon in it and is given the number two. January 20-21, 2019 is a Sunday-Monday when the two become one like in creation and how Adam and Eve started children. In creation the very first particle was one. It then broke in two and made two. The two then collided (big-bang) and made one and all particles in the Universes. With Adam and Eve God made first Adam as one. He then took a rib out of Adam when he was asleep (=outer space=nothing) and it made two. Adam and Eve then had sex, or became one, to make all people on earth just like creation. The sun is male and the moon is female as the days of Sunday-Monday can mean when they join as one as the bride and bridegroom at midnight that the U.S. has as joining of the two days. In the end satan stands inside the core of the sun to bring the end just as the beginning when the two become one.

Is the fifth angel sounding his trumpet and the half an hour of Revelation 9:1-2 and 8:1 five-six months and years from August 2013 to August 2018, plus five or six months to January 21, 2019? The half an hour in Revelation 8:1 would be a half a year from July-August of 2018 when smoke from a great volcano erupts and causes the tidal waves and smoke darkening the sun, moon and stars for the third part of the U.S. and the third part of the day and night as we read earlier in the book of Revelation chapters 8-9. Is the "fifth" angel the fifth month to the Bible's calendar, which is July-August when in 2015 or 2018 these events happen? Five months from August is January. Is the fifth also the fifth year of 2015? Will something happen in July-August of 2018, then some things else in December 24-25, 2018 and then other events and the end in January of 2019? The Bible does give those exact dates and scenarios. Are the earthquakes, volcano eruptions, tidal waves, smoke darkening the sun, moon and stars and all other events predicted in this book happen in January of 2019?

The Mayan's started their calendar in August 11 or 12 or 13 by some different authors. See *The Mayan Prophecies* by Adrian G. Gilbert and Maurice M. Cotterell page 184; *The Orion Prophecy* by Patrick Geryl and Gino Ratinckx page 154; and *The Mayan Factor* by Jose Arguelles page 72. That's awful close to August 10, 2015 or 2018 when this earthquake and/or volcano eruption and tidal waves could hit. Maybe time differences could put it August 11 or 12 or even the 13, or plus or minus three days. Is the exact date August 10-11?

If the volcano erupts and causes a great tidal wave that hits Charlotte, North Carolina and Virginia Beach, Virginia and kills Billy Graham (=if he lives there in Charlotte, North Carolina?) and Pat Robertson if he lives in Virginia Beach, Virginia, then that ancient prophecy will be fulfilled as Revelation chapter 11:7 and 14:13 predicted long ago. It predicted that the beast (=satan) that ascended out of the bottomless pit (hell=volcanoes) causes tidal waves (flood) and what kills (=satan is hell and fire where volcanoes come from) God's two witnesses (=Billy Graham and Pat Robertson). UFOs (beast-satan-antichrist) have been reported to appear near volcanoes near or during when they erupt. This was reported on the cable show *The History Channel* on a show called *Ancient Aliens* in 2011. So the prophecy could literally be true as hell causes volcano eruptions just as the book Deuteronomy 32:22-23 predicted. The "arrows" on those verses could mean bullets or missiles. And Revelation 14:13 predicts those who die at this time in Babylon (U.S.) will rest in heaven from their labors and their works of the gospel do follow them.

Revelation chapter 12 predicts satan tried to kill a child by a flood (storm=hurricane) at his birth from a woman who was born September 27 and fled into the south in 1981 some 27 years (hand=27 bones) after his birth. Revelation chapter one in chapter/year codes is our 1981 A.D. And Revelation 1:10 states John wrote or experience the book of Revelation on the Lord's Day, which is Sunday. Through my other books I state that the book of Revelation happened on June 12, 96 A.D. by the old Julian calendar, which was a Sunday (Lord's Day). Add three and a half months instead of years as time, times and a half or 1260 days as Revelation chapter 12 predicts a woman to travel to the south in that time to June 12, 1981 and it equals September 27, 1981, which was a Sunday (Lord's Day) and when me and my mom and dad traveled from the North East to Florida arriving in Ocala almost exactly at noon to 1 p.m. three and a half days from when we started counting each day. That day was my mother's birthday who gave birth to me in a storm or flood.

Add 35 years counting each year and it equals a time that satan (red dragon=12 month=August=red lava flow from erupting volcano) again tries to kill this same child, now a grown man, again with a flood (tidal waves and/or hurricanes) at this time in July-October (August 28-29?; September 26-27?; October 15?) of 2015 or 2016. That man could be called God's two witnesses and killed by these same great tidal waves (floods-hurricanes) that Revelation chapter 12 predicts caused by the volcano eruption. The "red dragon" of Revelation 12:3 is satan who is king of volcano eruptions that gives off red lava that are caused by him in hell. The sun, moon and 12 stars of the woman in Revelation chapter 12 could mean a Sunday-Monday on August 9-10-11, 2015-2016 when this flood happens. The "sun" is Sunday and the "moon" is Monday. The 12 stars could be August 12, 2013-2014-2015-2016-2018, or the Pisces zones that rule Florida where this man lives. Florida is also where the dragon's son was born there or off the coast in the Bahamas, which was part of the ancient city of Atlantis.

The red dragon, woman with the sun and moon and 12 stars could also have another meaning. That meaning is that the red dragon is a full moon lunar eclipse known as a blood (red) moon in the Chinese Year of the Dog polar opposite of the Dragon. And Revelation chapter 12 that predicts this red dragon, sun, moon and 12 stars has 17 verses in it. Could the chapter number 12 and the 12 stars along with 17 verses mean 12:17 a.m. in the morning on Sunday into Monday January 21, 2019, which is the start of a full moon and/or a lunar eclipse (blood moon)? The full moon then according to the book *Astronomical Tables of the Sun, Moon and Planets* by Jean Meeus page 197 states it happens at exactly 12:17 a.m. on January 21, 2019. It could be off a couple of minutes plus or minus, but is awful close to the exact dates and times given here and in my other books. See my book *The Divine Code 3* available by December of 2012. And both Revelation chapter 12 and 12 stars mentioned in it equals 21 reverse, which would be January 21, 2019 in the Chinese Dog Year in its 12th month (=12 stars and chapter 12) of the Chinese calendar, which would be January.

God saves this woman mentioned above in 2006 (=12 years= 2018-2019) who flees like an eagle into the south. The eagle is a bird or air sign of Libra. And September 25-27, 1981, when she flees into the south took three and a half days and is the Libra sign of the air and she arrives on her birthday of September 27, 1981 a Sunday just as August 10, 2015 is some 35 years later. She flees by car into the south with her son for exactly 3.5 days/years (1260 days, time, times and a half of time or 1260

Revelation 12:6, 14) till a flood tries to kill her son again on that date or in July-September. Delete the decimal point of the 3.5 days/years and it equals 35 years from 1981+35=2015, counting each year, or the year 2016. The "time, times and a half" or 1260 days or 42 months could also mean "time" as one decade, "times" as two decades and a "half" as five years (=half a decade). Add them together and it equals 35 years. See Revelation chapter 12, which predicts when satan, or that old serpent and dragon tries again to kill her son.

Is September 26-27 near her birthday and on her birthday when we see another predicted event happen 12 years later like what was suppose to happen on that date in 2003? Twelve years added to September 26-27, 2003=September 26-27, 2015. The book in the Bible, Colossians 2:16-17, predicts that future events happen on older dates as signs of the future dates. Are these exact dates September 7-8, 19, 26-27, 2015-2016?

Song of Solomon chapters 2 and 6:10,13 predicts travel in the year 2002 (=Chapter 2), plus 12 years in 2014. Then in chapter 6 of Song of Solomon equals 2006 the Chinese Year of the Dog Year in 2018-2019 when four returns or four years more added to 2014, which equals 2018-2019, which is when the end comes.

Daniel 12:11-13 predicts the end in 2625 years from the time the abomination of desolation occurs. The "abomination of desolation" is when the king of Babylon came to Jerusalem and stood in the Holy of Holies in the Jewish Temple there or placed a pagan statue there in 606-607 B.C. Subtract 2625 years from then and it equals 2019-2020, or counting each year 2018-2019 A.D. Is that when satan or the antichrist stands in the core of the sun where the Holy of Holies is in heaven causing it to go into a supernova making it very bright and killing him (satan and the antichrist and all demons) and is not only a very great abomination, but what causes desolation (=destruction) of the whole solar system. See Matthew 24.15.

Chapter Thirteen

Chinese Yearly Cycles

In the introduction of this book I told you how Chinese astrology has 12 yearly cycles instead of our astrology of 12 monthly cycles. I also show how going back in time by 12 yearly cycles can show us what will happen in the future by 12 yearly cycles.

The year 2015 counting backwards by 12 yearly cycles equals 2003, 1991, 1979 and 1967. Those years in history has some important dates and events. In 2003 on March 19-20 near a full moon came the second Iraq war. The year 1991 on January 16-17, near a new moon came the first Iraq (Babylon) war. Then in 1979 on January 31 and February 1 and November 4 came the over throw of Iran's leader and for the religious leader to return from France to take control on January 31-February 1, 1979. On November 4, 1979 Iranians stormed the U.S. embassy and took U.S. hostages for 444 days. Three Mile Island nuclear power plant had a melt down on March 28, 1979. Will in March of 2015 (=1979) we see another nuclear power plant disaster and/or be attacked like in Iran by Israel then Iran attacks Israel? And finally on June 5-10, 1967 was the Israeli six day war. Will Israel see some war or attack in June or July-August of 2015?

Martin Luther King, Jr., was assassinated on April 4, 1968 and RFK was assassinated on June 4-5, 1968. Will another political leader be assassinated in the White House or in the south, or by tidal wave or by plane crash in 2015 or 2016? The year 1968 is not exactly in the Chinese Yearly cycles of 12. It is one year off, but the prophecies can happen in that year plus or minus one year. Does these prophecies predict trouble with Iraq known as Babylon, or a spiritual Babylon of Turkey, Rome, Italy, the U.S. and Los Angeles in 2015-2016? And/or will Iran and Israel face trouble then? Is the third of the stars we saw in the first chapter of this book that which Revelation predicts be missiles or bombs at these times of July-August or some other month (March? June?) in 2015 on these nations of Babylon? Does Isaiah 40:1-2 predict double trouble for Jerusalem at these times. Was the word double predicting another war in Israel in June like in 1967, or some other months in 2015-2016? Are the "arrows" of Deuteronomy 32:22-23 and Zechariah 9:14 that of bullets that kills the U.S. or Israeli President or God's two witnesses or someone famous.

Chapter Fourteen

Coded earthquakes

Note: Before we begin this chapter remember what was said in the introduction that prophecies can give many details and dates to events, but then fail and come true later on on the dates given in that failure. If these two earthquakes fail to happen at these dates and years look for future earthquakes using the same method in the future for other earthquakes and predict when they or one might come. For example, if one earthquake happens on one date in one year and the one year anniversary of that quake happens the next year on a full moon then look for a earthquake then, plus or minus a day, but on or near a full moon. This may not always happen, but as this chapter documents it has already happened twice. Keep a diary of earthquakes happening each year on the exact date and hour if possible, then look for that date the next year to see if it is a full moon. This doesn't always happen because the full moon is different in each year.

Over the years I have noticed a pattern in earthquake (and tidal waves?) predictions. There is a code that can sometimes predict earthquakes. It doesn't happen all the time, but every once an awhile it does. The code is based on Song of Solomon 6:10 "banners" and the Greek word for commotion or earthquakes and the words near them, which are: "second", "Augustus", and "moon" or "brilliancy" (=full moon).

This code worked two times is the past 20 years. How it works is that a major earthquake happens somewhere in the world in one year than on the same date, plus or minus one day, the next ("second") year another major earthquake happens on the same date and on a full moon.

Like I just said this code has happen twice in the past 20 years. It happened once in the great Northridge, California earthquake of January 17, 1994. Then on January 16-17, 1995, a year later, in Kobe, Japan another earthquake happen almost to or on the exact date as the first and it was on or near a full moon.

The second time this code has come true was in December 26, 2003 when a major earthquake hit Iran the day after Christmas. Then on December 26, 2004 ("second") another major earthquake hit Asia along with great tidal waves the day after Christmas and that date was a full moon. I actual thought a week before Christmas if we would see another earthquake the day after Christmas in December of 2004.

If this code is correct and the Bible quote and Greek words mean anything then on August 10, 2014, plus or minus three days a major earthquake (and tidal waves?) will hit some where in the world. Another will strike somewhere in the world on August 10, 2013, plus or minus three days, a year earlier.

Song of Solomon 6:10 predicts this second earthquake as happening in the morning, fair moon or full moon, as the sun and as terrible as an army with banners.

> "Who is she that looketh forth as the morning, fair as the moon, clear as the
> sun, and terrible as an army with banners?"
> Song of Solomon 6:10 (Old King James Version)

When you look up the word "banners" in the Greek dictionary of the *Strong's Concordance of the Bible* it is near the word for memorial (anniversary). That word means on the anniversary of a past event another events happens on that date connected to when armies come with their flags (=banners) in victory.

Will a major earthquake strike somewhere in the world on August 10, 2013, plus or minus three days, then on August 10, 2014, plus or minus three days another great earthquake strikes somewhere in the world on a full moon ("fair moon")? And that second one is on a Sunday (clear as the sun) and in the morning (=EDT or EST or morning time of the place where the quake hits) on the second anniversary ("banners") of the first one. This is just as Song of Solomon 6:10 and Greek words 4579, 4580,4582, 4572 and Hebrew 226, 234, and 1713 in the *Strong's concordance of the Bible* in the Greek and Hebrew dictionaries predicted. The flag or banners used in these verses and dictionaries can mean a signal or sign of coming danger when many armies are approaching. Is that signal of the two armies of the past when Jerusalem was destroyed in July-August of 585 B.C. and 70 A.D.? Will earthquakes, wars, attacks, storms and commotion's such as school shootings or public shootings happen on these dates of July-August in 2013, 2014 and 2018? Are the exact dates from Zechariah 7:3,5 and 8:19 in the fourth and/or fifth month of Av in the Bible's calendar, in which two armies we will see attacked Jerusalem on the same date years apart? The fifth month of Av on the 9th day is when the fast and the two armies attacked Jerusalem. Will on those dates on the 17th of the fourth, or 9th of the fifth, or 19, 21, 26-27, 15 of the seventh month in 2013, 2014 and 2018 we seen again attacks, wars, earthquakes, tidal waves, storms, commotion's and public shootings? Those dates are June 25, July 16-18, 22-24, 2013, August 14-17, 2013, September-October 2013, July 5-7,13-16, 2014, August 2-6, 2014, September-October 2014, July 20-22, 28- 31, 2018 and August 19-22, September 19, 21, 26-27 and October of 15 or September-October 2018 or on new moons in those years and months as shown in a latter chapter. The other dates are July 16-17, 2013, 2014, 2018, August 2, 19 and 28-29, 2013, 2014 and 2018 and September 7-8, 19, 26-27, 2013, 2014 and 2018. July 16-17 has several past disasters happen from the sky on those dates. Like TWA flight 800. The comet that hit Jupiter. And JFK, Jr plane crash all happened on those days. August 2, 1990 was the Iraq invasion of Kuwait. August 19 is when Adam was created. And August 28-29 was when satan fell from heaven. And Zechariah 7:1 and 8:19, and Haggai 2:18 tell of the fourth day and 24th day of Chisleu, which is our months of November-December and when Hanukkah is in 518 B.C. and 520 B.C. The *New Living translation* of the Bible tells us that December 7, 518 B.C. was when the fourth day of Chisleu was. That along with Haggai's date when it was written in 520 B.C. equals the Chinese Year of the Snake on December 7, which in 2013 A.D. and is the fourth day from a new moon (December 3). Could December 6-7, 2013 be a time of double trouble and blessings as those books of Haggai and Zechariah predicts? The year 2013 is the Chinese Year of the Snake the same as 520 B.C. See my other book entitled *The Experiment at Philadelphia* for more details of these events. See the book *Armageddon* by Grant Jeffrey for documentation of this fifth month and ninth day when two great armies came and completely destroyed Jerusalem. For the date December 7 see the book *Today's Parallel Bible* with NIV;NASB;KJV;NLT page 2173 and look at the NLT version on that page and notes below.

The "these so many years" of the fifth month and seventh month that Zechariah 7:3,5 predicted the Jewish people fasted and prayed on was from the years 585 B.C. to 515 B.C. In 585 B.C. the Jewish Temple was destroyed on the ninth of Av (fifth month) and was the Chinese Year of the Rat. The polar opposite of the Rat is the Horse that rules 2014 A.D. and 70 A.D. was the Chinese Year of the Horse the same as 2014 A.D. In 515 B.C. the Jewish people had finished rebuilding the Jewish temple and dedicated it. That year is the Chinese Year of the Dog, which 2018 and part of 2019 A.D. is. These same 70 years from 585 B.C. to 515 B.C. are the "many years" predicted of Zechariah 7:3,

Daniel and Jeremiah and may also be connected to the same time period to the time of the end as shown in the chapter five. The moon phases in 518 B.C. when Zechariah chapter 7 was written is very close to the same moon phase as 2013 making the fourth day of the ninth month be December 6-7, 2013 just as I mentioned above. Moon phases are different each year making lunar calendars different each year along with their feasts and fasts days. The moon phase in 515 B.C. is very close to the same moon phase of 2019 when in January 21, 2019 there is a full moon and lunar eclipse. See the book: *Canon of Lunar Eclipses 1500 B.C.-A.D. 3000* by Bao-Lin Liu and Alan D. Fiala. And Zechariah 8:19 predicts the tenth month, which to our calendar is in December-January (=January 21, 2019?), is when something happens.

According to the book *As Above, So below,* by Alan Oken page 157 Emperor Augustus was born September 23, 63 B.C. The year 63 B.C. was the Chinese Year of the Horse the same as 2014 A.D. We get the name August from the name of the Roman Emperor Augustus. We also get the name Sunday from the sun and the full moon from the phase fair moon as Song of Solomon 6:10 predicts. See chapter 7 for names of the days of the week and month's names. On August 10, 2014 is a Sunday, full moon, August and the Chinese Year of the Horse exactly as predicted.

And as Song of Solomon 6:13 predicts the end will come four years (=four returns) after that on August 10 or August 28-29, 2018, or January 21, 2019, which is still the year 2018 to the Chinese calendar?

> "Return, return, O Shulamite, return, return, that we may look upon thee.
> What will ye see in the Shulamite? As it were the company of two armies."
> Song of Solomon 6:13 (Old King James Version)

The "four returns" of that verse can mean four years added to 2014, which equal 2018 into 2019. The word "return" can mean return to a new year four times or four years later. And the "shulamite" mentioned may be connected to Solomon's name that means "peaceful" and "complete, whole and full under Hebrew words 7999-8004 in the Hebrew Dictionary in the book *Strong's Concordance of the Bible.* The two armies Song of Solomon 6:13 predicts are the two armies that came in July or August in 585- 586 B.C. and 70 A.D. to destroy the Jewish Temple and scatter the Jews. It is called the ninth day of Av, or the month before on the Bible's calendar, and both times those events happened on the same date even though to our calendar it may have been different dates because the Jewish calendar is lunar and ours is solar.

These two earthquakes in August of 2013-2014 might be the only major events of those months of July or August. The wars, terrorist attacks, storms, shootings, volcano eruptions that darkens the skies, famines, pestilence's and other commotion's might come later on as the Bible predicts "by and by" and the beginning of sorrows starts then in 2013-2014. See Luke 21:9 and Matthew 24:8.

Chapter Fifteen

Other predictions for 2013-2014

The flu epidemic of 1918-1919 that killed millions in the Spring of 1918 and peaked in the Fall of 1918 may again happen in those months or December of 2014 into 2015. The years 1918 and 1919 are the Chinese years of the Horse (=2014) and the Year of the Sheep or Goat (=2015). Will we see a new and very deadly form of a flu on those years in which Jesus predicted as a pestilence or epidemic of diseases or flu, which He said would come around when great earthquakes are happening around the world in different (divers) places during a war (=WWI)? See Matthew 24:7:

> "For nation shall rise against nation, and kingdom against kingdom, and there shall be famines, and pestilence's, and earthquakes in divers places." Matthew 24:7 (Old King James Version)

The epidemic or pestilence maybe caused by horses, sheep or goats or birds (=Gemini=Horse=2014) and flying (=Gemini to) things as the Chinese Years of the Horse and Sheep or Goat may predict. Revelation 6:8 predicts a great out break of disease to happen caused by animals. And with the Horse of Chinese astrology being our Gemini sign it could mean birds that the ancient Egyptians believed was connected to the Gemini sign causes this epidemic to start. The world wide epidemic could be for 2018-2019. Read my books of predictions on those years in *Predictions for 2015, 2018 and 2019* coming between now (2011) and December of the year 2012. Will this sicknesses or pestilence's cause sores and fever as Revelation chapter 16 predicts? Or are those predictions of Revelation chapters 6 and 16 that of the "Black death" that hit Europe centuries ago and killed a third of all Europe? Revelation chapters 6 and 16 predicts a quarter of the population killed in which a third is very close to that. Revelation chapter 9 predicts a third of mankind killed by animals carrying disease coming from the bottomless pit where most UFO researchers claim UFOs come from. My book *The antichrist* shows how UFOs are demons coming up out of hell at the center of the earth where there is fire and brimstone. Brimstone can be translated sulfur in which some people claim UFO beings smell like and hell smells like and strange beasts seen on earth smells like (big foot?).

Revelation chapters 6 and 16 predicts people dying with high fever (heat) and black sores on them exactly as Revelation 6 and 16 predicted. It even predicted the disease coming from animal, which the black death was caused by fleas on rats. One cable channel claimed people saw lights in the sky releasing gases into the air and black shadowy figures at the edge of town in the fields (crops-sickle) shortly before the black death appeared. Was the lights UFOs or demons releasing the disease in gas in the sky. The people said shortly after they saw these things people soon began to die. Was the black shadowy figures where we get the term "the grime reaper?" from. And did they cause the black death by UFO beings who we just read are demons from hell at the center of the earth coming up from there (the bottomless pit) just as the book of Revelation predicted. See my book *The Experiment at Philadelphia* drawing 6 page 422 for a drawing of the bottomless pit.

Zechariah 9:14 predicts whirlwinds and arrows to hit the south in 2014. In chapter year codes of the Bible Zechariah chapter 9 is our year 2002 A.D. See Chapter 7: The Codes. Add 12 years of the Chinese cycle and it equals 2014 when great whirlwinds (=storms or hurricanes=plural) hit the south in the U.S. The "arrows" predicted in that same verse could mean an terrorist attacks, or bombs, missile or bullets hitting the southern U.S.. Or it could mean a school or public shooting in the south on a Thursday. Our day of Thursday is the blood covenant when Jesus died on the cross on that day as Zechariah 9:11,14 predicts. Are those predictions near or on a new moon (trumpet of verse 14) and when earthquakes and tidal waves, wars, attacks, shootings and storms are about to happen in July-August of 2013-2014 and 2018? The ancient Jewish people sounded a trumpet at the new moon each month and at the time when war was about to happen. The storms or hurricanes and attacks, wars, terrorist attacks and shooting may happen near each other when these earthquake strikes or the other dates given in this book.

Nostradamus in quatrain C6:Q24 predicts a war when Mars (Leo-or Tuesday) and scepter (=Jupiter=Thursday) happens in Cancer. Leo could mean the Leo sign from July 21-23 to August 22-23, plus a cusp of seven to August 28-30. It could also mean a U.S. President born in Leo as President Obama is. The Cancer sign starts on June 21 to July 21-23, 2014 and star time from July 21-23 to August 21-23, 2014, plus the cusp to August 28-30, 2014. In June of 2002 Pakistan and India were on the verge of war in that year, which is the same Chinese Year as 2014. Will we see them again on the verge of war then in 2014 or some other war or attack in July-August of 2013-2014? A strange thing is happening now (July 15, 2011) and that is India has just been attack by someone and they are already threatening to attack Pakistan if they were the attackers. And U.S. President Obama is reporting to make a deal with congress to raise taxes and wants the deal done by August 2, 2011. Add nine, the number of Mars, which we seen in that Nostradamus quatrain, to 2002, the year we seen connected to these ancient prophecies, and it equals 2011 in Leo sign or star time from July 21-September 23+7=30, 2011 or August 2, 19, 28-29, 2011. Is that when this plane crash could happen or the war between India and Pakistan happens? Is this what Daniel 11:19-20 was predicting as a vile man raising taxes and then takes a trip by plane (=eagle) around the world and it crashes into the ocean and his body is never found or hard to find? Both events are in the July-August-September-October time space a few years earlier than 2013-2014. Will they happen now or as Colossians 2:16-17 predicts are a sign of them happening in our future in 2013-2014, 2015, 2016-2018 in those same months, or March-April and in the same ways?

That same plane crash was predicted for President Clinton in April of 1996, but failed to happen. He was from Little Rock, which Obadiah 1-6 predicts a leader from a "small" (=little) and "rock" (=Edom) would fly like an eagle high in the sky (=airplane) and be brought down to the ground. Will this event happen to him sometime in the future or to another U.S. President in the future? Twelve years of Chinese cycles from 1996 equals 2008, plus six years as the polar opposite, equals 2014 when this plane crash with someone famous happens.

The ancient prophecies of that plane crash are predicted in Obadiah 1-6, Psalms chapter 99, Daniel 11:19-25, Zechariah chapter 11, Jeremiah 23:19-20 and 30:23-24 and Amos 2:14. Those predictions are that of an airplane crash with some leader on board and possibly in the ocean and his body never found or hard to find. This airplane crash maybe by accident caused by mechanical failure or by lightning or storm. These ancient prophecies predict an invention failure as Psalms 99:8 predicted for someone who sits between the Cherubs and is leader of a nation spiritually known as Babylon, which could be the U.S., Rome, Italy, Turkey or Iraq. He raises taxes and then takes a trip around the world and his plane goes down in the ocean on the way back. See Daniel 11:19-25. The Cherubs represents the sun that rule the double Pisces zones as the two longitude zones over the eastern U.S. where the White House is and in land. The middle of those zones (=sits between the Cherubs=sun) that go through almost exactly between New York City, Philadelphia and Washington, D.C.

These prophecies could also mean airplanes are again used in terrorists attacks on those cities or Chicago or Los Angeles or the White House. If President Obama is President in 2013 it maybe him at the White House whose attacked. He is born in the Leo sign that is ruled by the sun and Pisces, which rule the cities of Los Angeles, Chicago, Philadelphia, New York City and Washington, D.C. Twelve years added to 9-11-2001 when planes attacked buildings in New York City equals 2013 when they may again strike as Chinese cycles of 12 predicts. Or will this time they attack nuclear power plants or our electricity power source? If a woman is the U.S, President at this time it may be her that these ancient prophecies happen to. There are several prophecies of an end time woman leader of the U.S. See Revelation chapters 17-18; *Unusual prophecies being fulfilled* by Perry Stone page 67;and *The Book Of Angels* by Ruth Thompson, L.A. Williams, and Renae Taylor, pages 116-121. That woman President of the U.S. may come in 2012 or 2016 and be the U.S. President in 2013 and/or 2017 and rule until the end comes.

Chapter Sixteen

The Carving II

The ancient Egyptian carving on the ceiling of the temple Hathor in Dendera, Egypt dated 100-300 B.C. or earlier might predict the events in this book. See my book entitled *The Experiment at Philadelphia* page 462 drawing 45 for a look at part of that ancient carving. In it you see a kneeling woman, near three stars, one star, a pig, seven stars, a raft with a goat's head on it and the sun or moon disk between its horns, one star again and a table with four snakes on it. Near that table is a kneeling woman. The woman represents Cancer the woman sign that runs from June 21 to July 21-23 and star time from July 21-23 to August 21-23. Add seven days (=the seven stars) to the August 21-23 and it equals August 28-30.

The pig seen on the carving is the Chinese Year of the Pig which 2007 A.D. is. Add seven years (the seven stars) to the year 2007 and it equals 2014 in June 21 to August 30, which we just seen the kneeling woman meant. Add the four snakes seen on the carving near the pig to 2014 and it equals 2018. The snakes can also mean the Chinese Year of the Snake, which is 2013, plus one star (one year) added to that, and four years more as the four snakes, and it equals 2013+1=2014+4=2018. The polar opposite of Snake in Chinese astrology is the Pig. And the kneeling woman in Chinese astrology equals our Cancer sign and July and is ruled by the Chinese Sheep or Goat, which head (goat's head on a raft=waters=Cancer sign) is seen next to the kneeling woman on that carving. From these calculations we can conclude that on June 21-August 30, 2013, 2014, 2015, 2016 and 2018 certain events may happen then as documented in this book.

Chapter Seventeen

The Trumpets and Sun

The word "trumpet" or "trumpets" are predicted six times in the book of Revelation. Could this have been a prediction of some event or events happening on a new moon in which we seen the ancient Jewish people would sound a trumpet at the sight of a new moon or right after it? The new moons in June 21-August 30, 2013, 2014 and 2018 are July 8, 2013 and August 6, 2013 and June 27, 2014, July 26, 2014, August 25, 2014, July 12-13, 2018 and August 11, 2018. May 28, 2014 is also a new moon as well as November 22, 2014. Are these dates when a great earthquake strikes San Francisco and/or Seattle with possible tidal waves or a great earthquake and tidal waves strike somewhere in the world?

Revelation chapter 5 predicts a small book with seven seals (=seven chapters) to be open by the "Lamb" from the tribe of Juda and root of David. The "Lamb" is a sheep or goat in which we seen Chinese astrology rules our Cancer sign and month of July. It also is the star time of Cancer when certain events may happen in from July 21-23 to August 21-23. The tribe of Juda the lion equals Leo the lion sign that runs from July 21- 23 to August 22-23, plus seven day cusp to August 28-30. Leo the lion is ruled by our sun, which rules the eastern U.S. and possibly the Sun tabloid and National Enquirer. The "root of David" is David's father Jesse who was born in the Cancer sign. Were these ancient prophecies predicting a seven chapter book to be open by David (Perel?) or Jesse, John or Ed in the Sun and/or National Enquirer tabloids on the dates mentioned in 2013, 2014 or 2018? Is the "lamb" that opens the seven chapter book might be born on April 6 or 9, the dates of Jesus's death and resurrection (the slain lamb in Revelation chapter 5)? Or is he born on June 24-25 (Jesus's birthday), or on June 27, which is Jesse's birthday the father or root of David? Or is it June 20 the birthday of John the Disciple of Jesus who wrote down the Bible's book of Revelation in heaven on June 12, 96 A.D., which was a Sunday the same as August 10, 2014. And David's birthday the father of Solomon was September 7-8, 19 or 26-27 and Solomon's birthday was October 15. July 19 is the ancient Egyptian New Year, which could be the birthday of this editor. The lion (Leo) from the tribe of Juda that Revelation 5:5 predicts could be the editor or leader of the Sun and/or National Enquirer birth sign or star sign of July 21-September 23, plus or minus the cusp of seven days to September 30 or July 14. Are any of these names and birthdays connected to the Sun or National Enquirer? Will one of them named above or born on the above dates help open or publish an excerpt of this seven chapter book (seven seals) in the seventh month (September-October) of 2013?

You may ask what in the world does a seven sealed book opened in heaven have to do with a seven chapter book opened on earth? Psalms 84:11 states God in heaven is a sun and the Sun tabloid on earth is not only in the sunshine state of Florida, but in the Pisces zone that rules the sun and the tabloid is called the Sun. And if they decide to publish an excerpt from this book of seven chapters (=seven seals) they would open (publish or go public) one or more seals from this book when no one else would just as Revelation chapter 5 predicts they would. Revelation 1-5 states that God and the lamb in heaven shine as the strength of the sun (=Sun tabloid). And Revelation chapter 5 predicts two sevens, which could mean twice is this book excerpt published in July-August or later in 2013 and in July-August or later in 2014. The seven churches that the book of Revelation was sent to long ago were in western Turkey which was the end of the Virgo zone and near the beginning of the Libra zone. The great pyramids below them are exactly on the Virgo-Libra zones. Is that when Revelation's small book is opened (published) in the Sun or National Enquirer? The end of Virgo and beginning of the Libra sign is from September 14-23, plus the cusp of seven days to September 30, or into Libra, which runs from September 23-October 22. The ancient Egyptian New Year where the great pyramids were built as a starting point began on July 19, which is when some of these events in this book may happen on.

The "little book" that Revelation chapters 4-5-10 predict could mean a small 5x8 paperback written on the front and back of each page with seven chapters as those prophecies predict for this book. In ancient times books were large and only written on one side and so these prophecies were predicting a modern day book.

Chapter Eighteen

The end 11

The count down to the end was predicted by Hal Lindsey as a starting point when Israel (fig tree) became a nation again on May 14-15, 1948. See his book *The Late Great Planet Earth*. He claims the "fig tree" represents Israel and is the sign for the count down of the last generation. Matthew 24:32-34 predicts this:

> "Now learn a parable of the fig tree; When his branch is yet tender, and putteth forth leaves, ye know that the summer is nigh.
> So likewise ye, when ye see all these things, know that it is near, even at the doors.
> Verily I say unto you. This generation shall not pass, till all these things be fulfilled." Matthew 24:32-34 (Old King James Version).

The summer being "nigh" may predict the end in summer time as the months of July-August are. And the "generation" might be 70 years as Psalms 90:10 predicts for a life time that David the king of Israel (fig tree) is strongly connected to. Add 70 years to May 14-15, 1948 and come to May 14-15, 2018 when the signs come for the end sometime in summer.

The fig tree puts forth leaves and fruits in the spring and summer. *The Smith's Bible dictionary* on pages 192-193 states that the fruit always comes before the leaves and the figs harvest is in May-June the same month Israel became a nation.

The "sorrows" that Matthew 24:8 predicts as signs of the count down to the end Hal Lindsey claims that word can be translated "birth pangs." Virgo the Virgin in astrology and numerology is a woman and is given the number five. If the commotion's happened in 2013-2014 and you add five years to those years it equals 2018-2019. Matthew 24:7 predicts those commotion's as wars, pestilence's and famines in verse seven then the very next verse eight it predicts that they would be signs of the sorrows to come as birth pangs of a woman giving birth. Does those ancient prophecies mean the commotion's or attacks on 9-11-2001? And then two years (by and by=Luke 21:9) later the great second Iraq war happened. That war involved nation against nation, and kingdom against kingdom in a great war with great signs and fearful sights from heaven (=shock and awe). The shock and awe are the fearful and great signs from heaven that happened then causing earthquakes, famines and pestilence's in 2003, but it is not the end or the end is not in September 26-27, 2003 as Luke 21:9-11 predicted. Twelve years added to that date is September 26-27, 2015 when certain events may happen on.

Does the four returns of Song of Solomon 6:13 predict four years from when the earthquake happens on August 10, 2014 till the end in August 28-29, 2018? In my other books I show how in 26 A.D. was when John the Baptist and Jesus came proclaiming the kingdom of God is at hand. The Chinese Year of 26 A.D. is the Year of the Dog the same as 2018 and part of 2019 A.D. are. And Daniel 12:11-12 prediction of 1290 days and 1335 days added together equals 2625 days. Change each day to years as Ezekiel 4:6 tells us to do and you have 2625 years. Daniel 12:11-13 tells us to start the count down from when the king of Babylon came and stopped the daily sacrifice and did the abomination by standing in or putting a pagan statue in the Holy of Holies in the Jewish Temple at Jerusalem. The Book of Daniel starts at this time in Chapter one of that book in the third year of Jehoiakim, which was 606-607 B.C. Subtract 2625 days from then and it equals 2019-2020. Counting each year it equals 2018-2019 A.D. as the time of the end. Here's what the book of Daniel 12:11-12 prediction states:

> "And from thew time that the daily sacrifice shall be taken away, and the abomination that maketh desolate set up, there shall be a thousand two hundred and ninety days.
> Blessed is he that waiteth, and cometh to the thousand three hundred and five and thirty days." Daniel 12:11-12.

The vision that I had on August 29, 1982 at 1:18 am to 7:18 am-a Sunday, of God as a Cherub for almost exactly six hours might give the year and date of the end. Six (hours) times six equals 36 hours or years. Add 36 years to 1982 and it equals 2018 at 1:18 a.m. on August 29 as the end of days that Daniel predicted the end would come when many travel to and fro for their summer vacations, which happens mostly in July-August according to *The Travel Channel*.

In the book of Revelation and other parts of the Bible there is often mentioned the wrath of God happening in the end as wine or the vine harvest, winepress or grapes and vineyards. The grapes used for making wine come from a vine and are their harvest is from August-September and some have even claimed is from June to September as the harvest for grapes. See *Holman Bible Dictionary* page 610. Was this a clue for the end in July-August of 2018? Or is the half hour (=half a year=six months) from then till the months of January-February of 2019 is when the end comes? See Revelation 8:1 for the half an hour prediction. Is the half hour of Revelation 8:1 a prediction of 30 minutes, dropping the zero, equals three minutes or three years as the same three angels of Revelation chapter 14 come at the end when the wrath of the wine press of God happens? Are those three years July-August of 2013, 2014 and 2015 or 2018?

Chapter Nineteen

The Carving III

The ancient Egyptian carving from the temple Hathor at Dendera, Egypt shows the carving being held by four women standing up and eight bird headed men kneeling. Was this a prediction of when the end of the world would happen? The women could mean the female sign of Capricorn, which ends January 19. The woman could also mean Cancer a female sign and is ruled by the moon that is given the number two with a zero equals 20. Add the 20 and 19 together and you have January 19, 2019. Add two days (=moon) to that date and it equals January 20-21, 2019 as the time of the end.

Why two days are added to January 19, 2019 is because the four women holding the carving with two hands each could be the women signs of Capricorn and Cancer. The Cancer sign rules the breasts, which are two and the Cancer sign happens mostly in July the polar opposite of January. The two breasts along with the two hands of the four women on the carving are two days. The eight Gemini headed men kneeling, which is representing the end of that kneeling sign of Capricorn (January 19) and are Gemini (=bird headed). The Gemini sign is that of the twins or two again and the polar opposite of Sagittarius when the end comes. At the end of Sagittarius star time is January 19 the same as the end of the Capricorn sign. All the two's just mentioned are two days added to that date of January 19, 2019, which equals January 21, 2019.

The ancient carving also shows a circle with eight kneeling women in it near Capricorn with arm bands on them with 12 stars near the circle. Could the 12 stars along with the four women and eight bird headed men holding the carving equaling 12 again be the reverse date of 12 or 21 on a full moon two days after the end of the Capricorn sign and Sagittarius star time? That date would be January 21, 2019, which is a full moon (circle). The arms bands the kneeling women (=knees ruled by Capricorn) in the circle could be the death bands that many wear after the death of someone. In this case the death of all people in the whole (=circle) world. The eight kneeling women inside the circle near 12 stars might mean the Capricorn sign that is female or woman and given the number eight and the kneeling of those women represents Capricorn again because it rules the knees. The circle and 12 stars would be a full moon (circle) on a Monday (=moon and woman too) reverse the date of 12, or 21, and plus two days after the end of Capricorn on January 19+2=January 21, 2019, which is a Monday and is when the end of the world comes.

See my book *The Nativity* page 81 drawing 14 for a drawing of part of this ancient Egyptian carving showing the bird headed men kneeling and women holding the carving. See my book *The experiment at Philadelphia* drawing 34 page 451 for the circle with eight kneeling women in it near Capricorn and near the 12 stars.

Chapter Twenty

Matthew 24-25

Mathew 24:19-20 predicts that you should pray that the end not to be on a Sabbath Day nor in winter:

> "And woe unto them that are with child, and to them that give suck in those days!
> But pray that your flight be not in the winter, neither on the sabbath day:"
> Matthew 24:19-20 (Old King James Version)

January 20-21, 2019 is a Sunday, which is the Christian Sabbath Day and in winter time less than a month from Christmas Day when John the Baptist was born. Was the reference in Matthew 24:19-20 warning to those who give suck mean shortly after birth on December 25, would come the end in January on January 20-21, 2019? The "give suck" could also mean Cancer sign that rules the breasts and is mostly in July and is the polar opposite of January and Cancer rules the moon where we get the name Monday from that January 21, 2019 is.

As II Peter 3:2-18 and Matthew 24:48-51 predicts people will mock after the Christmas Holidays or during them that someone predicted the end of the world and nothing happened. Then when January 1, 2019 comes after they were just drinking and drunken with the drunkards, eating and partying they will mock God. They will say where is the promise of His Coming for since the fathers fell asleep things continue since creation. Then sudden destruction will befall them all. They also could say that after December 21, 2012 if nothing happens then.

Matthew 25:1-13 predicts the bridegroom (Jesus Christ) to return shortly after midnight and to be ready and know the hour and minute if possible. It is told in the form of a parable of ten virgins, five wise and five foolish. In the *Strong's concordance of the Bible* in the Greek dictionary of that book the word "ten" is or near the words numbered 1176-1177. The word 1176 defines "ten" as this: "ten:--[eight-] een, ten." The second word 1177 is "twelve". Put the two together and 12:18 a.m. a little after midnight. The 18 is the eight in brackets along with the 10 equals 18 as after the brackets is the letters "een" as added to 10 and eight in which we call eighteen. The word "twelve" could again be reverse as 21 on January 21, 2019 at 12:18 a.m EST as when the bridegroom cometh as a thief in the night when people are sleeping and they are unaware. One Bible verse tells us to watch because if we knew when the thief was to come in the night on that date we would be ready or else we will be left behind like the five foolish virgins in the night that weren't ready because they knew not the day and hour and minute of His Coming. Are the statements in the Bible of people not knowing the end has come because they are asleep and unaware of the time in the night? And is the cry at midnight that the bridegroom cometh predicted in Matthew 25:1-13 angels that tell of these books of mine that shows the time of His return so you be wise virgins and not the foolish virgins?

Job 34:20 predicts sudden destruction of people at the time of midnight:

"In a moment shall they die, and the people shall be troubled at midnight, and pass away: and the mighty shall be taken away without hand." Job 34:20 (Old King James Version)

The vision I had of God on August 29, 1982 at 1:18 a.m. Eastern Daylight Time would be 12:18 a.m. Eastern Standard Time in the U.S. on January 21, 2019. But, if the prophecies mean Israeli time, and they can, 12:18 a.m. Israeli time on January 21, 2019 it would be 5:18 p.m. Eastern Standard Time in the U.S. when people set down for sup or supper or dinner time. Is that what Jesus meant by He knocks on the door and comes in and "sup" with you and you with Him just as the time of His coming is called "the marriage supper of the Lamb" See Revelation 3:20 and 19:9, 17?

Matthew 22:2-14 predicts in the end times God would marry Jew and Gentile, male and female together as a she/male and the righteous Christian and Jews as guests invited to that wedding would refuse and be repulsed by it. So God would send his servants out to the streets and invite many guest both good and evil and the marriage of God would be set with many guests. Then the Lord would see one of the guests not in wedding garments, but naked or in his pajamas and say why he came here like that? The reason is because he was in bed at the time of the wedding as noted above and God will throw him out into hell. Be ready for the bridegroom as Matthew 25:1-13 also predicts because you may not be ready and miss out on it. For many are called but few are chosen.

Song of Solomon chapter 5 in the Bible also predicts this wedding of God as a door (=the time it happens=January?) as being part male and part female in one. Without sex we all wouldn't be here. The same is true in the beginning with the Big Bang. If that sexual encounter didn't happen nothing and no one would have ever been created ever.

The rumors of wars and wars, but the end is not yet and then kingdom against kingdom and nation against nation and earthquakes, famines and pestilence's are the beginning of sorrows just as Matthew 24:7-8 and Mark 13:7-8 might mean the opposite in order of those things and/or they all happen at one time or several times followed by people disappearing in the Rapture shortly before the end on a Sabbath Day (Sunday) and in winter as Luke chapter 17 and Matthew chapter 24 predicts. The wars and rumors of wars and kingdom against Kingdom and nation against nation may be the two Iraq wars were two kingdoms, the U.S. and the United Kingdom (England), and other nations fought after long periods of wars and rumors of wars in 1990-1991 and 2001-2003 to 2014. During these time those two kingdoms and other nations fought against Iraq twice. During the latter war there was a war with the terrorist in Afghanistan and Pakistan from 2001-2014 when it is suppose to end. All of those wars and rumors of wars were the beginning of sorrows that Matthew 24:7-8 predicted with earthquakes, famines and pestilence's happening in them with earthquakes, famines and pestilence's happening in them or in other (=diver) places around the world like in Iran (2003), Asia (2004), Pakistan (2005), Haiti (2010) and etc and may continue in 2012-2015 to 2019. Then wars and rumors of wars are happening now (2011-2013) with Israel and Iran that may just break out into a war in 2012-2013, but the end is not yet or by and by or in two years from then in 2014- 2015 when a tidal wave happens to the East Coast of the U.S. looking like the end is near, but isn't. And great earthquakes famines and pestilence's occur due to those events, but it also isn't the end. See Luke 21:9-11. Three and a half years after the tidal wave would be when the end comes in January 20-21, 2019 when our sun goes into a supernova and people disappear in the Rapture that Sunday-Monday. A light by the sun may give a sign of the sun is about to go into a supernova. A war and/or tidal waves and earthquakes, famines and pestilence's may also all happen at this time too, which would fulfilled all these ancient prophecies of Matthew chapter 24, Mark chapter 13 and Luke chapters 17 and 21. This seems to be the correct order of these things. It's confusing in these prophecies because they may be backwards and in different times and orders and events. That's why they are hard to understand and why many have given a different interpretation of them in order, time and place.

The evening and night of January 20, 2019 fix a great dinner time meal for you and all your family and friends. Then stay up fully dressed the whole night watching for Christ's return just as the ancient prophecies predicted. Try these same things in 2026-2030 and 2060-2061 on December 24-25 and on June 24-25, or the other dates given in this book.

Chapter Twenty One

The Mayan Code

The book *The Mayan Prophecies* by Adrian G. Gilbert and Maurice M. Cotterell pages 130-134 state that the ancient Mayans would go to the top of their pyramid at midnight on or around November 11, 1507 A.D. to appease the devil not to destroy the world. The number 52 years is used as to how often they had to do this. Other books along with that one give the time periods of 52, 520 and 5200 years. If those years are 360 day years, whereas ours are 365.24 days long, it makes 520 years shorter by about eight years or equal 512 years. Add 512 years to 1507 A.D. at midnight and it equals 2019 A.D.

The book that lists all lunar eclipses from 1500 B.C. till 3000 A.D. list a lunar eclipse on December 19, 1507 A.D. That would put a full moon, which lunar eclipses can only happen on, in January of 1508 A.D. as January 17-18. Add three months, counting each month, to November 1507 A.D. and three days to January 17-18, 1508, and it equals January 20-21, 1508 A.D. changed to January 20-21, 2019 as the time when a lunar eclipse happens and the end comes. The year 1508 A.D. is the Chinese Year of 2024 A.D., minus six as the polar opposite, and it equals 2018 A.D., which doesn't end to February of 2019 by the Chinese calendar.

Chapter Twenty Two

The Door

Ever since the vision I had of God on August 28-29, 1982 I began to hear knocks on my door in the morning. At first I thought it was dreams. Then I thought it was the wind, which does make sounds on the door like knocking. I would actually sometimes get up and answer the door to find no one there. This went on from 1982 to now (2011) and is still happening. In the Bible it predicts God's return and the end of the world as signs of the doors (plural) and door in these verses of Matthew 24:33 and Revelation 3:20 and 4:1:

> "So likewise ye, when ye shall see all these things, know that it is near, even at the doors." Matthew 24:33 (Old King James Version)

> "After this I looked, and, behold a door was opened in heaven: and the first voice which I heard was as it were of a trumpet talking with me; which said, Come up hither, and I will shew thee things which must be hereafter." Revelation 4:1 (Old King James Version)

> "Behold, I stand at the door, and knock: if any man hear my voice, and open the door, I will come in to him, and will sup with him, and he with me." Revelation 3:20 (Old King James Version).

Matthew 24:33 prediction that God's return is at the "doors" is interesting because it uses the plural word of doors meaning one or more doors as to the sign of His Coming and the end of the world when the marriage supper ("sup") of the Lamb happens with people of earth and Jesus Christ. After reading several astronomy books I notice one as saying the ancients believed that the constellation Capricorn was thought to be the gate way or door way to heaven. Is it where and when we go when God comes back to take you off the earth to save you from the sun supernova to some other place in heaven where we will be hid from danger for ever in paradise?

That makes one door. The other door may just be the month of January when the Capricorn sign rules and is the star time or cusp of that same constellation. The name of the month of January also means "Roman god Janus, protector of the gates." So that gives the second meaning of the word "doors" or gates when the end will come and God returns to take us to those doors in that sign and month. Remember that January 19, 2019 is the end of the Capricorn sign, but it also runs from then to February 18-20 as star time when the sun is actually in that sign. The cusp of the Capricorn sign also would run from its ending on January 19 to January 26.

The reason I may have heard these knocks on the door from 1982 till now (2011) in the morning is because that vision of God in 1982 started at exactly 1:18 a.m. and ended 7:18 a.m. in the morning eastern daylight time. The exact time of 12:18 a.m. eastern standard time on January 21, 2019 in winter is in the eastern U.S. where I was. That time equals exactly 7:18 a.m. Israeli time when the end comes and God returns to take us all to heaven (door or gateway) for ever from the danger that's coming quickly. See Revelation 22:20-21. August 29, 1982 was a Sunday as is January 20, 2019. The end may come in the morning in Israel on January 21, 2019.

Chapter Twenty Three
Dreams, visions and angel visitations

Parts of this chapter was included in my books entitled *The experiment at Philadelphia* and in *The boy who could predict earthquakes*. I enclosed it here again with some new information on some of these dreams, visions and angels visitations. Take another look. I left in some of the old dates to show you how ancient prophecies can predict certain events in detail, but be wrong or fail to come true. Sometimes their interpretations are right and true, but the end results fail to come true. They give exact dates, birthdays, sometimes names, places and events, but the end of them still doesn't come true and they fail. For some reason all ancient prophecies of the Bible, Nostradamus, ancient Egyptian and the Mayan seem to do this. For what reason I do not know. One time a wise man said that he thought God put the Universe in a great coded message or puzzle waiting for someone to decode it and tell or reveal its secrets. Jesus said He talked in parables to confuse the people that are ignorant, but the wise would know the secrets of the puzzles. He also said there would come a time when He would not talk in parables, but plainly talk about all things. We are very fast approaching that time.

Below are a number of dreams, visions, angel appearances and important events I have had over the years. You will learn by reading them how to interpret dreams, visions and angel appearances. Remember that dreams are also all day long when awake, not just for when you are asleep. In creation all is a dream as explained earlier in my other book. So how ever you interpret a dream you can interpret the same things while you are awake. Like the sight of birds, movies, songs, any kind of astrological and astronomical events, anniversaries and all things.

The sight of birds or hearing them chirp that I saw or heard is a good example of this when I was awake. I just put the dream interpretation to it even though in some cases I was awake. It is possible every thing in your life has a meaning. From a singing bird, to the date or numerology of dates and anniversaries in your life to songs, weather and even TV, movies, books and magazines-everything! You may have already been visited by angels and never really thought of it. Movies and TV is clearly a vision, or a dream also. You see it on the screen and hear it, but it isn't really there. Just like a dream or vision. Songs and their artist also have deep meanings telling of events of the present and future along with very great philosophical meaning.

Days of death can equal the day of birth in prophecies. If you dream of someone who has died look to their day of death, or things of that day, then look at that person's birthday for the interpretation. Also look at the age of the person and add it to the date you are looking for in the interpretation. And any person you dream of look to their birthday, or event that happened to them, or something that is in the dream. The Titanic, for example, would be the dates of April 14-15. The months and years of when the movie was made, or comes out, and different clues in the movies, along with the actors birthdays and death days, all gives clues to the exact interpretation of the dream. Also conception days can have a great meaning to an event. Counting back about 270-280 days equals sometimes near the day of conception. Jesus, I believe was conceived on September 19 the day Jacob, David and my dad were born on. It is not an exact science, but originally astrologers believed that conception times were the true spot to place you horoscope not on your birthday. But they knew since that the exact time of conception is almost impossible to find out and so they place your sign at the time of birth. Sometimes when you were born your brother may have been conceived. And some important people may have their day of conceptions on an important date. President Bush, for example may have been conceived on September 11 or 27, dates we will or have seen are important in future events.

Check all them out in not only our astrology, or astronomy, but also Chinese astrology. Certain animals in your dream could be that of a certain Chinese year, or hour, or month, the same as our astrology. Shot in the knee, for example, as one of my dreams had equals the Capricorn sign that rules the knees. You will get the hang of to how to interpret your dreams and life and be able to prophesied if you keep reading this whole book and all my books and use the code and information given in them. Read the book *The Dreamer's Dictionary* by Lady Stearn Robinson and Tom Gorbett and use its interpretations of each thing dreamt of.

What ever you dream you can look up those symbols and see what it may mean in that book and this book. But remember that that book may not always mean what your dream means. And also remember some dreams can mean nothing, or have great meaning, but fail to come true. Parts of a dream may predict you will be moving, at a time you are thinking of moving and your interpretation of the dream maybe to move. The dream may even tell you where to move to a place you were thinking of moving to. But the move may not be what you should do. See Ecclesiastes 5:7. Dreams can be deceiving, inspirational and even supernatural in knowledge, but fail and not be true. It is also possible the dream was to move to that place in meaning and is what you really should do.

When using that dream dictionary be sure to look up several parts of the symbols. For example, I had a dream of strawberry jelly. I looked up jelly and the interpretation was gloomy and I was depressed for dreaming of jelly. But the page before that under jam the interpretation was good. Jelly is jam, yet they are two opposite meanings.

I remember reading in Nostradamus about a man named Mark Anthony and pencil or writing connecting to him. At the time I was sending my book to publishers. One called me on it and his name was Mark Anthony. It seem clear to me that this was going to be my publisher. But he wanted $15,000 dollars to publish my book. I think shortly after that he went out of business. If I would of went with him as the prophecy seems to predict I may have been out $15,000 dollars and a publisher out of business. So just because some things seem to make sense in dreams, visions and prophecy it can be wrong to do what they say.

On the other hand sometimes things in dreams, visions and prophecy can be exactly what you should do and will change the world as we know it if you persist at it. It may not come true right away, but if you persist at it the end may be glorious. What you pray for and work hard at now may not come true for decades. A quick solution and answers to prayers don't always happen that way. I started these books in August 1976. They were published in 2001 and 2012. In 1978 I begged God and prayed with all my might for Him to deliver me from poverty and have my book published. Nothing happened. In 1982 I begged and prayed to God with all my might for Him to deliver me from poverty and publish my books. Nothing happened. These same things happened in 1992, 1995, 1997, 1998, 1999, with no results. In 2001 to 2012 they were published by me paying to have them published. I begged God and prayed with all my might to be delivered from poverty in 2001, 2002, with no results. I had spent 45,000 hours and $20,000 dollars for these books with little or no return. Hopefully they will sell in 2013. Yet they may not and the dream of me profiting from them, or the new ones published will not come true and I die at the time before I see the many events happen.

But you get what I am saying about dreams and hopes you have for the future and interpretations of dreams, that may, or may not be true, or come true exactly the way you think, or hope. That's true about all things. Every thing isn't exactly the way we think they are, run and exist and were created and are destroyed by. I don't mean to depress you or discourage you. When I first started these books

I never knew they would turn out so powerful the way they did and that I would learn so much and have the chance to teach others the mysteries kept secret since the world began.

And who knows maybe some day they will all sell billions of copies and teach all people true wisdom of all subjects and help and comfort all people. That is why I first started them, not for money and fame or credit, but to teach and help people in the search for the truth. The money may come later just as Matthew 19:29 predicts of someone giving up houses, lands, family, friends and children for the gospel of Christ (these books of mine) will some day (not right away) be given 100 fold of all those things. Of course as Ecclesiastes also predicts the works (books) of one (me) is given in a great inheritance (after I die) to another. That other is one who didn't work on them or share their wisdom and beliefs of those works (books). Yet he and she is richly blessed by them and isn't satisfied with riches, even though the one who done the work needed those riches all his life.

As stated in this book I gave up all those things to write these books in May of 1977. Now in 2012 I am still working on them and hoping and praying with all my might to have them be successful. That's 35 years later and a lot of stresses, problems, hard work, preserving and patience. What you do now is important whether they be lesser things, or great things, or in between things. All things can change the world five-ten or 20-30 years down the road for all time in a great, medium or small and in a good, or balance or evil way. Remember that! Watch and remember what the movie *It's a wonderful life* taught us. Now let's get down and do some dream, vision and angel visitation interpretation:

Vision of August 29, 1982 at 1:18 am to 7:18 am-a Sunday, I experience a vision of God as ball lightning and God as a Cherub for almost exactly six-seven hours. Add 24 years to 1982 and it equals 2006. Add four years and six months to 2006 from August and it equals January 18, 2010. Add 24 minutes to 1:18 a.m. minus seven hours equals 6:42-43 p.m. on January 18, 2010. The 1:18 a.m. could be a symbol of January our first month followed by 10 days of January 18. Why the 24, 4, and six-seven years, months, hours and minutes are added or subtracted is because Cherubs are elders, which Revelation claim are 24, 6, 7, 8 and four in number. And the six-seven months and hours added or subtracted are the time period in which the vision of the Cherubs or elders was seen on August 29, 1982 from 1:18 a.m. to 7:18 a.m. counting each hour or not.

Update: The date of August 29, 1982 at 1:18 a.m. eastern daylight time or 12:18 eastern standard time was a Sunday and when you add 24 hours (=24 elders) to it you come to Monday. When you multiply six times six it equals 36. Add 36 years to 1982 and it equals 2018 into 2019. The wings of Cherubs or seraphim's are sometimes six and it equals six times six or 36 years. They control time by rotation and gravity at the core of stars, planets and moons. Add six months (=six wings), counting each month, to August 29, 2018 and it equals January 29, 2019. Subtract seven or eight days (=cherubs-elders) from that date and it equals January 20-21, 2019 at 12:18 a.m. EST. That date is at the end of Sunday beginning of Monday going seven hours to 7:18 a.m. Israeli time as the exact time of the end. The vision of 1982 lasted six hours, but was Daylight savings time making it one hour more on eastern standard time in January 20- 21, 2019. Subtract six minutes from that time of the full moon then at 12:17 a.m., counting each minute, and it equals 12:12 a.m. January 21, 2019, which is exactly when a lunar eclipse starts. Add six minutes to 12:12 a.m. and it equals 12:18 a.m. January 21, 2019 or December 24-25 or June 24-25, 2060-2061.

I saw two angels on December 25, 2000-Christmas Day. Were they a sign of double trouble in December of 2012 exactly 12 years from the year 2000 and that date (=December 24-25, 2012)? Is that the time when Israel and the U.S. attack Iran and Iran attacks back? December 25, 2000 was a Monday the same as December 24, 2012 is when these events may start on. If these attacks start

Monday evening into Tuesday it equals the time of war on Tuesday, which is Mars in Latin and Mars is the god of war and the red planet and the year 2012 is the Chinese Year of the Dragon. Is that date the "early" that Psalms 90:14 in the Holy Bible predicts for God's servant? Instead of the attacks and wars happening August 10, 2013-2019 they happen then. And I am bless early with the sales of my books then and I receive double for my shame of two years in 2001-2003 for two years in 2013-2015. December 24-25, 2012 are a Monday-Tuesday, which are related to the moon and Mars or Leo and the sun as Revelation chapter 12 predicts a woman clothed with the sun (=Mars=Red= Leo=Lion=Tuesday) and the moon (=Monday) under her feet when the great Red Dragon pulls down a third (=3000 or 3) of the stars (=missiles). I saw these angels about 11 a.m. to noon to 1 p.m. Christmas Day in 2000. That time was Eastern Standard Time, which would make it 6-8 p.m. Israeli time in the evening ending Monday and starting Tuesday when missiles or stars start falling from heaven. It also could mean six hours (=six wings of the angels) from then and 12 hours added to it or between 6- 8 p.m. and 6-8 a.m. in Israel's or Iran's time or Eastern Standard time. Or are the six wings six hours added to 11 a.m.-1 p.m. is 6-8 p.m. Eastern Standard Time when these attacks start at 1-3 a.m. Israeli or Iran time? Are those angels the ones set out on December 24-25, 2012 to tell people of these books of mine and then August 10, 2013-2015 another set of angels are sent out to tell others of these books of mine? In Revelation chapters 4-5 predicts four beasts and 24 elders. Are they the symbol of December 24-25, 2012 after the fourth month (=four beasts) from September's Jewish Civil Calendar and our 24th day (=24 elders)? Satan is not only known as the Red Dragon in Revelation chapter 12, but also the beast in chapter 13 making that exact date when he causes trouble between Israel and Iran. The year 2000 and 2012 are Chinese Dragon Years. The polar opposite the Dragon is the Chinese Dog year of January 21, 2019 when it is soon ending. Revelation chapter 12 war in heaven and a third of the stars falling to earth are what Revelation 6:12-13 and 11:19 are predicting. These predictions of great hail is satan standing inside the sun's core and fighting with Jesus and His angels causing a great sun supernova. That causes the outer core of the sun to explode and fly into the earth as great hail and falling stars. Revelation chapter 12 is our year 2012 and its polar opposite 2018 into January of 2019 as the Chinese Year of the Dog. That same chapter number 12 can be reverse to mean January 21, 2019, which is the 12th month to the Chinese Dog Year. Satan as the red dragon in Revelation chapter 12 is Mars the god of war and January 20-21, 2019 is a Sunday-Monday as the woman is clothed with the sun (=Sunday=January 20, 2019) and the moon (=Monday= January 21, 2019) under her feet in that same chapter. Mars is Leo (lion) that the sun rules and where and when this great war happens in (=sun=Leo=Mars) after a solar eclipse and on a lunar eclipse in January of 2019 as Revelation 6:12-13 predicts.

On August 29, 1995 I saw a man riding a bike down the road with three birds on his back with one having two red tip wings. As I passed him I looked in my review window and saw him cross over the road to a side street. The side street was named Bates. I considered this man to be an angel and the birds and street to be prophetic in time of future events. When I thought of the street named Bates I could only make sense of it by connecting it to Norman Bates the fictional character in the famous movie *Psycho*. That movie was made in 1959-1960, which is the Chinese Year of the Pig the same as 2007 and its polar opposite is the Snake in 2013. The three birds on the back of the angel were that of the Gemini sign known to the Egyptians not as the sign of the twins, but as birds because it is an air sign where birds fly. The Gemini sign ends June 20. Add three years to 2007 and 30 days to the end of the Gemini sign as symbols to the three birds on the back of the angel who went onto Bates street and you come to July 19-20, 2010. Add another three years to that and it equals 2013 when the end may come. The movie *Psycho* was filmed in December-January. The polar opposite of January is July

19-20, 2010 when predicted events will happen. The polar opposite that date is January 18-19, 2010. Anthony Perkins who played Norman Bates in the movie was born April 4. Subtract three months from that as the three birds on the back on the angel showed, and it equals January 4, 2010. Multiply 2x7=14 days added to January 4, 2010 and it equals January 18, 2010 when predicted events begin to happen. Birds have two wings and in numerology equal the number 7, thus, 2x7=14. In the beginning of the film *Psycho* shows the date of December 11. Add 14 days to that and it equals December 25. Add 24 days to that as the angel I saw was a cherub or elder, which numbers are given as 24 in Revelation chapters 4-5, and it equals January 18, 2010. The three birds on the angel's back one in the middle with two red tip wings could refer to 30 days (three birds) before the end of Gemini (June 20=Gemini end and birds) equals May 21. Then minus two days (two red tip wings) equals May 19-20, 2010 when events predicted happen at 2:43 p.m. (seen at the beginning of the movie *Psycho*), 6:43 p.m. or 11:10-11:11 a.m. or some other times. The three birds on the back of the angel could refer to 30 days before the end of Gemini (=bird=wind sign) on June 20 and 30 days after the polar opposite of that date on December 21. Those time spans gives us the dates of May 21, 2010 and January 20, 2013 when adding three years to 2007 and 2010 as the three birds also represent. The two red tip wings on one of the three birds in the middle could mean minus two days from May 21 equals May 19, 2010 when predicted events happen on that day or the next on May 20, 2010. This angel visitation could also predict two other dates of trouble. Visions of birds, as the three birds seen on the back of this man (angel), could mean May 19-20, 2010, as we seen and also May 17-18, 2011 and May 30, 2012, plus or minus three weeks. The date of May 18, 2011 is subtracting 30 days from the end of Gemini the bird or air sign in symbolism to May 20. Subtract two-three days as the three birds with one with two red tip wings on it and you have May 17-18, 2011 when another great earthquake may occur. As for the third date of May 30, 2012 it is given by the three birds on the back of the angel as 30 days or the 30th day in Gemini (bird.) To our calendar that would be May 30, 2012 when two very famous people will die. The exact times of 11:10- 11:11, 2:43, 12:48, 1:18 may or may not be the exact times of these three events.

Update: The Cherub I saw on a bicycle in August 1995 that had three birds on his neck and one with two red tip wings cross over into Bates Ave, Eustis, Florida is connected to the *Psycho* movie with Norman Bates as we seen, which was filmed from November 11, 1959 to February 1, 1960. The year 1960 is the Chinese Year of the Rat the same as 2008. The three birds being five the number of Gemini an air sign or bird sign added three times to certain dates comes to the end. Add five years to August 2008 and it equals August 2013. Add five years to that and it equals August 2018. Add five months to that and it equals January of 2019 as the three birds or three times the number five is used in time periods. The two red tip wings equals the moon, which is the number two and being red equals a blood moon or lunar eclipse in that month of January 2019. That date is January 21, 2019 as the end. The Gemini sign as the birds on the angel's neck equals April-May-June of 2014 the Chinese Year of the Horse, which polar opposite is the Chinese Year of the Rat of 1960 when the movie *Psycho* was finished. Will at that time the final blessing of prosperity happens or a time to travel? And the middle bird on the angel with two red tip wings could mean half or three (=three birds) and a half years from two years added to 2013, which equals 2015 (=2+2013= 2015). The three birds being five each equals 15 days minus (=the red tip wings of the middle bird=minus=in the red) August 25, 2015. That equals August 10, 2015 plus three and a half years or 1260 days equals January 21, 2019 as the end on a lunar eclipse. I may have seen this angel with the birds on his neck exactly on August 25, 1995, in which minus 15 days or three times five equals 15 and August 10 (August 25-15=August 10, 2013, 2014 and 2015+three and half years equals January 21, 2019).

I had a dream on September 3, 2002, which I saw a dead rat on his back with blood, then I saw the island of Qatar in the Persian Gulf and then I saw the Hawaii Islands appearing in the Persia Gulf Ocean and then I saw a spider.

Update: The Hawaii Islands has in it or near it Pearl Harbor where the Japanese bombed on December 7, 1941. That year is the Chinese Year of the Snake and the day December 7, 1941 was a Sunday. December 7, 2013 is the Chinese Year of the Snake and a Saturday when blessings come as reported in other places in this book and my other books along with Haggai 2:18- 19 and Zephaniah 3:17-20. The spider in the dream is like a tarantula, which has eight legs in which is the number of Saturn that we get the name Saturday from which December 7, 2013 is. Also Qatar in the Persian Gulf is a very rich state and is in the Scorpio zone. Scorpio is the eight sign and Saturn (Saturday), which is when on December 7, 2013 riches (Qatar) comes, then four more months to March 7, 2014 and more riches come, then three or four months later on May-June of 2014 more riches come. The year 2014 is the Chinese Year of the Horse, which polar opposite is the Rat and its four legs and the blood in the dream equals four months, counting each month, from December 7, 2013 to March 7, 2014. Add four years to 2014 and it equals 2018. Gemini as the twins or two added to December 7, 2013 equals December 7-8, 2015 when a double blessing happens as royalties. The Chinese Rat equals our sign of Sagittarius that star time runs from December 21 to January 19. Opposite Sagittarius is Gemini the third sign and twins of the number 2. Adding two months, counting each month or not, from November-December of 2018 and it equals January 19, 2019. Add two days and it equals January 21, 2019 the time of the end and that date is a lunar eclipse of which the Bible calls a blood moon as the blood on the rat in the dream four years after 2014 (Rat) equals 2018 into January of 2019 by the Chinese calendar.

One night I had a dream of me, my mom and dad picking up a foreigner at Orlando Airport and driving over a bridge with a large alligator or crocodile under it and to the side of it was a young alligator or crocodile climbing aboard a 4x8 piece of plywood. I then found myself in the back seat with this foreigner with my dad driving the car and my mom up front going very fast through tunnels with light. I then found my self in Chicago airport in a store looking at magazines.

This dream means the foreigner coming over waters with a great dragon below it known as satan that is black (see Song of Solomon 1:5) is representing Africa the nation of blacks over the waters (=Atlantic Ocean) that causes a flood or tidal wave from there or off its coast from a red volcano (=red dragon of Revelation chapter 12=red lava) to hit Florida and the Eastern U.S. Coast.

To the side there is a little dragon getting up on a 4x8 pieces of plywood. Then, in the dream, me, the foreigner, and my mom and dad up front of the car are suddenly going through tunnels with many lights in it and I then find my self in the Chicago airport looking at magazines. The tunnels represents death of my mom and dad. You have heard of life after death cases where they reported tunnels and lights, which is what was meant by those tunnels and lights in this dream. It also means dates of birth coming through the birth canal into the light. My Dad's death was on January 18, 1985 and his birth was on September 19, 1919. The year 1919 was the year of the Chinese Sheep or Goat, which August 10, 2015 is. My mom died on July 30, 2006, which is the Chinese Year of the Dog the same as January of 2019 is. The little dragon getting on the 4x8 plywood equals four, plus eight, equals 12 days added to July 30, counting each day or not, equals August 10-11, 2015, when a flood (=tidal wave) from the great dragon and little dragon comes from the coast of Africa from an earthquake and/or volcano to destroy Florida. Chicago is ruled by the Leo the lion sign in which this flood happens on August 10-11, 2015 or July-August, 2015 in the Leo sign in the Chinese Sheep or Goat sign. My Dad's death in January 18, 1985 and my mom's death in July 30, 2006 equals the

Chinese Year of the Dog (=2006) in January (my dad's death) of 2019 (=Dog). My dad being born September 19 is the Virgo sign, which cosign is Gemini the third sign and twins or the number two. And the 4x8 plywood adding the four as four years added to 2015, when the flood happens, equals 2019, on January 18 (=dad's death) plus two- three days (=Gemini) equals January 20-21, 2019, when the end comes. The dragon in the dream can mean crocodile or alligator or serpent or snake at the time when he (=satan) fell in August long ago and may again at that time. The 4x8 piece of plywood could equals 4x8=32 years added to 1981 when we all first moved to Florida to when the tidal wave hits two years later on the exact date of August 10, 2015. See Amos 1:1.

On August 10, 2013 and December 25, 2013 a 1000 angels will be sent out at night to speak to a 1000 people in the U.S. telling them where and how many of my books to buy. The following Bible verses predicts these things:

> "He that hath an ear, let him hear what the Spirit saith unto the churches."
> Revelation 3:22 (Old King James Version)

> "But thou, O Daniel, shut up the words, and seal the book, even to the time of the end: many shall run to and fro, and knowledge shall be increased." Daniel 12:4 (Old King James Version)

> "The chariots of God are twenty thousand, even thousands of angels: the Lord is among them, as in Sinai, in the Holy place." Psalms 68:17 (Old King James Version)

> "Solomon had a vineyard at Baalhamon: he let out the vineyard unto keepers; every one for the fruit thereof was to bring a thousand pieces of silver.
> My vineyard, which is mine, is before me: thou O Solomon, must have a thousand, and those that keep the fruit thereof two hundred.
> Thou that dwellest in the gardens, the companions hearken to thy voice: cause me to hear it.
> Make haste, my beloved, and be thou like to a roe or to a young hart upon the mountains of spices." Song of Solomon 8:11- 14. (Old King James Version)

> "How should one chase a thousand, and two put ten thousand to flight, except their rock had sold them, and the Lord had shut them up.
> For their rock is not our Rock, even our enemies themselves being judges.
> For their vine is of the vine of Sodom, and of the fields of Gomorrah; their grapes are grapes of gall, their clusters are bitter.
> Their wine is the poison of dragons, and the cruel venom of asps.
> Is not this laid up in store with me, and sealed up among my treasures?"
> Deuteronomy 32:30-34 (Old King James Version)

Those verses from the Bible predict that a spirit that is a bluish-white light that sparkles and makes you smile ear to ear travels to and fro at summer vacations (August 10-11, 2013) and Christmas vacations (December 24-25, 2013). At those times are when many people travel (to and fro) and the angels speak to a thousand or 10,000 people as to where they can find knowledge (my books) on the end times that Daniel was seeking in Daniel chapter 12. The vine and vineyards Deuteronomy and Song of Solomon predicts are the grape harvest in August in the Chinese Year of the Snake (=asps), which is the year 2013.

In Deuteronomy 32:30 it predicts how "one chase a thousand, and two put ten thousand to flight..." and Song of Solomon 8:11- 14 predicts a thousand or ten thousand angels the same number "many" means in Daniel 12:4 that travel and speak to people where to buy my books. See also Isaiah chapter 7. They all predict a thousand and then ten thousand and one twenty thousand in Psalms 68:17. The meaning of these prophecies could mean a set of a 1000 angels are sent out in August 10-11, 2013 and tells 1000 people in Florida where to buy my ten copies of my 14 books and keep one and give the others to nine other people God shows you. Then on December 24-25, 2013 the second set of angles numbering 10,000, this time are sent out to certain people to tell them where to buy one copy of each of my 14 books. That would make 20,000 people altogether just as the Bible predicted. II Kings 2:11 predicts the prophet Elijah to have been taken by a great chariot (Auriga) of fire and horses and a whirlwind to heaven. His birthday is December 24-25. Is that when the 10,000 angels appear to tell and make known to 20,000 people altogether all 14 of my books and it all happens by July 2014. The Chariots of God in the Bible's Psalms 68:17 could be that of the constellation Auriga The Charioteer. It appears over head at midnight to 5 a.m. on December 25, 2013 when the second set of angels appear shortly after their first appearing on August 10-11, 2013. The first set of a thousand angels telling 1000 people to buy 10 copies of each of my fourteen books and the second set of a 10,000 angels that appear to them or new people later that year on Christmas morning would say that the author is in error or a heretic, crazy and his wisdom despised, but you are warn not to say that to the angel and buy copies of his books. This could also refer to a woman or women and/or men (=one or thousands) that may say that to the angels at their first coming or their second coming. Acts and Joel chapters 2 in the Bible predicts when the Holy Ghost comes 5000 would be save, then 3000 would be saved, then multitudes would be save, which means 10,000 or 20,000 the same number that Psalms 68:17 predicted as Chariots of God and by angel visitations. Auriga the Charioteer is not only over head at night in December 25, 2013 when angels come, but is over head near the sun in May-June when the Holy Ghost came in 30 A.D. That year is the Chinese Year of the Tiger the polar opposite of the Monkey. The Chinese Monkey rules Leo and August. That is when in August 10, 2013, or July-August of 2013, the first set of angels are sent out to tell of these books. And by that time in May-June-July of 2014 the 20,000 people will have been given or bought these books. Mount Sinai (Psalms 68:17) when Moses went up to shortly after Passover and was given the law many believe was in May-June of that year which was 1484 B.C. the Chinese Year of the Ox. The polar opposite of the Ox is the Sheep-Goat, which is our 2015 A.D. when people are to run for their lives in certain places in July-August. It is the time to flee by car on the mountains of spices (spring or summer time) in 2014 or 2015 or 2016 from Florida if you live there or from the U.S. East Coast. These verses predict these things:

> "Suffer not thy mouth to cause thy flesh to sin: neither say thou before the angel, that it was an error: wherefore should God be angry at thy voice, and destroy the work of thy hands?" Ecclesiastes 5:6 (Old King James Version)

> "Then said I, Wisdom is better than strength: nevertheless the poor man's wisdom is despised, and his words are not heard." Ecclesiastes 9:16. (Old King James Version).

When those certain people the angels had contact with that are in Florida and/or on the Eastern

Sea Coast of the U.S. see a person (angels?) on the rooftop or appears to you at night and warns you of these events in the summer of 2014-2015-2016 and/or January of 2019 then run away from those areas don't even stop to take things just drive away inland as far as you can and away from Florida. Take I-75 in Florida up through Georgia then connect with Road 24 through Tennessee and Kentucky then Road 65 to Indiana and stay there till all is clear or if Florida is totally destroyed find a new place there or inland.

In Israel the same thing applies on those dates, but run to the mountains east of the city of Jerusalem, or Petra, Jordan. These same things apply in August of 2015-2018 or March 12, April 12, plus or minus three days in 2015-2018 and in January of 2019. Those times are when Acts and Joel chapters two predict a darkened sun and blood moon as eclipses in January of 2019 and/or volcano ash and smoke and/or great troubles as wonders in the heavens above, and signs in the earth beneath (earthquakes-volcanoes, comet or asteroid impact, wars) blood and fire and vapour of smoke (volcano-nuclear bombs?) in July- August or March-April and January of 2015-2019.

The "one week" of Daniel 9:27 might just be literally one week before the end at January 21, 2019, or January 13-14-21, 2019, when the sun increases light, stormy seas or tidal waves, earthquakes, wars, attacks-nuclear and volcano eruptions and all that is predicted above and in this book and my other books happens. This is what is predicted in the Bible for Israel and the Eastern U.S. to do at this time:

> "Then let them which be in Judaea flee into the mountains:
> Let him which is on the housetop not come down to take any thing out of his house:
> Neither let him which is in the field return back to take his clothes.
> And woe unto them that are with child, and to them that give suck in those days!
> But pray ye that your flight be not in the winter, neither on the sabbath day:"
> Matthew 24:16-20. (Old King James Version)

Do not look for your beloved at this time. See Song of Solomon chapter 3. For as Isaiah chapter 54, Matthew chapter 24 and Ecclesiastes 5:6 predicts as the days of Noah one woman born on May 19 (Noah's Flood) and/or other women and men will mock the angel saying the author was insane (=error). Thus, God may destroy the works of their hands, that is their houses or apartments or condos, cars and all material things and possibly their lives by the tidal waves (flood) this author warned about. See Ecclesiastes 5:6. Noah's flood happened in 2341 B.C. which was the Chinese Year of the Monkey that rules our month of August and the Leo sign. August 10, 2015 or July- August 2015, or that same date or July-August in 2014 or 2016, is the Chinese Horse or Monkey Year. On March 12, April 12, plus or minus three days 2015-2018, or in January of 2019 these events or others may happen. Zephaniah 3:17-20 predicts a time when all troubles are undone when people gather for a solemn assembly. The solemn assembly could be a funeral and/or a fast and be my dad's funeral that happened between January 18-28, 1985, which is the same calendar as 2019. The fast is in the fifth month, or our July-August of 2014-2019 as Zechariah predicted. The solemn assembly could also be Pearl Harbor Day of December 7, 1941, which we seen has important events happen on that date in 2013. The predictions of Ecclesiastes 9:16 that the poor man's words are despised and not heard may mean all of the predictions from 2013-2019 don't happen and people mock and despise him for his predictions and wisdom in his books (=words) and he remains poor as Isaiah 57:12 predicts his works (=books) shall not profit him and no one or few read or buy his books, but his righteousness and truth and wisdom stands. These prophecies could also mean I die before the events happen or before I wrote all these books in the war of 1982-1985, 1992, 1996-1997. Or between now (October 2011) and up till when these events start happening in July-August of 2013. If I die I don't profit from these books because I am dead and the wisdom or the inheritance of these books goes to someone else as Ecclesiastics 7:11, 11:2 predicts.

During these times in January of 2019 there maybe a strange event that causes the earth's rotation to stop by stopping Venus' rotation. This will leave some of the world in total darkness for three days and part of the world in sun light for three days and some of the world in the evening or morning times for three days. A storm and tidal waves may also happen during these times fulfilling Luke 21:25-27 perfectly as signs in the sun, moon and stars and the seas and waves roaring and on earth distress of nations with great perplexity and then the son of man returns. In Daniel 2:21-22, Ecclesiastes 12:2, Zechariah 14:6-7, Matthew 24:22 and Luke 21:11 all predict these events. The only way time could be shorten is by the rotation of the earth to stop as Matthew 24:22 predicts along with the other verses. The reason this may happen is because Venus right now it rotating positively making a curse on the earth, human aging and all kinds of troubles. If after three days of no time the earth and Venus starts rotating again, but Venus is then rotating negatively then the curse and aging on humans will be gone and people will live long lives like in the Old Testament. This will make way for not a sun supernova to happen in January 21, 2019, but delay that event for a 1000 years. But instead of a supernova Christ comes back right after this event in January 2019 and rules the earth in peace for a 1000 years. This is what the Bible meant by strange and fearful signs in the heavens and time being change darkness at noon, evening or morning time, seasons being changed and the alterations of the solstices and equinoxes because once the three days are up it will only be the next day even though three days happen, thus, shortening the days as Matthew 24:22 predicted. The end of the world would be the end of the age at this time. Then after the 1000 year Kingdom reign satan is let lose and then shortly after our sun goes into a supernova and then the end of the world happens. And then people are taken off the earth to a new one with the new Jerusalem in heaven to live there forever in peace. See Revelation chapters 20-22 and II Peter chapter 3. What this time shorting does to the date of January 21, 2019 is not clear at this time. Does the rotation stop on that date or before or after it or at all?

This leads us to the writing of my books in which I tried unsuccessfully for 21 years to get published. Over that time period well over 750 rejections of it. In the year of 1997 I was trying the hardest ever to get it published without success. The years of no salary and stress of writing these books had taken its toll. I went up to Florida's Silver Springs attraction Park to take a break. I was really depressed about it.

When a got into the glass bottom boat I really was low and cried out in my mind for help from God and from my dad who died some years earlier. All the pain and trouble over this book was taking its toll over all those 21 years since I started writing it in August of 1976. I have lost my friends, some of my family and much humiliation and frustration because of it. I have given up my promising job as a carpenter and all the glories of life (wife, children, lands, houses, cars and material things) and career for it. My life savings was spent long ago over this book. I had nothing to show for it.

As I sat in the glass bottom boat I really was in need of some hope I cry in my mind Lord help me! Dad help me!! Out of this misery I heard a still small voice say *Field of Dreams*. I had started that movie the day before that day on Sunday. So when I went home after Silver Springs I finish the movie *Field of Dreams*. At the end Kevin Coster's dad eases his pain. A powerful personal message I right away seen coming from this movie to me. I looked up Kevin Costner's birthday. It was shocking the very day my dad died on January 18 from colon cancer that moved into his liver. He died at 11:10-

11:11 a.m. and was born 1919, which was the Chinese Year of the Sheep or Goat. Kevin Costner's birthday was January 18, 1955, which was near the Chinese Year of the Sheep or Goat. My dad died in 1985 near the Chinese Year of the Ox the same as January 18-19, 2010 is at the end of the Chinese Year of the Ox. And when I first viewed the movie *Field of Dreams* it was the Chinese Year of the Ox on September 7-8, 1997 and was a Sunday-Monday. January 18, 2010 is a Monday.

I looked up James Earl Jones' birthday and found it January 17. I then looked up Amy Madigan and found it to be September 11, very near when I was viewing the movie on September 7-8, 1997. It also maybe when many events happen on 9-11-01. September 8, 1997 was a Monday as is January 18, 2010 is. And Amy Madigan birth year was 1950 the Chinese Year of the Tiger the same as 2010 when in May predicted events happen.

I looked up the writer and director of the movie and found he was the son of Jesse. My father was the youngest son of Jesse the same as David the father of Solomon. I looked up Gaby Hoffman, the little girl in the movie, and found her birthday as January 8, 1982. January 9, 1982 was a lunar eclipse.

In verse 19 of Psalms 89:19 is the day in September when my father was born the youngest son of Jesse on September 19? Just as David was born on who wrote Psalms. Psalms chapter 89 is our year 1989 when the movie *Field of Dreams* was released. The vision of that verse of Psalms could mean a movie. Movies are pictures that aren't really there as a dream in our heads at night are and is what the Bible calls here as a vision. Was it predicting motion pictures? Psalms 89:19 predicts God to talk to some one through a vision (movie). The "horn" of Psalms chapter 89 could refer to the Capricorn sign, which is a sea goat with horns. Opposite Capricorn is Cancer, which July 19-20, 2010 is in the sign of Cancer. The carving from the temple Hathor in ancient Egypt shows a goat's head and horns with a Sun and Moon disk between them near a kneeling woman with seven stars and 12 stars next to her. And both the books of the Bible Revelation chapter 12 and Song of Solomon 6:10 predicts a woman with the Sun and Moon in the morning. On July 19-20, 2010 the Sun use to be leaving Cancer the Moon and entering Leo the Sun and as we read July 19-20, 2010 are a Monday (Moon=day) and a Tuesday (Mars=Leo=Sun). The goat could also refer to Capricorn just mentioned as the end time month or its polar opposite July when end time events happen. The seven and 12 stars where the woman is kneeling equals 19, or July 19, 2010. Capricorn rules the knees and the raft the goat's head is on in the carving represents waters or seas as Cancer is a water sign.

In the movie *Field of dreams* it shows two dates being 1919, and 1922, which are the years when my dad and mom were born.

In the movie Kevin Costner is trouble with his life and hears a voice to build a baseball field in the middle of his corn field. The full Moon in September 1997 when I was first watching this movie was called the Full Corn Moon. In the movie a character called Moonlight Graham, played by Burt Lancaster comes and heals Kevin Costner's (birthday January 18 when my dad died) little girl, or virgin (Virgo sign equals September 11, 2001) daughter.

The "go the distance" that the man hears and sees on the score board of the baseball game next to Moonlight Graham could be that of 12 years and 12 months from when I was watching the movie to be strengthen then like he is in the movie. In the movie he builds the baseball field and Christmas comes and goes meaning 12 months pass till the next corn harvest in September or when the movie was made in July. That is why we add 12 years and 12 months to 1997, which equals July 2010.

There is also a 16 year time span in the movie from 1972 in July when the movie *The Godfather* came out to its time of 1988. Add 16 years to 1997, when I first saw the film, and it equals 2013 as the time of the end harvest when I go the distance and see my dead father again.

My mom was born in 1922 and September 7-8, 1997 is in the Virgo sign, which is rules Boston where the base ball game was being played and the 1922 and Moonlight Graham is seen who is Burt

Lancaster born in November. The Moon rules Cancer, which is given the numbers 2-7 or 27, or September 27, 1922 when my mom was born in the cusp of the Virgo sign (Boston).

In the movie Kevin Costner's dad worked in the naval yards. My dad worked in the shipyards.

Was this movie the vision or movie David wrote about not to help ease his pain, but his son's? (Solomon's birthday October 15 same as me). "To go the distance" and "ease his pain" in July of 2010? Daniel 10:17 even predicted "how can this the servant of my lord talk with my lord?"

Was Daniel and David in Psalms 89:19-20 telling of this unusual talking between father and son in this movie (vision)? Were those verses numbers 19-20 equals July 19-20, 2010? And was Psalms chapter 89 the year 1989 when *Field of Dreams* came out and was filmed in July when I am strengthen in 2010 on the 19-20th day of July? Or its polar opposite on January 18-19, 2010 is when I am strengthened? Or is it April-May of 2010 when I am strengthen? The movie *Field of dreams* came out in April of 1989, which was the Chinese Year of the Snake. The Chinese Snake rules our sign of Taurus and month of May when end time events may happened on in 2010. One writer claimed that Psalms 1-100 were predictions of our years of 1901 to 2000 after each chapter as one year. And with Psalms being the nineteenth book in the Bible Psalms chapter 89 with 19 before it equals 1989. My dad died on January 18, 1985 about 11:10- 11:11 a.m. Will some event happen at that time on January 18- 19, 2010? Zephaniah 3:16-20 predicts that someone would be strengthen at a time when a solemn assembly is happening. The solemn assembly could be the funeral of my dad who died on January 18, 1985 at 11:10-11:11 a.m. At that time God will undo all that afflicts me as Zephaniah predicted in the Bible.

In this movie the character that James Earl Jones plays says at the end of the movie that people will come and pay $20.00 to see the old dead ball players play a game. And at the very end of the movie when Kevin Costner's dead dad appears to have a catch with him ends with a long line of cars coming to the field. The two disc DVD's on this movie and how it was made says that there were more than 1,500 cars used in the end coming to pay $20.00 each to see the field of dreams. My 14 books sell for about $20.00-25.00 each including shipping and handling or not. That's the same amount James Earl Jones character said the people in the cars would pay. And 1,500 is close to 1000 people the Bible predicted to pay a 1,000 pieces of silver for 14 books. Maybe they buy 10 copies of each book to make $550-600 dollars altogether and by the end 1,500 people have bought these 14 books of mine. Deuteronomy 32:30 predicted 1000 and 10,000. If a 1000 buys 10 copies each of these 14 books of mine it equals 10,000 copies of the 14 books given to 9 other people by each of the first 1000 people be 10,000. And we read how 1000 pieces of silver equals .55-60 cents each multiplied that by a 1000 and it equals $550-600 dollars. That is what the 1000 people pay for 10 copies of each of my books exactly as the Bible predicted in Song of Solomon 8:11-14; Deuteronomy 32:30; and Isaiah 7:23. It even predicts it by a publisher of employees of about 200 who publish three books from an author in the Southeast (Baalhamon or Edom southeast of Jerusalem, Israel). Authorhouse, where these three books are published by, we seen had about 200 employees in 2003.

I don't know when the screenplay was done, or if it was started or done before January 18, 1985. I guess it could be a wild coincidence. My dad often in life wondered about and researched life after death communications. There was even one phrase I heard used in this movie that I never heard in any other movie that my dad often spoke.

And as in the end of the movie the writer is told by Kevin Costner to give a full description of the heaven out there in the corn field. I plan to give a full description dad in this book. And possibly the two witnesses will as well.

Thanks for the vision Dad!

Update: I saw this movie *Field of Dreams* for the first time on Sunday-Monday September 7-8, 1997, which was a Sunday into Monday and the full moon with a lunar eclipses happened on September 16, 1997. Add the 16 years in the film "to go the distance" to 1997 and it equals September 7, 2013. September 7-8, 1997 was the Virgo sign that has as it cosign Gemini as the third sign and twins or the number two. Add three months to September 7, 2013 and it equals December 7, 2013, which in my other books show is an important date with double blessings and possibly double trouble. Add three months (=Gemini) to December 7, 2013 and it equals March 7, 2014, and again a time of a great double blessing or trouble. Add five years (=Virgo) to September 16, 2013 and it equals September 16, 2018. Then add five months, counting each month to that date and it equals January 16, 2019. Add five days (=Virgo=five) to that date from which we came all the way from September 16, 1997 when there was a lunar eclipse and it equals January 21, 2019 when there is another lunar eclipse. The film *Field of Dreams* was filmed in July of 1988 and released in April of 1989. Opposite July is January and 1989 is the Chinese Year of the Snake, which on December 7, 2013 and December 24-25, 2013, seen in the movie at Christmas time, is when I go the distance and ease my pain when as Ecclesiastics 9:7 states God now accepts your works (books). In that verse "merry" could mean Merry Christmas (December 24-25, 2013), the "wine" meaning the wine harvest of August 9-10-11, 2013, and the "bread" being a great feast day with turkey and stuffing (=bread) as Thanksgiving is near the end of November and Hanukkah on November 28-December 5, 2013, which is also a feast day with bread. See Zechariah 7:1, Haggai 2:18-23 and Jeremiah 30:19. The last verse in Jeremiah 30:19 has the very words merry, or our Merry Christmas, and thanksgiving, as our Thanksgiving Day in November. Both are great feast days and days to make merry on. Are the chapter and verse numbers of Ecclesiastes 9:7 the ninth month to the Bible, or our month of December, and the seventh day as our December 7, 2013 when God "now accepteth thy works" (my books). And then my dad's death on January 18, 1985 is a Friday the same as January 18, 2019. Add three days from Virgo and its cosign of Gemini, that is the third sign, to my dad's death and it equals January 20-21, 2019 the time of the end. Zechariah 7:1-3 prediction of the ninth month and fourth day which we read in my books means December 7, 2013 as the Bible's ninth month and fourth day of Chisleu in 518 B.C. according to *The Ryrie Study Bible* in the chapter 7 verses 1-3 of Zechariah and its notes and the *Parallel Bible* under the *Living Translation*. The Year 518 B.C. equals the Chinese Year of the Sheep the same year that 2015 A.D. is. The book of Haggai predicts three be strongs or three years of blessings ending on the ninth month and 24th day, which in Hebrew calendar's is December 6-7-8, 2015 the time that the Jewish Holiday Hanukah starts in the Chinese Year of the Sheep. Will 10,000 or 20,000 people be told where to buy these 14 books on August 10, 2013 and August 10, 2015, equaling 20,000 people that Psalms 68:17 predicted with 20,000 chariots or cars that travel to and fro on summer vacations in the fifth month of the Bible in July-August of 2013-2015? See Daniel 12:4,7. The "early" of Psalms 90:14 may mean the angels and sales of these books happen in July-August of 2013-2015, in the wine harvest, but the royalties don't come until December of those years. And Malachi 3:11 predicts books not to be revealed before its time when the vine of the field or the grape or wine harvest happens in July-August of 2013-2015 and the royalty checks not until winter house (=December of 2013- 2015) and time of Elijah (=born December 24-25 or December of 2013-2015) as Malaci 3:10-11 and 4:5-6. Malachi 3:1 predicts a messenger or angels to be sent out at the time of that chapter and verse number. Put the chapter and verse number together and you have 31. Reverse that number and you have 13, which year ending in those numbers is 2013 when angels are sent out. In Year/Chapter codes Malachi chapter 4 would be our year 2009. The Year 2009 in Chinese astrology is the Year of the Ox. The polar opposite of that year is the Year of the Sheep which is 2015 when angels (messengers) are again sent out. The "sun of righteousness" and "calves" in Malachi chapter 4 are the sun that rules Leo the lion. The dates of August 10, 2013 and 2015 are when angels are sent out and those dates are in Leo the lion sign ruled by the sun. The "calves" equals the Ox family or its polar opposite the Chinese Year of the Sheep in 2015 on August 10. Malachi 3:7-11 predicts someone to give all their money and then sometime later at the right time God will open up the heavens and pour out a blessing that there's not room enough to receive. See Malachi 3:10. The "storehouse" in that verse equals winter house or autumn house when people lay up their food in storage for the coming winter and next year. In October (autumn store house) of 1982 I withdrew all my money from the bank and gave it all to the TV preachers after this verse command. Will in the fall or winter (=storehouse) of 2015 after the fruit of the vine time is ripe and the right year in August 10, 2015 will I see a blessing to much for me to comprehend? Is it a 100 million copies sold of each of my 14 books? The "book of remembrance" that Malachi 3:16 predicts at this time of August 10, 2015 could be that of all my 14 books written years before (remembrance=years before) that year will sell a 100 million copies with one of those book of mine giving the exact date and events of the volcano, earthquake and tidal wave hitting Florida and the U.S. East Coast? That book is entitled *Predictions for 2015*. The seven seals of the book of Revelation chapter 5 equals seven eyes and seven horns, which we seen equals 14 books on the world wide web or WWW. Or are the numbers 20,000 in one or two years of 2013-2014 and 100 million in 2015 as Revelation chapter 5 along with Daniel chapter 7 predicts? The "wings" of Malachi 4:2 are two as equaling two years and times the many (=1000) angels (=wings=messengers) go out from 2013-2015. The wings could also mean travel of the angels by wings and people by planes on summer vacations and winter Holidays. The "double" blessing of Isaiah 61:7 and Zechariah 9:10-14 might be the angels that are sent out at these two times to tell people where to buy my books on August 10, 2013 and August 10, 2015 and the royalty checks come on December 7, 2013 and December 7-8, 2015, which are dates we read in my books as special times predicted in the Bible, dreams and angel visitations.

On September 25-26-27, 3005 are dates near Rosh Hashanah the Jewish New Year and a new moon as was September 26-27, 2003. The Year 3005 is the Chinese Year of the Ox which the ancient Egyptian carving from the temple Hathor shows Ox horns on figures near Libra, which starts on September 21-23 to October 20-23. Could that have meant the grime reaper on that day in 3005 A.D.? Nostradamus quatrain C1:Q56 predicts when the angel (new moon) is approaching Libra changes are made in the times and dates "sooner and later", like the times and dates in my other books and this book and a great vengeance comes. And does the date in this book and my other books for the end in January 21, 2019 mean the Rapture when Jesus comes back as a thief in the night (secretly) and takes all (or one?) the Holy Christians to heaven followed by a seven year period of trouble on the earth as Daniel 9:27 predicted? Seven years added to January 21, 2019 equals the year 2025 A.D. when the Second Coming of Christ happens to reign a 1000 years or the end of the world happens then. If He reigns for a 1000 years from 2025 it equals 3015 A.D. when on June 24 there is a lunar eclipse and the end comes. The 1000 year reign of 360 days for each year equals 15 years shorter from 2025 to 3010 A.D., plus five years satan is let lose for equals 3015 when the end comes as II Peter chapter 3 predicts. The exact date maybe on June 24-25, 3015, the Chinese Year of the Pig, the same as 2019 A.D. which is when the great Rapture happens and both times (2019 and 3015) are times of Christ's return, one in secret (=thief in the night) and one in full view (=seen in the sky with great glory as the sun goes into a supernova).

II Samuel 11:1-2 predicts when the year expires is when kings go to war at eveningtide. There are many times to different calendars as to when the "year expires" or New Year's Day begins. In December 31, 1982 into January 1, 1983 were important dates for prophecies. Those dates are the year of the Dog in Chinese astrology. Will in December 31, 2018 into January 1, 2019 or later in that month will we see kings (Presidents) go to war? Or does the Rapture happen then or in that month and seven years later in January of 2025 the kings go to war when the year expires to the New

Gregorian calendar? Will prisoners be released then as in January 1, 1983 they were in Louisiana? Will there be river flooding then as was in January 1, 1983?

If you see a person on the rooftop or an angel appears to at these times then flee from Florida or inland from Florida's East Coast about 50 miles and from the East Coast of the U.S. In Israel flee to the mountains in the East or Petra, Jordan. Once there, if these events happen, store up quickly food and water and try to find a place with a fireplace and store up wood.

Burt Lancaster seen in the movie *Field of Dreams* was born in 1913 and died in 1994. The Chinese Year of 1913 was the sign of the Ox which rules our month and sign of January and Capricorn. The Chinese Year of 1994 is the Year of the Dog which January of 2019 is the ending of the Chinese Year of the Dog.

At this time in January or March 12-April 12, August 10, July-August from 2013-2019, or the other dates given in my other books could see great earthquakes, storms, tidal waves, attacks, wars and volcano eruptions happen on those dates in those years or the years 2011-2019. In fact, August 10, 2014- 2015-2016 is when these prophecies predict the volcano to erupt in the Canary Islands off the West Coast of Africa. That would cause a great tidal wave to hit Florida and the U.S. East Coast in August 10, 2014-2015-2016, plus or minus three days, or July-August, along with a war or some kind of attack on the U.S. and/or Israel at that time. See my other books *Predictions for 2013-2014, Predictions for 2015, Predictions for 2011-2019* and this book, which are included in this book.

Revelation 16:10 predicts the beast's kingdom (the U.S.?) be full of darkness. Was this referring to the volcano ash of the volcano in the Canary Islands blowing over to the U.S.? Or is it Yellow Stone Park volcano erupting making all or most of the U.S. dark even at noon as Isaiah 16:3 and Amos 5:8 causing great earthquakes, famines and pestilence's just as Jesus predicted in Matthew 24:7-8 and Luke 21:9-11. The "by and by" of Luke 21:9 and Jeremiah's 51:46 predictions of rumors of wars and then a year or two later war and great destruction may be these events. Or it may be war or attacks like a EMP bomb exploded over the middle of the U.S. that causes all electronic and electricity to stop throwing the whole U.S. into darkness and causing great cold, heat, earthquakes, great famines and pestilence's.

The movie *Field of Dreams* was released sometime in April 1989 (=Snake) and was mostly shot in July of 1988 (=Dragon). Was these things predictions of July-August of 2012, the Chinese Dragon Year the same as 1988, and April 2013, the Chinese Snake Year, the same as April 1989, when events happen and travel happens at both times like the roes and hinds of the field running or skipping upon the mountains of the highways as cars do after the voice of the beloved is heard the July-August before then in 2012 in the wine or vineyard harvest time. See Song of Solomon 2:7-13, 8:13-14, Revelation 2:29. The great constellation Auriga The Charioteer appears in the East in the early morning before dawn (4 a.m.-6a.m.) July 27-31 and August 1-13, 2012-2013-2019 and beyond. Is this what Psalms 68:17, Song of Solomon 8:11-14, 2:8-17 and Amos 5:8 meant by morning, angels and voices, Chariots running down and up the hills of highways at the time of a vineyard harvest (=July-August) in the south in 2012-2013-2019 or beyond. Daniel 12:4 predicts a time of summer vacations when many travel (=20,000 chariots) and knowledge is increased by books revealed then by the voice of angels. July-August are the two months when most summer vacations are taken in the U.S. One star of the constellation Auriga The Charioteer is apart of the Taurus constellation known as the seven stars and has seven stars in it known as the seven sisters. And Orion and Gemini are right near Taurus and Auriga. Gemini is ruled by Mercury that is associated with messengers or angels from God who tell men and women things.

Chapter Twenty Four

2012

Note: The dates and years given in this chapter may not happen then, but in years to come on those same dates but different years. They are set as a foreshadow of things to come as Colossians 2:16-17 and Ecclesiastics 1:9 predicts just as the ancient Egyptian and Mayans believed things that happen in the past will come true in the future and things that look like they will happen now are foreshadows of times, dates, places, people of things that will come true in our future.

The Mayans' calendar ends December 21-22, 2012. Many speculate that the world ends then and/or a new age begins, but what does the Bible say about that date?

Revelation chapter 11 predicts three and a half days after God's two witnesses are dead that a great earthquake or quakes strike Jerusalem, Israel and/or the U.S. when people give gifts one to another all over the world. We know that time as Christmas Eve and Day as when people all over the world give gifts one to another. The three and a half days added to December 21-22, 2012 equals December 24-25, 2012, which are Christmas Eve and Day when gifts are exchanged all over the world.

Ecclesiastes 7:14 predicts the day of prosperity is the same day as adversity (trouble). Was it predicting that December 24-25, 2012, three and half days after the death of God's two witnesses, that a great earthquake strikes the city of Jerusalem, Israel killing seven thousand men and destroying a tenth of the city? See Revelation chapter 11.

Daniel 12:4,7 predicts when many people travel to and fro that knowledge of end times will be shown by angels to certain people. December 21-25, 2012 is when many people all over the world travel to and fro for the Christmas holidays. And Revelation 3:22 predicts that an angel (spirit) speaks to certain people on those dates telling them where to buy books on end-time prophecies. This angel is a bluish-white light that makes you smile ear to ear. Daniel 12:7 predicts time, times and half as three and a half years from the Christmas holidays in 2012 to the end. In fact, Daniel 9:27, Revelation chapters 10,11, 12 and 13 also mention that same time period of three and a half years to God's time clock as a countdown to the end by 360 day years, which to us is 365.24 day years. The prediction of 1260 days, 42 months and time, times and a half all equals three and a half years from December 24-25, 2012 to the end on June 24-25, 2016.

Revelation chapter 12 predicts a great red dragon and a woman clothed with the sun and the moon under her feet with 12 stars. Are the 12 stars and chapter 12 codes for the year ending in 2012 in the 12th month of December when it is the Chinese Year of the Great Red Dragon? The red planet Mars (red Dragon) predicted in Revelation chapter 12 is the Latin name for Tuesday, which is December 25, 2012. The sun the woman is clothe with that is also predicted in Revelation chapter 12 rules Leo the lion and is Mars, which, as stated is the Latin name for Tuesday. See Appendix A: The Codes in my book *The boy who could predict earthquakes*. And the moon under the woman's feet in Revelation chapter 12 is Latin for Monday, which December 24, 2012 is. Thus the sun and moon in Revelation chapter 12 means Monday-Tuesday December 24-25, 2012, in the Chinese Year of the Dragon (2012). Also the moon is given the number 2 or 20 and the sun is Pisces the 12th sign and 12 backwards is 21. Put it all together and you have December 21, 2012.

Matthew 24:19-20, 32-33, 37, 48-51, Luke 17:26 and II Peter 3:2-18 may also predict these dates plus three and a half years. Matthew 24:19-20 predicts trouble on a Sabbath day in winter time when a woman gives birth and suck as the date of end time events. Friday-Saturday to the Jewish People is the Jewish Sabbath on December 21-22, 2012. It is also the start of winter time. And December 24-25, 2012 is a Monday-Tuesday when a woman gives suck (breasts) to a newborn (=Christmas Day=Christ's birthday). The word "suck" can also mean breasts, which is when summer begins and the Cancer sign is on June 20- 21, 2016. And December 24, 2012 is a Monday, which is named after the moon that rules Cancer and the breasts (suck). June 24-25, 2016 is also a time of giving of gifts one to another on the true Christmas Day of June 24-25. (See my book titled *The Nativity*.)

Cancer and the moon rule the breasts which newborns suck on and the Cancer sign begins June 20-21. Shortly after that counting three and half days equals June 24-25, 2016. This is what Matthew 24:32-33, 37, 48-51 mean by the Lord "delayeth" His coming in December of 2012, and then people mock and scoff at the prophecies that God's two witnesses claim for so long were coming and didn't. See Matthew 24:48-51 and II Peter 3:2- 18. June 24-25, 2016 is a Friday-Saturday (=Jewish Sabbath) shortly after summer begins and just as prophesied we would know the end is soon when summer draws nigh (=June 20-21.) See Matthew 24:32. And there are exactly three and a half years from December 24-25, 2012 to June 24-25, 2016, which is the Chinese Year of the Monkey that rules our Leo the lion sign that Revelation 5:5 predicts as the sign of the end.

The "root of David" that Revelation 5:5 and Revelation 22:16 predict as the root and offspring of David and the bright and morning star all connect here to Jesse the root or father of David born in the Cancer sign (June 20-27, 2016). And David's offspring is Solomon born October 15 as the Libra sign that is ruled by Venus, whose Latin name is Friday, which both December 21, 2012 and June 24, 2016 are. The "door" that Matthew 24:33 and Revelation 4:1 predict is that of the Capricorn sign that begins on December 21-22, 2012. To the ancients Capricorn meant "gateway" or "door" to the heavens. And when Matthew 24:37 and Luke 17:26 predict the end as the days of Noah it means the time of the end is in the Monkey Year of 2016. Through computer software we now know that the flood happened May 19-20, or November 10-11, 2341 B.C., which was the 17th day of the second month as Genesis 7:11 states. And creation happened in May-June according to my other book *The Experiment at Philadelphia*. So when II Peter 3:2-17 predicts scoffers to come like a flood of Noah and creation he was referring to May-June and 2341 B.C. when it was the Chinese Year of the Monkey the same as 2016 A.D. on June 24-25.

Both these dates of December 24-25, 2012 and June 24-25, 2016 are birthdays as we have and will read of certain Bible prophets. Matthew 24:7-8 predicts earthquakes at a time when a woman is in labor pains. One birthday is the birth of John the Baptist on December 24-25, in the Chinese Year of the Dragon and the other birthday is on June 24-25 for Jesus Christ, which in 2016 is when the end comes. The word "sorrows" in Matthew 24:8 can be translated as "pangs" or "birth pains" showing us these two dates of births of John the Baptist and Jesus Christ as the dates of future events in 2012 and 2016.

The two witnesses of Revelation chapter 11 that are killed by an earthquake, attack, sickness, natural causes or an airplane crash could be both political and/or religious leaders in the U.S. and/or Israel. II Peter 3:2-6 predicts when the fathers fall asleep (die) and no end comes scoffers will come. They will shout how they (fathers) died and the end had not come after their preaching the end is near for so many years, yet things continue as they were from creation and the flood (May-June.) They will shout how the end still hasn't come even after the 2012 date so why bother to look for the end and Second Coming because it is foolishness.

Creation happened in the Chinese Years of the Sheep or Goat and Snake. Those same years are 2013 and 2015. The waters or the flood of Noah that those verses state previously would be in May-

June or November-December of 2013-2015. It also could be December 21-25, 2012 when these two great witnesses die as predicted in my book *The boy who could predict earthquakes*. The years 2012 and 2013 are water years in Chinese astrology and could be what II Peter 3:2-7 means by waters and the flood. Noah's flood happened either May 19-20 or November 10-11. The Chinese water signs mean winter or autumn when these events could happen. The Bible also calls winter autumn. And remember Matthew 24:19-20 prediction of end times in winter? The Greek word for "winter" (December 21-25) is near words for "1000, cherubim, manuscript and hand." Those words in Greek could be predicting 1000 or 20,000 angels or cherubs appear and speak to certain people telling them where to find books (=manuscripts) on December 21-25, 2012 (winter). It also may predict the end as the hand 10 years (10 fingers) from the Chinese Year of the Dog in 2006+10=2016, which equals June 20- 25, 2016. See these words in Greek numbered 5494-5507 in the Greek dictionary of *the Strong's Concordance of the Bible*.

The identity of these two religious witnesses of God could be Billy Graham and Pat Robertson both born in the Chinese Year of the Horse. The Chinese sign of the Horse rules our Gemini sign of the twins. The twins equals two as the two witnesses of Revelation chapter 11 that are the two olive trees (or branches) and two candlesticks or lamps. Hal Lindsey and/or Perry Stone may be one or two of the two great witnesses of Revelation chapter 11 instead of Billy Graham and Pat Robertson. Do they both die on December 21-25, 2012 and/or June 20-25, 2016?

The three woes of Revelation chapters 8,9 and 11 with the second woe happening as the earthquake in Jerusalem after the dead two witnesses of God lay there for three and half days could mean that nothing happens in December 21-25, 2012 and people scoff. Then in June 20-21, 2016 the two witnesses of God die and then earthquakes happen three and a half days later. Then people scoff and mock the prophecies and very quickly the end or third woe comes. That is when the end of the world happens on June 24-25, 2016. It could happen either way, meaning the death of God's two witnesses happens on December 21-22, 2012 or June 20-21, 2016.

Revelation chapter 12 predicts the great red dragon and three and half years to the end starting from the 12 month (December) and 12th year (2012=Dragon). We have calculated that three and a half years from December 24-25, 2012 equals June 24-25, 2016 as the end. I don't know why the last two woes come quickly if three and half years happens between the two except that the dates are polar opposites making them the same time and date, thus they quickly happen on those dates or they happen in June 20-21, 2016 and then three and a half days later comes the great earthquakes and then the end quickly follows. This would be three and a half years after 2012 when everyone thought the end would come, thus they scoff from then and from these times and in June 20-25, 2016. And as I stated Revelation chapter 12 in reverse is 21 in the 12 month of our calendar in the Chinese Year of the Dragon, which is December 21, 2012 at winter time on the Jewish Sabbath.

Luke 21:20-36 and Matthew 24:15-21 predicts a time of the end when you see armies in the city (Jerusalem?) and people are partying over the Christmas holidays on December 21-25, 2012. Those verses tell the Jews at that time to run to the mountains in the south. Revelation chapter 12 tells of a Dragon who will shoot two or three stars (a third) from heaven down on Israel and that the Jews at that time should flee into the wilderness, which means the south where Petra is. Petra is a great city carved out of the mountains south of Jerusalem. The current President of Iran right now (July 2010) has his birthday in the Chinese Year of the Monkey the same year as 2016 is. And Revelation chapter 12 predicts him to draw down two or three missiles or bombs on Israel in the 12 month of December and in the Dragon Year of 2012. That time of December 21-25, 2012 is when it's winter, a Sabbath, and a famous birthday (Christmas Day and John the Baptist birthday of December 24-25, 2012). At that time is when people are over eating, drinking and going about the cares of this life as people do during the Christmas holidays. Three and a half days before Christmas Day and Eve are

December 21-22, 2012 a Friday-Saturday (Jewish Sabbath) and is the beginning of winter just as those prophecies predicted.

Revelation chapter 12 predicts three and a half years from the Year of the Dragon, will come stars falling down from heaven as wars in heaven happens. Those Years are 2012-2013 (Dragon) and 2016 (Monkey) when two or three missiles are fired by Iran at Israel and the sun goes into a supernova with parts of its outer layer flying and hitting the earth. Both are as predicted in Revelation chapter 12 as stars falling from heaven and war in heaven in the Dragon and Monkey Years in Chinese astrology. Revelation chapter 12 predicts the Dragon (2012- 2013) and mentions the serpent, which tempted Adam and Eve in the Garden in 3997 B.C., which was the Year of the Monkey (2016).

Hal Lindsey once stated about the prophecy of II Peter 3:3- 4 that it must have been written to the Church because the world could care less about the Second Coming and the end. If Israel is destroyed in 2012-2013, then the years 2013, 2014, 2015 come and go without Christ's return, then many in the Church would probably say "where is the promise of his coming for since the fathers (the many Jews killed in the war of 2012- 2013) fell asleep (died in that war) things continue as from creation." They may even say that about this book in 2012- 2013, 2016 and later on in 2050, 2054, 2055 and 2060.

The reason they may say that is because the Bible predicts Jesus' Second Coming is at the end to save Israel before it's destroyed. If Israel is destroyed in 2012-2013 and things continue as they were in 2013, 2014, 2015 then the Christians in the Churches, the remaining Jews and Rabbi's in the many synagogues around the world will begin to mock and scoff at the Bible and its predictions. They scoff at it because no Christ came to save it. And it continues as a desolate place where briers and thorns grow up and the only thing that can live there are demons and weird animal that are unclean. Isaiah chapters 7 and 13 predicts this of Israel after many arrows (missiles or bombs) are shot at Israel (a spiritual Babylon) by the Medes (Iran) and/or Syria and Russia at the end times.

Hal Lindsey said once that Israel has a Samson complex and that is if it is destroyed it will destroy all its enemies all around it as Samson did in the Bible. Along with Iran's nuclear missiles Syria may launch a massive amount of scud missiles with biological and/or chemical warheads on Israel. These great weapons of Iran, along with Syria and Russia are described in Zechariah chapter 14. They would make, as Isaiah chapters 7 and 13 predicts, Israel to be a complete desolation that is uninhabitable for years to come that only briers and thorns can grow there. This maybe what Luke chapter 21 means by the times of the Gentiles in the end times. It could of meant that Israel is destroyed and only Gentile nations live on in the world for three and a half years later or longer as Isaiah 13:19-22 predicts from generation to generation. A generation of 40 years added to 2012-2013 or 2016 equals 2052- 2053-2056. Then the next generation starts in 2052-2056 and the end of the world and the Second Coming of Christ happens then shortly after those dates.

If this great war happens in 2016 along with all the other signs and prophecies Jesus predicted in Matthew chapter 24, Mark chapter 13 and Luke chapter 21 then one generation will pass till the end and the Second Coming of Christ. Those prophecies will be signs as the beginning of sorrows that come first then one generation later the end and Second Coming happens. See Matthew 24:7-8, 34. This makes 2016 the start and count down to the end and Second Coming by one generation. A generation can be 40 years give or take five-six years. Add 40 years to 2016 and it equals 2056. Add or subtract five or six years to that year and it equals 2050-2060 or 2062 when the end comes and the Second Coming of Christ happens.

If the wars, attacks, earthquakes and death of the two TV preachers doesn't happen in 2012-2013 or 2016 and 2020-2062 comes and the fathers fall asleep (die) by that time then the end and Second Coming of Christ comes quickly in the years 2050-2062. Many will scoff during the years 2016-2062 claiming where is the promise of His Coming since the fathers fell asleep all things continue as from creation. They say the Lord "delayeth" His Coming and "is slack" concerning His promises. See Matthew 24:48 and II Peter 3:9. By 2050-2062 many of the old TV preachers and writers on Bible prophecy predicting Christ return is near since 1940-2016 will have died of old age or sickness by then. They are the "fathers" that fell asleep (died) not the two witnesses or the many Jews and/or Americans killed in the war or attacks of 2012-2013 or 2016, if those events happen. Those fathers who die of old age or sickness have often said the end is near and the Rapture and Second Coming is near from 1940 till 2012-2013 and beyond and nothing happened. In fact, Matthew 24:48-49 predict them as saying "my lord delayeth his coming and they go and eat and drink with the drunken." If December 21, 2012 comes and goes without the Second Coming of Christ and the end of the world happening people may go and over eat and drink then. That time would be the time during the celebration of Christmas and New Year's on December 24-25 and December 31-January 1, 2012-2013. And exactly as II Peter 3:3-4, 9 predicted they would then be mocking, laughing and scoffing at that date and prophecies of the Mayans, Egyptians and Nostradamus.

The book of Psalms in the Bible is divided into five books and has 150 chapters. One man stated that Psalms chapters 1- 100 are prophecies after our years 1901-2000 A.D. If you count the rest of the chapters of Psalms you come to 2050 A.D. as the end and the Second coming of Jesus Christ. The Year 2050 is the Chinese Year of the Horse and 2060 is the Chinese Year of the Dragon. If you add the 10 virgins of Matthew 25:1-13 as 10 years to 2050 you again come to the year 2060 when Sir Isaac Newton predicted the end to come and the great Second Coming of Christ would happen. If nothing happens in 2016, or the end or Second Coming of Christ doesn't happen then people will begin to scoff as II Peter 3:2-7 predicts when 2020, 2030, 2040, 2050 and 2060 comes. They will mock and scoff this book like crazy if the end and Second Coming of Christ doesn't come in 2016 and anyone trying to set dates or warning of those events in 2050 and 2060 will be utterly laughed at.

Nostradamus in his quatrain C3:Q94 predicts 500 years after his writing and publishing of his quatrains a new age will begin. Nostradamus wrote and published his quatrains the Centuries in 1554 and 1555. Add 500 years to those years and it equals 2054-2055, which are the Chinese Years of the Dog and Pig. The Chinese Year of the Dog I have stated in my books is after 26 A.D. and 2006 A.D. as the special time when events happen like the Lord's Prayer says: "hallowed be thy name, thy kingdom come…" God's name spelled backwards equals Dog or the Chinese Years of the Dog that 26 A.D., 2006 A.D. and 2054 A.D. are. The "hallowed be thy name and thy kingdom come" is related to His name (God) spelled backwards as we just stated means "Dog," or the Chinese Year of the Dog, or its polar opposite the Chinese Year of the Dragon in 2012 and 2060 when His kingdom comes.

There is one other interpretation of these prophecies of God's two witnesses and that is two people other than Billy Graham, Pat Robertson or Hal Lindsey and/or Perry Stone come to Jerusalem, Israel and preach and prophesied for three and a half years from December 21-25, 2012. They then are killed three and a half years later and then three and a half days later they are resurrected and a great earthquake happens and then the end comes quickly on June 24-25, 2016. These two witnesses would be born June 20-27 and the other December 24- 25. Or the two witnesses are one joined together as one man born in the Chinese Year of the Horse who writes about two parts of good and evil in books for three and half years from December 21-25, 2012 to June 20-25, 2016 and then dies then. The people become aware of these books and man by angels appearing to them in December 21-25, 2012. It's possible movies are made of his books in which many see over that time period of three and a half years or a small group of people about 20,000 buy the books and learn their information on end times just as Daniel 12:4 predicts. Those people or others will mock and scoff at this book if nothing happens between now (2010) and 2016 into 2050-2062, when the old fathers have fallen asleep (died) by that time and there is no end or the Second Coming Christ doesn't happen.

There are at least three places in the Bible where it predicts a time period of two years, or some period of time would past from when certain events happen to an another time which is not the time of the end. See Matthew 24:7-8, Luke 21:9-11 and Daniel 10:19. The "by and by" of Luke 21:9-11 and Daniel's 10:19 "two be strongs" and Matthew's 24:7-8 "beginning of sorrows" may mean two years from December 21-25, 2012, plus or minus 21 days, could see certain events predicted then, but the end does not happen two years (by=one+by=two) from those set dates. The certain events these prophecies predict are earthquakes, wars, attacks, storms, famines, diseases, fearful sights in the sky and commotions happening in either December 21-25, 2012-2013, plus two years, equals 2014-2015, but it's not the end in those years of 2014-2015. The II Peter 3:2-7 prediction may come true then, but instead of the death of God's two witnesses (fathers), the fathers who fell asleep (died) are the Jewish people killed in the war of 2012-2013 or 2016. If nothing happens in 2012-2013 or 2016 then people will begin to mock, laugh and scoff at the prophecies of the Second Coming and say the end of the world is not happening just as Peter predicted.

If these certain events of earthquakes, wars, attacks, famines, diseases, storms and the death of two famous TV preachers happens on December 21-25, 2012 into 2013, then plus two years equals 2014-2015, which is not the end either. Some preachers and I have placed the end in 2015, but 2016 looks more like the correct year for the end. The "fearful sights and great signs from heaven" that Luke 21:9-11 predicts could mean missiles attacks and/or comet, asteroid impacts, plane attacks, sun nova or flares from our sun or another sun or something else strange or fearful in the sky. If nothing happens in December 21-25, 2012, plus or minus 21 days, or in 2013, then look to 2016 for these events. And Daniel chapter 10 predicts these events and tells of trouble with Iran (Persia) and/or the U.S. and Israel at one of these times of December 21-25, 2012 into 2013 and June 20-25, 2016, plus or minus 21 days each. Daniel chapter 10 predicts Israel will attack Iran (Persia) then Iran will attack Israel, then Israel returns to attack Iran again three weeks/three months/three years after the dates of December 21-25, 2012, or June 20-25, 2016. But Iran could attack first and then Israel attack it.

There's still another possibility and that is that nothing happens on December 21-25, 2012-2013, plus or minus 21 days, but Iran gets a nuclear bomb or bombs and targets Israel with it on June 20-25, 2016 killing many. Then, as II Peter 3:2-7 predicts, many will soon begin to mock and scoff. They will say where is the promise of His Second Coming and the end since the fathers fell asleep (the many Jews who died in the war of 2016) that things continue as they were since creation and from 2016 to 2020-2040-2060. Again the "fathers" in this other interpretation are not two famous TV preachers, but the many Jews killed in the Iranian attack in the war of 2012-2013 or 2016.

Another possibility is that the war and attacks by Iran, Israel and Syria happen between now (July 28, 2010) and 2013. Then when December 21, 2012 comes they will scoff and mock the date. They do this because of the Mayan date of the end on December 21, 2012 and nothing happened, but the two witnesses die and many Jews die in the war and attacks before then and Jesus didn't come back to save Israel. Then they say "where is the promise of His coming since the fathers fell asleep (died) all things continue as from creation." The "fathers" are all the Jews killed in the war when Israel is destroyed between now (July 28, 2010) and 2013 making many scoff at the date saying the very words just mentioned that II Peter 3:2-4 predicted. The two earthquakes may happen and God's two witnesses die between now (July 28, 2010) and 2013. The "by and by" in Luke 21:9 and the two be "strongs" of Daniel 10:19 written in 535 B.C., which was the Chinese Year of the Tiger the same as 2010 into 2011, may mean two years from 2010-2011 yet the end will not happen then. Two years from 2010-2011 equals 2012-2013 when the Mayan date comes and nothing happens two years after 2010-2011 when the wars, attacks, earthquakes, pestilence's and famines happen. Matthew 24:7-8 also predicts these same things as the beginning of sorrows yet the end is far in the future.

Daniel chapter 10 predicts attacks and wars between Israel and Iran (Persia) in the first month and 24th day plus or minus 21 days. If a Israel attack on Iran (Persia) happens in 2010 or 2011 that date of the first month and 24th day would be October 1-4, 2010, April 26-27-28, 2011 and October 20-21-22, 2011, plus or minus 21 days. Then the by and by happens from 2010 or 2011 to 2012-2013 when the end doesn't happen but Israel is already destroyed and the Mayan end date came and went without the end of the world or the Second Coming of Christ happening as II Peter 3:2-7 predicts.

On October 15-16, 1962 and November 22, 1963 marked the start of the Cuban missile crisis in 1962 on October 15-16 and the JFK assassination on November 22, 1963. The year 1962 is the Chinese Year of the Tiger and the year 1963 is the Chinese year of the Rabbit. In 2010 it is the Chinese Year of the Tiger and in 2011 is the Chinese Year of the Rabbit. Will we see, as we did in those same years in 1962-1963, a nuclear crisis and a assassination in 2010-2011 on October 15-16, 2011 and November 22, 2011 or the other dates just given?

Isaiah chapters 7 and 13 predicts Iran and Syria to fight against Israel with arrows (missiles-bombs) the same as the book of Deuteronomy 32:22-23 does also. Of the 12 zodiac signs Sagittarius is the archer of arrows and starts from November 22 to January 19 as the Sagittarius sign and sun time when the sun is actually in Sagittarius. Will between November 22-Jaunary 19, 2010-2011-2012-2013 we see these arrows (missiles) shot at each nation of Israel, Iran and Syria?

Chapter Twenty Five

The Dates of the Book of Revelation

The Smith's Bible Dictionary states that the book of Revelation in the Bible was written between 95-97 A.D. How we know it was 96 A.D. is because we know it was written on a Sunday (the Lord's Day=Sunday) in the Chinese Year of the Monkey in the creation (Alpha-first) month of June, so it must have been written June 12, 96 A.D., which was a Sunday and the Chinese Year of the Monkey. Revelation 5:5 we have seen in the chapter before relates to Juda the lion, or our Leo the lion sign, which in Chinese astrology rules the Year of the Monkey. The Chinese Year of the Monkey only happens every 12 years in Chinese astrology.

The books of Isaiah and Revelation in the Bible state the phrases "first-last, beginning and end, Alpha and Omega" as the time of the end, which is creation and destruction. Isaiah 46:10; 48:3 and Isaiah 48:12 state that God declares the end from the beginning meaning both creation (first-Alpha) and the end (last-Omega) come in the same month. We have also seen in the first chapter how II Peter 3:2-18 predicts this same thing. My book entitled *The Experiment in Philadelphia* states that creation and Noah's flood started in May-June. Thus the beginning (June) and the end (June) are one and the same times these two events of creation and destruction happens.

The World Almanac and book of facts list June 12, 96 A.D. as a Sunday. It also mentions that date as the old Julian calendar. Today we use the Gregorian calendar in which it is 13 days ahead of the old Julian calendar making June 12 be June 25 (June 12+13=June 25) when the end comes in the Chinese Year of the Monkey in 2016 A.D. Both 96 A.D. and 2016 A.D. are the same calendars meaning the days of the weeks are the same in each. This only happens every so often.

The left and right hands of God are the dates of December 21-22 and 24-25 and June 20-21 and 24-25. See Song of Solomon 2:6. Jesus stands on the right hand of God in heaven and Satan stands on the left hand of God in heaven making them polar opposites just as those dates are on our calendars. Those dates symbolize the birthdays of Abraham, Elijah, Moses and John the Baptist on December 24-25 and Isaac, the first antichrist and Jesus on June 24-25.

In the book of Revelation it mentions several times the four beasts and 24 elders. Were they a code for the fourth month and 24-25th days of two polar opposite calendars that are the Bible's and the Jewish civil calendars? The Bible's calendar starts in March-April as the first month making the fourth month June-July and the 24-25th days to our calendar are June 24-25 or July 24-25. The Jewish civil calendar starts in September-October making its fourth month December-January and the 24-25th days to our calendars are December 24-25 and January 24-25.

The book of Haggai in the Bible predicts great joy on the ninth month and 24-25th day. Again to the above calendars of the Bible and the Jewish civil calendar that would make the dates of November-December 24-25 and May-June 24-25 to our calendar. It is a time when God shakes the heavens and the earth just as the book Haggai 2:6 predicts. The book of Haggai in the Bible represents when the Jewish temple at Jerusalem was finished and dedicated in 515 B.C., which was the Chinese Year of the Dog. Daniel 9:27 predicts a week, or seven days (7x360 =2520 days) changed to years 2520 years. Subtract 2520 years from 515 B.C. and it equals 2006 A.D., not counting the year zero and 2006

A.D. is the Chinese Year of the Dog. Add seven years to that (=Daniel 9:27) and it equals 2013 A.D. And on December 21-25, 2012, plus three and a half years added to it equals June 20-25, 2016 when the end happens. The three be strongs of Haggai 2:4 could be three years added to 2013 equals 2016 A.D. in the ninth month (June) and 24-25th day (June 24-25, 2016).

Chapter Twenty Six

The Dog Year/10-Year Delay

The year 2006 is the Chinese Year of the Dog the same Year as 26 A.D., when John the Baptist came and Jesus started His great ministry. Both of them came claiming the kingdom of God is at hand and the acceptable year of the Lord was then. (See in the Bible Isaiah 61:1-3; Matthew 4:17; Mark 1:15; Luke 4:18- 19; Revelation 1:3.) Jesus began His ministry in June on the third day after the new moon as the gospel of John noted when He went to a wedding feast at Cana. We have the term "June Bride," which may relate to the marriage of Christ and His church the bride in June of 2016.

Jesus was baptized by John in the Aries sign of March 21- April 19, which is the sign of a Ram or Lamb of God just as John called Jesus "the lamb of God." Jesus then went out in the desert for forty days to be tempted and then returned and started His ministry in June of 26 A.D., which was the Chinese Year of the Dog the same as 2006 A.D. is.

In the Lord's Prayer we say: "…Hallowed be thy name, thy kingdom come…" Was this relating to spelling God's name in reverse, which is Dog or the Chinese Year of the Dog in 26 A.D. and 2006 as the day of His coming in June 10 years after 2006, which equals June 24-25, 2016. The hand we learned earlier was important in the Bible and they have 10 fingers, which can mean 10 years from when both John and Jesus claimed the kingdom of God is at hand in 26 A.D.(=Dog) to the end in 2016 ten years after 2006, which is the Chinese Year of the Dog (26 A.D.).

Revelation 1:3 predicts the time is at hand when John the disciple wrote down the book of Revelation on June 12, 96 A.D. He didn't mean that the end is soon after that date or year, but the end is that date of June 24-25 in the same Chinese Year of the Monkey as 96 A.D was, which we stated is the same as June 24-25, 2016 is? It's also the same calendar as we have seen.

The change or delay for 2006 is recorded in Matthew 24:48; 25:1-13 and Daniel chapter 12 as a 10-year delay from the Chinese Year of the Dog in 2006. Daniel's time, times and half, or 1260 days, plus 1290 and 1335 days added together, equals a 10-year period delayed or a countdown from 2006 to 2016. And Daniel chapter 1, Matthew 25:1-13 and Revelation chapters 2-3 all give 10 days for the end to come or a 10-year delay to the end from the Chinese Year of the Dog. Ezekiel 4:6 tells us to change a day for a year.

The five wise virgins of Matthew 25:1-13 could have meant five delayed periods of time of 10 are wrong and the second five or the fifth date mentioned is right as the five foolish virgins were wrong about the dates and times and the five wise virgins were right. Were they talking about the five dates I give in my books that are wrong for the end time dates in 2012- 2013, 2018-2019 and 2015 and the fifth date is in the fifth book, which is this book and is the right date. Moses wrote the first five books of the Bible and Psalms is divided into five books. Remember the Bible in Ecclesiastes states that in dreams, visions and words there are many vanities (inspired deceptions and great falsehoods). And the 10 virgins can mean "brides of Christ" in a June wedding when the bridegroom (Christ) comes for His Church the Bride and Virgin. That time will be a little after midnight Israeli time as Matthew 25-1-13 predicts. The exact time of 1:18 or 12:18 a.m. I show in my book *The boy who could predict earthquakes* explaining that the word "ten" in Greek means 12:18. This time would make it be 5- 6-7 p.m. Eastern time as the marriage supper (5-7 p.m. on the eastern U.S. is dinner or supper time) of the lamb happens at the end with the June Bride. The great "bridegroom" (Jesus) is mentioned twice in Matthew 25:1-13 as Coming then or shortly after 12 a.m. Is this why several prophecies tell us to be awake and clothed for the wedding of God because it comes late at night? Is it also why these ancient prophecies stated He (Christ=bridegroom) will come upon you unaware because you are sleeping? Is it a time when you are unaware and not looking because your asleep? Is this why Bible prophecies state one is in bed and taken and one at the mill grinding for food at supper time? Those times would be 12:18-1:18 a.m. Israel time when many are asleep in bed and 5-7 p.m. Eastern time in the U.S. when it's supper time. See Luke 17:34-36.

The 10 virgins in Matthew 25:1-13 have lamps with olive oil in them to light them. The olive oil comes from olive trees ruled by the moon and Cancer sign, which June 24-25, 2016 is part of the Cancer sign. And every time the word "lamp" is used in the Bible you can translate it candlestick or vice versa. See Zechariah chapter 4, Revelation chapters 1-5 and 11. The prediction of two candlesticks can also be found on an ancient Egyptian carving dating back to 100-300 B.C. that shows the 12 zodiac signs on the ceiling of the temple Hathor in Dendera, Egypt. There are 12 figures holding the carving. Four are women standing up with their hands around the carving and eight are bird-headed men kneeling holding the carving. On the carving two candlesticks or lamps can be seen. Drawing a imaginary line between the two, you have one line from the lamps or candlesticks going through the end of Taurus the bull or ox horns and entering Gemini the twins. The opposite candlestick has the imaginary line going through the end of Libra and enters the beginning of Scorpio. Were these predictions of the end when the sun is leaving Taurus the bull or ox horns and entering Gemini the twins on or near summer on June 20-25, 2016? Are Libra and Scorpio the days of Friday and Saturday June 24-25, 2016? Libra is ruled by Venus, which in Latin is Friday June 24, 2016 and Scorpio is ruled by Saturn, from which we get the name Saturday from and June 25, 2016 is Saturday.

The women holding the carving along with the kneeling bird-headed men could also mean these same things. Women are a female sign of Taurus and birds the ancient Egyptians linked to Gemini. On June 20-25, 2016 the sun is leaving Taurus the bull or ox horns and entering Gemini the twins. The Taurus sign is also known as the seven stars, which Revelation chapters 1-5 predicts as the end. The same as Amos 5:7-8 in the Bible also predicts seven stars and Orion near it to be the time of the end. Orion, Taurus (seven stars) and Gemini are all near each other as drawing 44 at the end of my book, *The Experiment at Philadelphia* shows. The time of when those three constellations are seen overhead are at midnight on December 21-25, 2012 and behind the sun at noon overhead and not seen then on June 20-25, 2016. Taurus rules Israel and Jerusalem. The Gemini sign is the sign of the twins and rules the Chinese Horse sign that both of God's great two witnesses are born under who are the two candlesticks or lamps.

The kneeling of the eight bird-headed men holding this carving is referring to Capricorn and Cancer because Capricorn rules the knees and its polar opposite is Cancer. The date December 21-25, 2012 is the Capricorn sign (kneeling) and June 21-25, 2016 is the Cancer sign (=opposite Capricorn.) See Appendix A: The Codes in my book *The boy who could predict earthquakes* and see my book *The Antichrist* at drawings numbered 9,13,14 and my book *The Nativity* at drawings 14 and 16 to see that ancient Egyptian carving and the Cancer constellation of drawing 16. Drawing 16 of those drawings in my book *The Nativity* shows the Cancer sign (=June 21-25, 2016) and the manger, which has a group of stars named the beehive. The Greek translation of Sphinx is beehive. The sphinx is where the great pyramids are in Egypt and are below the seven churches the book of Revelation was written to in western Turkey in the Virgo zone (=women-Virgo-Gemini-Taurus.) The book *The Orion Mystery* claims the great pyramids at Giza, Egypt and other places of Egypt are aligned to the constellation Orion, which we read are near Taurus and Gemini. Were the sphinx and pyramids declaring the end date? Was that ancient carving also showing the end date by the two lamps or candlesticks and the 12 people holding the carving?

The women seen on that ancient Egyptian carving can also represent Virgo the Virgin woman and its cosign Gemini along with another woman in the sign of Taurus. June 20-25, 2016 is, as we have seen, when the sun is leaving Taurus and entering Gemini. And Virgo, which the woman is, has the polar opposite of Pisces the sun. The sun may go into a super nova or explode at that time as the sphinx in Greek can also mean or the symbol of joining (wedding=bride and groom) together the good (Christ= matter) and evil (satan=antimatter) in the core of the sun. This happens at this time in the end to cause a super nova that destroys the sun and the whole solar system shaking the heavens and earth just as predicted. The sphinx is a body of Leo the lion that rules the sun and is Mars the god of war and violence and the head of Virgo the woman virgin who is pure and good.

Chapter Twenty Seven

The Monkey Year

June 24-25, 2016 is in the Chinese year of the Monkey. Remember in Chinese astrology each of the 12 signs rules once every 12 years, not each year. The 12 Chinese signs also rule two-hour periods for each day and night.

Many ancient Egyptian drawings show a monkey or baboon pictured in them along with the scales (Libra). See drawings 14,15,19,21,22,23 at the end of my book *The Experiment at Philadelphia*. Were they predicting the end in the Chinese Year of the Monkey in 2016 and a Friday, which is Latin for Venus that rules Libra (scales?) Many past events happened in the Chinese Year of the Monkey. Noah's flood began the second month and 17th day in 2341 B.C. According to astronomical soft ware that date was the Chinese Year of the Monkey and May 19 or November 11. Jesus often claimed the end time "as the days of Noah." Was he referring to 2016 in May-June? When Jesus often mentioned the end time prophecies He said that they would be like "the days of Noah," what did He mean? In the days of Noah the people bought, sold, built, married and were given in marriage all the way until Noah and his family entered the ark and the flood came and destroyed them all. Will the end in June 24-25, 2016 be the same way? Will the people scoff and mock date setters and the Bible prophecies all the way past 2012, because nothing happen then, till June 24-25, 2016 when the end comes quickly? People in Noah's days may have done the same thing: mocking, scoffing and laughing at Noah for a long time seeing there was no rain and flood and things continue as they were since creation and everything continues on. Then the flood came quickly and destroyed them all. Will our end come the same way? Or will a long time come like in Noah's days till the end comes and people mock, scoff and laugh at the preaching of the end and Second Coming from 2012-2013, 2016- 2060? By the way the mention of "marriage" in these prophecies could mean June, which we call "the June Bride" when the end comes in 2016. See Luke 17:26-27 and Matthew 24:37-51. The Rapture predicted in Matthew 24:40-41 happens just before the end on June 24-25, 2016 as noted in another chapter of this book. And Matthew 24:48 claims people of our times will say their lord delayeth His coming, then the end will come quickly without warning when they are unaware of and not looking for it and are not ready for the wedding. There are other parables that predict the time of His Coming as people unaware and undressed for the wedding. See Matthew 22:1-14. Is that again referring to the end in June 24-25, 2016 as a June Bride at a wedding or some other time other then that in 2050-2060?

The Book of Revelation was written in 96 A.D., which was the Chinese Year of the Monkey. The year 1776 when the U.S. was born was also the Chinese Year of the Monkey. The creation of Adam and Eve and their fall in August-September happened in 3997 B.C., which was the Chinese Year of the Monkey. Were all these important events in the Chinese Year of the Monkey that of signs of future events in the Year of the Monkey in 2016?

In 2004 many prophecies came to pass as Colossians 2:16-17 predicts would be signs of future events just as September 26- 27, 2003 was. September 26-27, 2003 was a Jewish Sabbath, a new moon and a holiday or solemn day of the Jewish New Year. Then the next year mostly in September three of four great hurricanes hit Florida in 2004, which was one of the most bizarre hurricane seasons ever. That same year volcanoes around the world began erupting, or acting up, including Mount St. Helens. And the great Asian earthquake and tidal waves happened as one of the greatest earthquakes to ever strike the earth. The year 2004 was the Chinese Year of the Monkey.

The big question is: will these same events happen again in 2016? Or will we approach June 24-25, 2016 without them? The prophecies suggest both ways. The prophecies of the books of Matthew chapter 24, Mark chapter 13, Luke chapters 17 and 21 all predict the end times as coming without warning or signs, while they and others claim they come with many signs and warnings. This is confusing, but maybe on purpose to fool or trick us from knowing the truth. People may just give up looking for the end and go about their cares of life as predicted exactly "as the days of Noah."

Chapter Twenty Eight

War in Heaven

The famous Bible saying of "the abomination of desolation" may mean satan standing at the core of the sun causing war there between satan and his angels and Jesus and His angels resulting in a sun nova exploding the sun's outer layers causing them to fly with great force like hail or stars falling upon the earth. See Revelation 6:13 and 16:21.

Satan may do this by killing himself and the sun and whole solar system at the very end. Part of satan is an antimatter dung hill and in the core of the sun there is a great shield surrounding heaven and paradise where God is and His angels are in the Holy of Holies as pure matter. If satan were to stand in that place the antimatter and matter would explode with great violence. See Psalms 84:11 for God being a sun and a shield near its core protecting the paradise inside the sun from the evil, wrath and heat.

One preacher stated that the ancient Jewish temple at Jerusalem corresponds to things and places when put over the map of the United States. The Holy of Holies on his map where the ark of the covenant would be was Los Angeles. Will in December 21-25, 2012 and/or June 20-25, 2016 we see a great earthquake in Los Angeles and quickly followed by the end with pieces of the sun smashing the earth as hail and stars falling as Revelation 6:13 and 16:21 predicted? Zechariah 14:5 also predicts a great earthquake in Jerusalem when Christ appears. And in Revelation 11:19 it predicts that earthquake and/or the earthquake in Los Angeles to be followed by great hail. That hail could be pieces of the sun exploding when the ark of His testament (ark of the covenant) is seen in heaven as predicted in the Bible in Revelation 11:19 and chapters 18-19. That event and place will cause the smoke of Babylon (Los Angeles) and the sun to rise up forever.

Abraham, John the Baptist and John the disciple all relate to these two great earthquakes and the two witnesses of God. Abraham, as told in my book *The Experiment at Philadelphia* was born in the Chinese Year of the Rat. The Chinese Year of the Rat is polar opposite of the Chinese Year of the Horse and rules Gemini and Sagittarius, which are polar opposites. When I mention polar opposites I mean the same date, time, place and event. We have stated earlier that God's two great witnesses predicted to die at one of these times would be Billy Graham and Pat Robertson, both born in the Chinese Year of the Horse that rules Gemini and its polar opposite is the Rat and the Sagittarius sign.

Gemini rules the arms, which the hands are connected to in which we mentioned the dates of December 21-25, 2012 and June 20-25, 2016 relate to the left and right hands of God. John the Baptist was born December 24-25, 5 B.C., the Chinese Year of the Dragon, the same as December 21-25, 2012 is. And John the disciple was born June 20, which is the Gemini sign. See my book *The Experiment at Philadelphia*. Gemini rules the earth and is an air sign in which John and his brother were known as sons of thunder. Putting these two together you would have earthquakes on the arms or hands in December 21-25, 2012 and/or June 20-25, 2016. The Earth equals Gemini as told in Appendix A: The Codes at the end of my book *The boy who could predict earthquakes*. And Gemini being an air sign where great thunder happens equals a great earth (=Gemini) quake (=thunder) and a great shaking of the heavens and earth. Shortly after those two earthquakes the whole earth and solar system shakes because of a sun nova when satan stands in the Holy of Holies at the core of the sun. Gemini we also read was that of twins and connected to God's two witnesses who preach and die at one of these two times, places and events.

The Chinese Year of the Dog we stated earlier equals 26 A.D. and 2006 A.D. The year 26 A.D. was when John the Baptist came preaching the kingdom of God is at hand and he was born in the Year of the Dragon (5 B.C.) The polar opposite of the Chinese Year of the Dog is the Chinese Year of the Dragon in 2012 when a earthquake or two hit Jerusalem, Israel and/or Los Angeles then and/or in June 20-25, 2016. June 20-27 is the Gemini and Cancer cusps represented by John and Jesus as their birthdays. Those dates are when the end is coming as the right hand of God on the true Christmas Day. That day is when people give gifts and summer is near when people travel to and fro on summer vacation as Daniel 12:4 predicts as when the end comes. See my book, *The Nativity.* Remember nothing may happen on December 21-25, 2012 causing many to scoff and mock end day dates. Then three and a half years later from December 21-25, 2012 the end comes quickly on June 20-25, 2016.

At that time as Matthew 24:30-31 predicts the angels will come and take people off the earth and into another heaven and paradise where no harm comes to them. This is the Rapture many have been talking about.

Chapter Twenty Nine

World War II

Over the 34 years of studying Bible prophecy and the end time tribulation period, antichrist, wars, brutal persecution I have come to the conclusion that it has already happened in World War II. Cable documentaries have claimed that Hitler changed times and laws. That he had three allies including Germany. He hated and killed the saints (Jews). His war went seven years and conquered 10-20 nations. Hitler was a leader born in the Ox sign and Year and was demon possessed. He was the fourth beast who was very terrible to come and caused the closet thing to hell on earth that we ever witnessed. All of this was mentioned by secular media (non-religious) and not religious people. The only religious comment was by Hal Lindsey, who said he thought Hitler was demon possessed. All the other statements were by secular (non-religious people) media.

Daniel chapters 2 and 7 predict the revived fourth beast will make a kingdom out of the revived fourth kingdom from Daniel's time. It would have three nations subdued by the revived fourth beast to revive that fourth Roman kingdom of Europe. The fourth revived leader or fourth beast would be born in The Chinese Year of the Ox (1889) and in Taurus the bull or ox sign of April 20 and start a war in the year 1939. The war would last seven years and be the deadliest and ugliest war ever seen, killing many Jews.

World War II began September 1, 1939 by Germany, which had two allies, Italy and Japan, to make three total. Germany conquered about 10-20 nations mostly in Europe the same places as the Old Roman Empire. Hitler was the revived fourth beast of Daniel chapter 7 and revived the fourth kingdom exactly as prophesied in Daniel chapter 2. In Daniel's prophecies the fourth beast is the fourth king or leader from the Babylonian king and kingdom as the first, then the Persian king and kingdom as the second, then the Grecian king and kingdom as third and then the Roman king and kingdom as fourth, and then Hitler as the fourth revived king of the fourth revived kingdom of Rome. The fourth ancient kingdom of Rome ended by breaking into pieces then was revived under Hitler as 10 toes part clay (10) and iron (10). See Daniel chapter 2.

Ezekiel chapters 38-39 predict these events too. Ezekiel 39 would be our year 1939 under codes. Those same chapters of Ezekiel also predict the evil leader as having hooks in his jaws, which is a sign of a bull or ox where we put hooks into their jaws or mouth to lead them. Those hooks equal a bull or ox and are when Hitler was born in the Chinese Year of the Ox and Taurus the bull sign (April 20, 1889).

The 10-20 nations Hitler conquered is predicted in Daniel 2 and 7 and Revelation 13 as 10 horns (10 kings or nations) plus 10 crowns (10 more kings or nations) minus the three allies of Germany, Italy and Japan. See Revelation 12:3.

Ezekiel 39:6 predicts fire to fall upon the "isles" of Gog and Magog, or two cities on an island (=isles) in World War II. When the Bible mentions fire it sometimes can mean atomic or nuclear fire. In WWII the U.S. dropped two atomic bombs on two cities of Japan, which is a great island and the third ally of Germany.

WWII lasted for approximately seven years (1939-1945), which was the great tribulation for the

Jews who would come out of it and become great again and have their own nation. See Daniel 9:27. That was the time of Jacob's (Israel's) trouble and that he would come back to his land and be healed and blessed by God, and in June of 1967 the Jews recaptured the city of Jerusalem and the times of the Gentiles were over exactly as prophesied. See Jeremiah chapter 30 and Luke 21:24.

Daniel 7:25 predicts the antichrist or fourth revived beast to change times and laws. Hitler changed the law so you could legally kill Jews. He also changed times by making Christmas Day be December 21, the first day of the winter solstice. He also tried to make a one world government and religion. Every nation he conquered he made to be govern totally by him and his master race. He also made agreements with the churches that they could continue as long as they made alliance to him just as Revelation chapters 13, 17-18 predicted.

There are several books that list the numerical value of Hitler's name as being 666 predicted in Revelation chapter 13 as the end time antichrist. But that fails to give him a mark equal to that same number and name as predicted. I show this mark, number and name as being Venus Virgo Libra in several of my books. Could that prediction of Revelation have not meant the actual name of the antichrist, but the name, place and time of the antichrist in astrology and numerology? Hitler was born April 20, 1889 in Austria. In astrology Venus (Jesus and His angel) gives all male children their souls. That's why the ancient Egyptian ankh means "life" as Venus is Life (Jesus.) And Austria is partly in the Virgo zone and is ruled by Libra. Thus: 666, Venus Virgo Libra and the marks or symbols of those three. See my book *The Antichrist* and see drawing 4 at the back of that book for the 666 mark.

Revelation chapters 4-6 predict one leader (=one crown) to come as one of the four horsemen or cherubs. One of those cherubs is described as a calf (bull or ox) in Revelation chapter 4. Hitler, being born April 20, 1889 was a Taurus sign born, which is the bull or ox sign. And if the four horsemen are the four cherubs or four beasts of Revelation and mark the starting point of the four seasons it could mean Hitler's birth day. And then with the precession of the equinoxes over 2000 years would make March 20-21, the first day of spring, come April 20. That is when the sun would be in Aries (=ram=lamb= false prophet) and spring time by sign not by seasons. That would make April 20 Hitler's birthday be a symbol of the white horsemen and a lamb as Revelation chapters 6:2 and 13 predicts as one of the four cherubs of Revelation chapters 4-6.

The false prophet of the book of Revelation comes up out of the earth and predicts over a seven year time period that their leader and people would reign for a 1000 years, just as Jesus Christ is predicted to do. The female sign of Taurus, in which Hitler was born, would make him both the beast coming up out of the sea and the false prophet (she-female) who predicts for seven years (Daniel 9:27) a 1000-year reign of him the Supreme leader (=God) and his people of Germany as the master race, a perfect fulfillment of those ancient prophecies.

Hitler became supreme leader of Germany and in 1938-1939 went seven years (=seven year tribulation period for the Jews and world) conquering and claiming he and the Germans were the master race and would reign 1000-years and were to kill all Jews. This is exactly what was prophesied in the Bible and what happened in WWII.

In the Greek dictionary of the *Strong's Concordance of the Bible* it lists the number "1000" near words for "Cherubim." And Ezekiel chapter 28 calls satan a cherub, which we stated in Revelation 6:1-2 predicts to come as one of the four cherubs with him as a calf or bull or ox, the Taurus sign of April 20, 1889. Taurus is also the number 6 along with Libra. Libra is a male sign and Taurus is a female sign. Those two joined equals the joining of Christ and His bride that satan tries to copy, but fails in Hitler. The sphinx we read is connected to the end-time date of June 20-25, 2016. We also read stars in the Cancer constellation are known as a beehive, which is Greek for Sphinx. But the Sphinx also means "joined" as the late James Kennedy states in his booklet about the gospel in the stars.

Will satan standing at the core of the sun at the end- time date join the two as in the beginning and as a bride and groom in a June wedding? Then will the end happens when Los Angeles is completely destroyed by a sun nova and the marriage supper of the lamb happens? See Revelation chapter 19. The Sphinx, being that of a woman's head and the body of a lion joined together equals Virgo the woman and Leo the lion (man). We have and will read how the woman of Virgo has the cosign of Gemini and is the female Taurus sign. We also read how the lion is Leo that the sun rules, which on June 20-25, 2016 is leaving Taurus and entering Gemini when good and evil join to end in a sun nova.

That end date is when the sun is leaving Taurus and Taurus is also an earth sign, which in Revelation chapter 13 predicts the false prophet to come up from as Hitler born on April 20, which is the Taurus the earth sign. And Saturday, April 20, 1889, when Hitler was born, is the day we get Saturn from. The planet Saturn rules Scorpio and is a water or sea sign as the beast of Revelation chapter 13 predicts the beast and fourth antichrist to come up out of the sea with 10-20 nations and seven heads. The seven heads in Revelation chapter 17 are predicted as seven hills that are Rome, Italy, one of three nations controlled by Hitler and his ally during WWII.

Many look for future Bible prophecies that won't come because they have already happen in WWII as shown in this chapter. And some look at past prophecies that they think happened, but didn't happen yet, but will in our future. One example of this is the great 40 year generation Hal Lindsey predicted from 1948 to 1988 as the time of the end as Jesus predicted in Matthew chapter 24 and Luke chapter 21. If you add a 40 year period or generation to 30 A.D., when Jesus made those predictions, it comes exactly to 70 A.D. when the temple and Israel was destroyed by the Romans. They may have even read those prophecies and fled to the mountains as Matthew 24:16 predicts along with the dead sea scrolls, which was found in the 1940's in a mountains near the dead sea.

The end-time antichrists that appear miraculously (UFO landing) and deceive the world with two books may not happened as predicted in Isaiah chapter 48 and by the book *The end of the days* by Arthur E. Bloomfield. By declaring those things as I did in my two books: *The Antichrist*; and *The Experiment at Philadelphia,* no one would be deceived by him or his appearance or his books because God showed them in advance taking away the power of them and possibly even stopping them. Thus, WWII fulfilled all the prophecies of the end-time antichrist.

So then with all the prophecies fulfilled in World War II the only events left are the death of the two witnesses of God and the great two earthquakes. Those events can come very quickly as Revelation chapter 11 predicts. Are you ready? The next chapter will tell you how to survive the end and arrive in heaven.

Chapter Thirty
Spring-Summer of 2007

A note here before will begin this chapter and that is it was written by January 8, 2007. The Chinese Year of the Pig was 2007 when certain events were suppose to happen. The polar opposite of the Pig is the Snake which is 2013 when events in this chapter may happen or counting each Year equals 2012. Add 12 years to 2007 the Year of the Pig and it equals 2019 when events may happen. The Year 2016 as the Year of the Monkey is one other possible date of the end as this chapter will document and my dream showed in a interpretation as the end and/or the time of a flood by tidal wave, Nor'Easter or hurricane.

Did Nostradamus, ancient Egyptian art and the Bible predict on June 9-12, 14-25, 2007, plus or minus 30 days, terrorist attacks, along with earthquakes (U.S. West Coast?), tidal waves (U.S. West Coast?), wars (Iran?), volcanic eruptions, storms (Florida's panhandle or central Florida?), three days of darkness or strange events in the skies and assassinations in the U.S. and Israel? Nostradamus in his quatrain C9:Q83 predicted trouble in the land of the "saints" or "angels" in the "infidel" year of the pig when the "sun is in 20 degrees of Taurus." The sun is 20 degrees in Taurus approximately June 9- 25, 2007 and that year is the Chinese Year of the Pig. The name Los Angeles means "the city of angels," which God's saints are known as and is ruled by the sign of Taurus. Opposite Taurus is Scorpio, which rules Washington, D.C. Will an earthquake and/or terrorist attack happen there or somewhere in the U.S. and/or Israel at that time? Nostradamus in that quatrain predicts an earthquake and "ruin" when "the theater is full." Los Angeles is part of or near Hollywood where movies are made. The time when movie theaters are full may give the time of this earthquake and/or terrorist attack in the evening.

Nostradamus predicted in C6:Q24 that after a great war in the Cancer sign by a Cancer sign leader, peace will come for a long time by another leader elected soon after. The Cancer sign begins June 20-21. President Bush was born July 6, which is also the Cancer sign. That quatrain predicts when Mars (Scorpio=Pig in Chinese astrology) and Jupiter (sceptre) are together on a Thursday (=Jupiter=June 21, 2007), war comes upon that U.S. President. Jupiter is the "sceptre" and is Latin for Thursday and 2007 is the Chinese Year of the Pig. Then shortly after that date a new Pig King (=President born in the Year of the Chinese Pig=1947=Hillary Clinton) would come "who brings peace to the earth for a long time (1000 years?)" shortly after this war, earthquakes and troubles occurs. She may usher in the 1000 years or peace, joy, hope, prosperity and good health.

I have often wondered why Amos 1:1 predicted, "two years before an earthquake." But when I considered June 15, 2005 an earthquake hit off the western U.S. coast and a possible tidal wave may hit and put that event and timing for a warning of another earthquake and tidal wave to hit there in two years on June 14-15, 2007, it makes sense. Those dates are of a new moon when several Bible prophecies predict times of trouble. See Amos 8:1-5.

Amos chapter one in Year/Chapter codes would be our year 1995, the Year of the Chinese Pig, the same as 2007. The year 1995 marked the times when Prime Minister Rabin of Israel was assassinated and hurricane Opal hit the Panhandle of Florida. Will the year 2007 include these same events with an assassination in Israel and/or the U.S. and a hurricane striking Florida's panhandle?

Amos chapter one also tells of the Charles Manson murders of actress Sharon Tate, who was stabbed to death while she was pregnant, just as Amos 1:13 predicted by "children" or the family of Charles Manson. Charles Manson was born November 11 and Amos chapters/year codes end 2003-2004. The latter year of 2004 was the Chinese Year of the Monkey when, on November 11, 2016 the end may come on his birthday 12 years after 2004, or as Amos chapter one has 3-4 transgressions, which equals 3x4=12. So in fact it gave the Pig and Monkey years as times of these great end time events, along with certain dates of earthquakes and other events happening. Amos 5:8 gives the exact time by star positions, as we will see, as 12 noon June 20-21, 2007.

The Book of Revelation in the Bible and ancient Egyptian art also predict earthquakes and attacks near when the sun is in Taurus known as the seven stars, which the book of Revelation calls the Taurus constellation. The book of Revelation was written June 12, 96 A.D., which was a Sunday, or the Lord's Day, as John wrote in Revelation 1:10. Ancient Egyptian drawings often show a sun or moon disk between bull's horns and snakes. (See drawing 42 at the end of my book *The Experiment at Philadelphia*.) Were they predicting trouble when the sun is in Taurus in June of 2007 (=Pig Year, the polar opposite of the snake)? The Pig time is from 9-11 p.m. when these events happen, or 7-9 p.m., which is the Dog time. The dog, or jackal, is also often seen in ancient Egyptian carvings and art. Was it giving the time of 7-9 p.m. when the theaters are completely full then "ruin" as Nostradamus predicted in C9:Q83? The 12 Chinese signs not only give certain years, but also certain hours of the day.

The "door" of Revelation 4:1 may be what the ancient Mayans and Egyptians believed was Orion, which is near Taurus and Gemini, whose star time runs in June. Amos chapter 5 may also predict this door opening when the sun (star time) is in or near Orion and the seven stars. In fact, Amos chapter 5 can relate to November 11, 2016, as well as June of 2007. June 20- 22, 2007 the sun at noon is in or near Orion, Taurus and Gemini. Then on November 11, 2016 at 12 a.m. those same constellations will be nearly overhead in the night sky. The ancient Egyptians built their great pyramids at Giza in positions that align with the constellation Orion. They believed Orion was the symbol of "the door." (See the book *The Orion Prophecy* by Patrick Geryl and Gino Ratinckx, page 155.) The ancient Mayans also believed those same constellations being overhead in November marked an important time.

Isaiah 40:1-2 predicts a "double" time of trouble for Jerusalem. The Israeli six-day war began June 5, 1967 and ended June 11-12. Will Israel and Jerusalem face double trouble then, one in June of 1967, and the other in June of 2007? Jesus predicted a 40-year period until when the end- time events would come. Forty years added to June 5-12, 1967 equals June 5-12, or 14-25, 2007. The same generation of 40 years came from when Jesus first predicted it in 30 A.D. till when the temple at Jerusalem was destroyed and the Jewish people scattered in 70 A.D. The Julian calendar in 70 A.D. is the same one as our year 2007. Same calendar years are very important in prophecy. By same calendar I mean both years have the same day of the week on the same dates. Each year the date and day of the week change, but every so often they align again.

The 2007 calendar is the same calendar as 1945, 1962, 1973, 1979 and 2001. These years were important years when attacks, troubles, or wars, possibly nuclear wars, happened, or could of happened. Psalms 79:11-13 predicts trouble with prisoners in the 11th verse, then a "bosom" or breasts and a "sevenfold judgment" in verse 12. Psalms 79:11 would be our year 1979 and 11th month of November when Iran took U.S. hostages (prisoners). The "bosom" or breasts are ruled by Cancer sign, which is given the numbers 2-7, or the year 2007, with two zeros in between. That year is the "sevenfold judgment" and "the seventh trumpet" of the book of Revelation when the little book and other books reveals God's great mystery as Revelation chapter 10 predicts. Is the sevenfold judgement and seventh trumpet that of our year ending with the number seven in 2007? Is it also the number 27 with two zeros in between to make the year 2007 when judgment comes? In 1979 we had trouble with Iran. Will in 2007 we again have trouble with them? Both years are the same calendar. Also is the knocking of Christ on the door that the Bible claims that of the Orion (door) constellation seen in June near the sun (God in heaven) in 2007? And the mention of God's hand so often in the Bible could mean the bones in the human hand, which are 27, with two zero's in between equals our year 2007 in June when He knocks on the door (Orion) of your hearts and minds to reveal (revelation) great hidden truths and mysteries.

Malachi chapter 4 and Revelation chapter 11 predicts two of God's witnesses born June 20 and December 24 to appear near the end times. Those birthdays are that of John the disciple, Jesus and the fourth beast of Daniel chapter 7 on June 20, which is the Gemini sign and Cancer cusp. Gemini is an air sign the symbol of wings, feathers and birds. The December 24th birthdays are that of John the Baptist, Moses, Nostradamus and Elijah and one of the witnesses of God in Malachi and the book of Revelation chapter 11.

The prophet Elijah was prophesied to come back from the dead as Malachi chapter 4 predicted shortly before the return of the Lord and to preach and prophesied till the end as Revelation chapter 11 predicted. Malachi chapter 4 may predict Jesus manger scene when He was born and mentions healing in His wings. Our Medical healing sign of Caduceus represents Mercury that rules Gemini and Virgo that has snakes wrapped around a staff with wings (=air sign=Gemini=June 20-21). Was this what Malachi meant by "sun of righteousness" and "healing in his wings?" June 21, 2007 plus three days equals June 24, 2007, which is a Sunday the name of which we get from the sun and is the Gemini cusp where we get healing from. The snakes seen on the Caduceus in Chinese astrology is polar opposite of the Pig, which year is 2007. And Virgo is ruled also by Mercury, which in Latin is Wednesday. The staff is ruled by Jupiter, which in Latin is named Thursday. June 20-21, 2007 is a Wednesday-Thursday when many are healed then, or three days later, on a Sunday morning. See Isaiah 58:8, Psalms 110:3, 121:1-8.

Mercury is also the symbol of messengers or angels from God who come and appear to people at night telling them what to do. Revelation 22:16-17 predicts the angels coming and appearing to people in the month of June when the Book of Revelation was written down and is a symbol of the door when the sun is in Orion. The seven churches the Book of Revelation was written to, and the great pyramids of Egypt, are in the Virgo-Libra zones, or Wednesday-Thursday, when these angels appear as a bluish-white light that makes you smile ear to ear. Malachi's book predicts these messengers to appear at the ox (calves) time, which in Chinese time is 1-3 a.m. The book of Revelation was written down June 12, 96 A.D., as we seen by the old calendar, and with the new calendar would be June 21-22, 2007, when these angels appear on a Wednesday-Thursday at 1-3 a.m., which is June 20-21, 2007.

The ancient Egyptian carving from the temple Hathor shows a pig near Taurus, three stars, seven stars, one star and 12 stars. (See drawing 45 at the end of my book *The Experiment at Philadelphia*.) Was that predicting June 7-12, 14-25, 2007 as the date of when great earthquakes, wars, terrorists attack, assassinations and storms will come upon the U.S. and Israel? The seven and 12 stars could represent the days in June from 7-12. The Pig is the Chinese Year of the Pig in 2007, when on June 7-12, 14-25 troubles come.

The pig on that same carving could also be President Ronald Reagan's birth Year of 1911. He died on June 5, 2004. Adding three years (three stars) to that date equals June 5, 2007 when troubling events begin to happen. The moon is in Aries-Taurus on June 9-12, 2007 according to one astrology book. Is that why an ancient Egyptian carving and art shows a sun or moon disk between bull and goat's horns predicting these events at this time period? Near the pig on that carving shows a goat's head with a sun disk or moon disk between its horns. Also seen near the pig are three stars, which symbolizes three years from when President Reagan died on June 5, 2004, when the sun (disk) was in Taurus, till the time of future events in June 5-25, 2007 when the sun (disk) and moon (disk) are in Aries or Taurus. This is shown in the seven (days) and 12 stars (days) near a pig on the carving, which is Reagan's birth year. He died on June 5 so you then add the +7+12 stars to that date and it equals June 5-25, 2007. Those dates on the ancient Egyptian carving near the pig and is the same time that the two candlesticks/lamps point to in June when Orion, Gemini and Taurus are seen in a certain position, date and time.

These stars on the carving of 1,3,7 and 12 could also mean three months (stars) and four years (stars=1+3=4) after the second Iraq war; 12 years (12 stars) from the first Iraq war (1991), would come these predicted events. The second Iraq war that started near a full moon (disk) near Aries (goat) on March 19-21 in the year of the Goat in 2003, plus three months and four years (=1+3=4; the stars seen near the pig) would predict future events on June 19-21, 2007. The pig seen on the carving near 12 stars represents the hours of 9-11 p.m. when the second Iraq war started at 9:30-38 p.m. ET March 19, 2003 exactly 12 years after the first Iraq war.

Matthew 24:32, Mark 13:28-30, and Luke 21:29-32 all predict trouble near when spring begins in March-April-May or near when summer begins in June of 2007. March-April-May of 2007 is the time when the spring leaves form on the trees. There are also lunar and solar eclipses in March of 2007. Joel chapter 2 and Acts chapter 2 both predict solar (darkened sun) and lunar (blood moon) eclipses as the time of the end when many events begins to happen. (See also Revelation 6:12-13.)

Jesus ascended into heaven in May of 30 A.D., 40 days after His death on the cross and resurrection on April 6-9, 30 A.D. The angels claimed His return will come the same way as lightning from heaven making clouds. (See Acts 1:11.) Was that predicting incoming missiles, bombs and planes causing clouds or smoke and mushroom clouds as the books of Acts and Joel in the Bible predict with blood in the first month of March-April 2007?

Nostradamus also predicted a quake, war or trouble in April-May. He predicts them as trouble in the milk moon month and April when the pope and/or Rome has trouble when a comet or comets rip the skies and/or missiles or planes attack. Each full moon of each month has a name. The full moon of May is the full milk moon. See quatrains C6:Q66; C2:Q46;C10:Q67.

It is possible that these events begin in March-May and go into June as attacks and wars. Or should we look closely at the news during March-May of 2007 for these events that come in June when summer is near or begins? The summer solstice, which begins summer, usually falls on June 20-22 each year. Those dates are the birth days of Jesus, His disciple John and the antichrist or fourth beast of Daniel born in Atlantis, possibly in the Pig Year long ago. At his birth the planet Wormwood, which is where he came from, blew up and he took Venus by force causing a reversal of its rotation after three days of darkness because all rotations of all planets stopped. (See Matthew 11:12.) Is this what Nostradamus in his quatrain and Amos chapter 5 meant as darkness in the air? See C9:Q83 and Amos chapter 5; Luke 21:11,25; Wisdom of Solomon chapter 7:17-21; chapter 11:17-20 in the Apocrypha; and Daniel 2:21. The "alterations of the solstices," the fearful signs in the sky and changing of seasons in those sources all refer to time stopping for three days on or near the summer solstice, thus making the beginning of summer season change by three days because the summer solstice would then begin on June 24 instead of June 21. The word "solstice" means "the sun has stood still." Will that happen in June 21, 2007?

Haggai's ninth month and 24th day when all good comes could be translated as June 24, 2007 by the Jewish Civil calendar to ours. Also Matthew 24:6-8, 19 prophecies as "birth pangs ("the beginning of sorrows") and those with child and give suck could mean the birthdays of Jesus and John His disciple, on June 20- 24, 2007 as the dates when these events happen possibly with the rotation of Venus and the earth stopping.

Venus rules all life and used to rotate counterclockwise, as the earth does, making long life spans exactly as Genesis claimed. But when the fall came and in Noah's flood Venus' rotation stopped for three days causing all other planets, including the earth, to stop rotating for exactly three days. (See Matthew 11:12; *Astrology: The space age science*, page 143.) After three days Venus and all planets began rotating, but Venus was then rotating clockwise making it the opposite of good and long life span for people of earth exactly like what happened after Noah's flood, the lifespan of people became shorter.

When the first antichrist was born in Atlantis on June 20- 22, the summer solstice, Venus was stopped for three days because evil was then on the earth. That evil was satan coming from Venus (6) to earth, first at Giza, Egypt the Virgo (6)-Libra (6) zones, to make 666 in September, and then born near Florida on the summer solstice. Venus rotating clockwise is a curse and evil on the earth and with it rotating counterclock wise is good and blessing on the earth. Will it again spin counterclockwise on the summer solstice making restitution for all good again as Acts 3:21 predicts in the spring and summer of 2007 exactly what was prophesied long ago? Or will these prophecies fail for 2007, but some come true in 2016? Amos 5:8 predicts this strange darkness in the daytime caused by the rotation stopping as the "shadow of death" in the morning when Orion and the seven stars are overhead at noon or in the east in early morning. Is that the early morning that was prophesied? Or is the morning in Israel making around midnight or 1 a.m. (1:18 a.m.?) in the eastern U.S. when time is stopped on June 20-21, 2007? This makes the day dark as night even at noon. (See Isaiah 16:3.) Or does it mean the stoppage is at noon in Israel and morning in the eastern U.S.? If the earth stops rotating at nighttime it would make the next three days dark even at noon as the prophecies predict. If it stops in the morning in Israel's time it would make evening come for three days when it is still light as Zechariah 14:6-7 predicts. That same chapter of Zechariah also predicts the same earthquake two years before it happened as we have seen Amos 1:1 predicted for Jerusalem or Israel and/or the U.S. (See Zechariah 14:5-16.) Those verses also mentions war or trouble for Jerusalem and Israel at that same time. Zephaniah 1:15-18 and Isaiah 58:8 predicts the Day of the Lord as one of great darkness and three days later in the morning our health shall be made good speedily. Venus rotating counterclockwise, along with the tree of life, cures all diseases and aging. The three days of darkness is done at this time to change all things and make these good things happen then. The curse on all people and the earth will go away that day if these things happen; if not they will continue on as they are till the end in 2016. If the rotation does not stop at this time the darkness may be due to the earthquake and/or volcano eruptions, wild fires, comet impact, storms, bomb, missile or plane attacks. Both Acts and Joel chapters 2 predict smoke and blood at this time.

The book of Daniel tell us from the start of the second Iraq war on March 19-21, 2003 to add 1335 days to it, which equals November 13, 2006 to the end times. This date is from when President Bush made a covenant with many to go to war with Iraq over lies (abominations) that they had weapons of mass destruction (desolation) just as Daniel 9:27 predicted would come in the end times.

The year 2006 is the Chinese Dog Year the same Year as 26 A.D., when John the Baptist came and Jesus started His ministry, both claiming the kingdom of God is at hand and the acceptable year of the Lord was then. (See Isaiah 61:1-3; Matthew 4:17; Mark 1:15; Luke 4:18-19.) Jesus began His ministry most likely on Halloween or the day after as moon phases for 26 A.D. show October 28-29 was a new moon making the third day October 31-November 1, 26 A.D. when He went to a wedding as the gospel of John claims.

In the Lord's Prayer we say: "Hallowed be thy name, thy kingdom come." Was this relating to spelling God's name in reverse, which is Dog or the Dog year of 26 A.D. and 2006 as the day of

His coming on Halloween on October 31, 2006. We get the word "hallowed" as part of the name "Halloween." See Amos 5:13 and Revelation 11:18 that predict the Lord's return as an evil day or day of the dead, which we have come to know as Halloween, the time of the dead spirits, ghosts, evil demons and witches.

Due to calendar changes Halloween on October 31 has the date of old Halloween on November 11, 2006. Nothing happened then as Nostradamus claimed changes in dates will come when the sun is in or near Libra. (See C1:Q56.) On November 11, 2006 the sun is directly in the middle of Libra at noon, which is also prophesied in an ancient Egyptian carving, as we will see, as well as Mayan prophecies which also give that same date. The Mayans gave the time of midnight when Taurus, Gemini and Orion are overhead on November 11, 2006. The changes in dates maybe September 26-27, 2003, September 7-8, October 31, November 11, 2006 to June of 2007 and November 11, 2016.

That change for 2006 is recorded in Matthew 24:48; 25:1-13 and Daniel chapter 12 as a 10-year delay from this Dog Year of 2006. Daniel's time, times and half, or 1260 days, plus 1290 and 1335 days added together, equals a 10-year period changed from 2006 to 2016. The 10 virgins of Matthew 25:10-13 are 10 years and 10 hours added to November 1, 2006, which equals November 11, 2016 at 11:11 a.m. That date is the date of the old Halloween when the kingdom of God comes delayed 10 years from the Dog Year of 2006.

The five wise virgins of Matthew 25:1-13 could have meant five delayed periods of time of 10 from Halloween of 2006 to 2016. The amount of those five delays is 10, the number of the virgins. Adding 10 years 10 days 10 hours 10 minutes and 10 seconds gives us the exact date of November 11, 2016 at 11:11 p.m. and 11 seconds as the end. At that time a comet or asteroid, sun nova, volcano eruptions or earthquakes will strike the earth as Revelation 6:12-13, Amos chapter 5 and Daniel 9:27 predict as the end. The antichrist or beast standing where he ought not as Mark 13:14 predicts is satan standing at the core of the sun causing a sun nova showering the earth with parts of its outer layers destroying the whole earth and solar system. The Wormwood of Amos 5:7 could be the remains of satan's planet called Wormwood between Mars and Jupiter where the asteroid belt is now, which along with comets and/or volcano eruptions could strike the earth at this time. This all started with the birth of the fourth beast or the great antichrist in Atlantis long ago who created the animal monsters in hell and the dinosaurs on earth, which were destroyed by the remains of Wormwood exploding and/or volcano eruptions when he was born June 20-22 in the Pig Year long ago.

November 11, 2016 is the Chinese year of the Monkey. Remember in Chinese astrology each of the 12 signs rules once every 12 years, not each year. They also rule two-hour periods for each day and night.

Many ancient Egyptian drawings shows a monkey or baboon pictured in them along with the scales (Libra). See drawings 14 and 19 at the end of my book entitled *The Experiment at Philadelphia*). Were they predicting the end in the Chinese Monkey Year of 2016? Many past events happened in the Chinese Monkey Year. Noah's flood began the second month and 17th day in 2341 B.C. According to astronomical soft ware shows that date was the Monkey Year and November 11. Jesus often claimed the end time "as the days of Noah." Was he referring to November 11, 2016?

The scales have women seen next to them in the many ancient Egyptian drawings and carvings, which could refer to Wednesday- Thursday as those days in Latin, meaning Mercury-Jupiter that rule Virgo (woman) and Libra (scales). The snakes often seen in ancient Egyptian and Mayan drawings and carvings could also mean the Chinese Year of the Pig in 2007 and Taurus and Scorpio that rule the Chinese Snake and Pig. The places of Los Angeles and Washington, D.C. are ruled by Taurus and Scorpio. The date of June 20-21, 2007, as we will see is important, and is a Wednesday-Thursday (=Virgo=Mercury; Libra=Jupiter). And November 11, 2016 is the Scorpio sign and on a Friday, which is

Latin for Venus. The many ancient Egyptian drawings and carvings show not only the scales of Libra, snakes and women, but the women sometimes holding the mark of Venus they called "ankh."

The Book of Revelation was written in 96 A.D., which was the Chinese Year of the Monkey. The year 1776 when the U.S. was born was also the Chinese Year of the Monkey. The creation of Adam and Eve and their fall in August-September happened in 3997 B.C., which was the Monkey Year. Were all these important events in the Chinese Year of the Monkey that of signs of future events in the Year of the Monkey?

In 2004 many prophecies came to pass as Colossians 2:16-17 predicts would be signs of future events just as September 26- 27, 2003 was. Four great hurricanes hit Florida in 2004 and was one of the most bizarre hurricane seasons ever. Volcanoes around the world began erupting, or acting up, including Mount Saint Helens. And the great Asian earthquake and tidal waves happened as one of the greatest earthquakes to ever strike the earth.

The big question is: will these same events happen again in 2016? Or will we approach November 11, 2016 without them? The prophecies suggest both ways. The prophecies of Matthew chapters 24, Mark 13, Luke 17 and 21 all predict the end times as coming without warning or signs, while they and others claim they come with many signs.

The ancient Egyptian carving from the temple Hathor shows two candlesticks or lamps that go through a circle with a man in it with a jackal on top in the middle of Libra. It also starts near a monkey or baboon, with a jackal's head with a sun or moon disk on top between a goat's horns. (See drawing number 47 at the end of my book entitled *The Experiment at Philadelphia*.) The other end of the line drawn through these two candlesticks goes through Gemini and Taurus. The pyramids at Giza, Egypt were believed to have been built on a pattern of the constellation Orion, which is near Taurus and Gemini. Amos 5:8 predicts the end time is when we see these same constellations at certain times and, as we will read in the next chapter, the Mayans also predict the end with those same constellations overhead at midnight on November 11, 2006. With the 10-hour delay as mentioned earlier, it comes to 11:11 a.m. The two candlesticks or lamps on the ancient carving are the same ones mentioned in Revelation chapter 11. They also give the same dates of June 20-24, 2007 and November 11, 2016. (See drawing number 13 at the end of the book *The antichrist*.)

The carving with these two candlesticks has bird headed men kneeling and women holding the carving. (See drawing 26 at the end of my book *The experiment at Philadlephia*.) Gemini is an air sign, which the ancient Egyptians often shows as a bird or bird-headed men. Taurus is a woman sign, which the ancient Egyptian shows as women. The mark or symbol of Venus known as the ankh the ancient Egyptians showed in their carvings and drawing as Venus, which rules Libra and Taurus. Is that when the sun is in Libra and Gemini-Orion and Taurus are overhead at midnight on Halloween November 11 in 2006, but is delayed to 2016 at 11:11 a.m. November 11, 2016? That date is a Friday, which is Latin for Venus that rules Libra, Taurus the bull and is the seven stars and a woman sign, which ancient Egyptian art often shows the scales, women, monkey and ankh as mentioned earlier. On that latter date the sun is in or near Libra-Scorpio the same as where the two candlesticks point to on one end and on the other end it is near Taurus-Gemini, whose star time is in June of 2007. (See drawings 44 and 47 at the end of my book *The Experiment at Philadelphia* and on star and planet locators at June 20-25 and November 11 at 11 a.m. for star positions at those dates.)

The one candlestick shown by a monkey or baboon next to a jackal's head and a sun and moon disk between the goat's horns could relate to these prophecies and dates. (See drawing 47 at the end of my book the experiment at philadelphia.) Was this predicting the Chinese Monkey Year of 2016? The date of November 11, 2016 has the moon in Aries (goat's or ram's horns). That is the moon disk between the goat's horns. The sun disk on top of a jackal at that time is directly in the middle of Libra at noon. The jackal is a Dog and in Chinese astrology rules Libra the scales, and the sun is directly in the middle of Libra on November 11, 2006 at noon. In 2016 on November 11 the sun at 11:11 a.m. is near the end of Libra and beginning of Scorpio just as the carving shows where the two candlesticks point to. (See drawings 27 and 47 in my book *The Experiment at Philadelphia* and planet and star locators on November 11 at 11 a.m.)

The circle on top of Libra directly in the middle of it with a man in it and a jackal on top also shows these same things with the sun (circle) in the middle of Libra (=dog= jackal) on November 11, 2006 at noon or near the end of Libra and the beginning of Scorpio at 11:11 a.m. The circle also is the moon, which would be in Libra's cosign of Aries as noted above for November 11, 2016 when the moon is in Aries. The Dog is known as dogma, or commandments, or the 10 commandments, and is the symbol of 10 years from the Dog Year of 2006 on Halloween, or Old Halloween, till the date of the Old Halloween on November 11, 2016.

The Mayans had a covenant with the devil that expires every 52 years, 520 years and/or 5200 years. When it expires the world may end if they do not appease the Devil. Many believe the last 5200 years ends in our year 2012 A.D. They start at approximately 3113 B.C., but if you start at 3109 B.C and deduct 5124 years from that date you come to November 11, 2016, not counting the year zero. Both 3109 B.C. and 2016 A.D. are Chinese Years of the Monkey. Why 5124 years are used instead of 5200 years is because the Mayans, as does God in the Bible, and many ancient cultures uses 360-day years instead of our 365.24-day years. Multiplying 5200 years by 5.24 days equals 75.68 years, or approximately 76 years shorter then our 5200, making 5124 years subtracted from 3109 B.C. to be 2016 A.D. not counting the year zero.

The book *The Mayan Prophecies*, by Adrian G. Gilbert and Maurice M. Cotterell pages 130-134 predict that in 1507 A.D. the Mayans went up to their temple to plead with the devil not to destroy the world for the next 52 or 520 years. They may have done this as well in 1503 A.D. When adding 520 years to that year, it comes to 2023 A.D. Subtract seven years from then and we come to the year 2016. Why I deducted seven years is because 520 years at 365.25-day years makes it seven years shorter by 360-day years.

The year 1503 A.D. was the Chinese Year of the Pig, the same as 2007. Both Nostradamus and Solomon were born in the Year of the Pig and died in the Year of the Ox or Tiger. The polar opposite the Tiger is the Monkey. Were Solomon and Nostradamus prophets from the beginning (birth) to the end as predicting end-time events in the Pig year, Ox Year or Monkey Year? Nostradamus predicted in C3:Q94 that 500 years from his birth would come end-time prophecies and revelations. Was he predicting 520 years from his birth in 1503 A.D. till the end of the world in 2016 A.D., the same as the Mayans? Also Daniel chapters 9 and 10 written in 538 B.C. and 535 B.C. are the Chinese Years of the Pig (2007) and Tiger, whose polar opposite is the Monkey (2016). He predicts end-time events strongly in those two chapters. Will they come true in 2007 and 2016?

Jesus was also born in the Year of the Snake 4 B.C. the polar opposite of the Pig (2007), and He died 30 A.D., the Year of the Tiger, the polar opposite of the Year of the Monkey (2016). Were His birth and death, like Nostradamus and Solomon, predicting those two years of the Pig (2007) and Monkey (2016) as important years in prophecies?

The book *The Mayan Prophecies* by Adrian G. Gilbert and Maurice M. Cotterell, pages 130-134, claims the Mayans had this covenant with the devil (serpent-snake). They would go up to the top of their temple on November 11. At that time is when Orion, Taurus and Gemini are overhead, or nearly overhead, at midnight. They would then try to appease the devil so that he will not destroy the world every 52 years, 520 years or 5200 years, which started in 3109 B.C continued in 1503 A.D., 1964 A.D. and ends 2016 A.D. This gives the date of the end of the world by all these sources as…

November 11, 2016 at 11:11 a.m.

Chapter Thirty One

End Time Dates

A book I wrote in 2001 put the end of the age or world or Second Coming in June 20-21, 2001 a Wednesday into Thursday. Matthew chapter 24 predicts a generation from the main sign of Israel becoming a nation, which was on May 14-15, 1948. Psalms chapter 90 puts a generation as 70 years. Add 70 years to 1948 and it equals 2018 in 2019 when the end would come. But If you count 2000 years from when Jesus predicted the end in April of 30 A.D. it equals exactly 2030 A.D. when the end of the age or world or Second Coming or Rapture will happen. That year is the Chinese Dog Year the same as 2018-2019. If you count years as 360 days, as God does, then the 2000 years would come to June 20-21, 2001. And if you count the beginning of this age at 4480 B.C. and subtract 6480 years or one age it comes to 2001 again. Hosea in the Bible predicts after two days He will revive us and the third day raise us up. Many have concluded this meant a day for a 1000 years as Psalms chapter 90 and Peter stated in the Bible as a time period to God. Two days would be two thousand years to our Gregorian calendar would end in 2001 and then the third day would start. According to what New Year's Day you use it makes several dates in 2001 as the time of the end, but nothing happened. June 20-21, 2001 was a new moon with a solar eclipse near noon (blackened sun) seen south of Israel at that time (=noon hour=creation of the stars) on a Wednesday-Thursday the exact time of creation of the stars as Genesis chapter 1 states. Revelations seven churches are located in Western Turkey where the end of the Virgo zone ends and the beginning of the Libra zone begins. That is Mercury or Virgo and Jupiter or Libra in astrology, which equals our days of Wednesday-Thursday. June 20-21, 2012 is also a Wednesday- Thursday. It could also mean Virgo-Libra in September of 2012 when these events of Iran and Israel happened or the royalties of the books sales come in if Israel attacks Iran in April-May- June of 2012. June 12, 2012 is when the book of Revelation was written down long ago and could be when Israel attacks Iran and then in September (Virgo=Revelation's seven churches) of 2012 the royalties come in from the book sales in May-June.

Daniel chapter 12 of 2625 days (1290+1335=2625) subtracted from 606 or 605 B.C. equals 2020 A.D. plus a 40 year generation equals 2060 A.D. when the end comes. Psalms chapter 90 (=our 1990) with 70 or 80 years or more added to 1990 equals 2060- 2070 when the end may come. Adding 2000 years as Hosea 6:1-2 predicts to 26-30 A.D. when John the Baptist and Jesus came claiming the end is at hand and the kingdom of God is at hand, equals 2026-2030 A.D. when the end of the U.S. occurs by a super volcano eruption in Yellowstone Park and/or a comet or asteroid impact on the U.S. or in the Atlantic or Pacific Oceans or wars and attacks happening then. It wouldn't be the end of the world by the end of the U.S. And the Americans, Christians and Jews left alive around the world will suffer persecution, prison and death for years to come and only faith and patience will help them as Luke 21:12-28 predicted.

At that time of this great disaster the books The Book of Angels by Ruth Thompson, L.A. Williams, and Renae Taylor and Unusual Prophecies Being Fulfilled Prophetic Series/Book 3 by Perry Stone tell of angels and minister that predicted the U.S. future and its end to George Washington and some old minister in the U.S. The story of the angel and George Washington took place right before the big battle to start the U.S. An angel supposedly a woman appeared to him and showed him how great the U.S. would become in visions. She also predicted its end. Was she also predicting its end when a woman rules the Union (U.S.)? The old minister in Perry Stone's book had seven prophecies that seem to all come true except the last which predicted a woman President of the U.S. and in her term the U.S. is destroyed. Is the great whore of mystery Babylon in Revelation chapter 17-18-19 that of a woman President of the U.S. or Rome, Italy or some where else?

II Samuel 11:1-3 predicts when the year expires kings will go to war. This could mean the Old Julian calendar New Year's Eve and Day, or the new Gregorian calendar New Year's Eve and Day. It also could mean the Bible's New Year's Eve and Day. And also the Jewish Civil calendar New Year's Eve and Day as to when Israel attacks Iran or some other war, or the Rapture, the end of the world and the Second Coming happens. These dates are March 1, 20-21, 24-25, December 31-January 1, Rosh Hashanah (September-October) and June or July (19) as creation's first month and even October 31 and November 1-2, 11, as the Anglo- Saxon calendar.

I Samuel 2:5-10 also predicts a time when God's maketh poor and then maketh rich and wars and other events happen in the time of the "horn". The Taurus sign of a bull with horns runs from April 20-May 20 and star time from May 21-June 21. I left my job in May of 1977 (=Snake Year=2013) and became poor then. Will God make me rich then too in March-May of 2012-2013? Will it be on Pentecost in those years, or May 28-29 in those years of 2012-2013 when the first Pentecost came in 30 A.D. which could be the same dates as in 2012 on May 27-28, 2012 if you count from April 6, 30 A.D. or from April 9, 30 A.D. Is the "double blessing" that Isaiah 61:7 predicts for shame that of a April-May-June as the blessing in 2012 then a August 10, 2013 blessing that comes on December 7, 2013. Do angels go out on those dates or December 24-25, 2012 and August 10, 2013 and the blessings come March 7, 2013 and December 7, 2013? March 7, 2013 is a Thursday and same calendar and date I came out of prison as Zechariah 9:10-14 predicts "double" for like Isaiah 61:7 also predicts. One year is 2012 and one year 2013 or double. Or the two or double blessings are both in 2013 as being not 10,000 but 20,000 double the people the angels are sent to. Deuteronomy 32:30-31, chapter 33, and Jude 14 all claim 10,000 sometimes with an "s" on the end. Could this mean a change from 10,000 people to 20,000 people informed at this time of these books? And as Ecclesiastes 9:16-18 predicts the wise heard or read words in quiet more than those who proclaim out loud and that this wise man from the south has his wisdom despised by the religious leaders as they will tell you when they shows them my works (=books). It may be best to you who read these books not to mention them to others except for witnessing Jesus Christ to others is good, but don't tell them of these books.

Zechariah 9:10-14 prediction of double blessing as Isaiah 61:7 predicts also might mean March 7-8, 2002 and March 7-8, 2013, which are both Thursdays and Fridays and the exact same calendars. These times are times of shame followed by times of double blessing as Psalms 90:14-17 predicts the days and years of trouble shall be numbered as the same days and years of double blessing. Or the times of riches comes in the times of poverty, which we read was May of 1977, the Chinese Snake Year and May-June of 2013 the Chinese Snake Year.

The predictions for 2013-2014-2015 of a volcano eruption and tidal wave may not happen then, but in January of 2019 if at all. Those books of mine entitled Predictions for 2013- 2014, Predictions for 2015 and Predictions for 2011-2019 may all fail or only parts come true. This is true of all ancient prophecies as I often explain in my 14 books. Sometimes things don't happen the way they appear even when they are written under inspiration. Psalms 68:17 twenty thousand angels as chariots might mean December 24-25, 2012 when Israel attacks Iran angels tell 20,000 people of these books of mine when Auriga The Charioteer is over head at midnight to morning. Or it could mean Auriga is near or behind the sun in May-June of 2012 when angels are sent out to tell 10,000 or 20,000 people of my books then in July-August 10, 2012 three months (21 days or three weeks=three months) after

Israel attacks Iran Iran attacks Israel and angels are sent out to tell 10,000 more people of my books to make 20,000 or more altogether as Psalms 68:17 predicts. Or it's 20,000 people both times as a double blessing. Song of Solomon predicts 10,000 women and possibly 10,000 men that are told of this wisdom making it 20,000 altogether in 2012-2013 (in May-June of 2012 or December 24-25, 2012 and July-August of 2013) making double trouble and double blessing in those two years. The angels come in May-June of 2012 and/or July-August or December 7, 24-25 of 2012 as the double blessing when Auriga is seen behind the sun or over head at night. Then in the fall the blessing of 2012 comes and in March 7, 2013 the second blessing comes. The three weeks could also mean a attack in April-June 2012 or December 24-25, 2012 then three years (=three weeks) later in 2015-2016 Iran attacks and angels are sent out and another blessing with trouble as Ecclesiastes 7:14 predicts. The 1000 pieces of silver and a 1000 vineyards in Song of Solomon chapter 8 may fail as well as its 200 keepers (workers) of the publisher which is now (2012) 1100 people not 200 as predicted for 2003 when it was 200 people at the publisher Authorhouse where all my books were published. Both those things may fail. March 7, 2013 is a Thursday the same as March 7, 2002 when I was released from jail (prison). If on December 24-25, 2012, plus or minus 21 days, is when Israel attacks Iran and then Iran attacks Israel and the U.S.? That time period is when 20,000 angels are set out to tell people where to buy these 14 books of mine and I receive the royalties on March 7, 2013 or May-June of 2013 as I Samuel chapter 2 and Zechariah 9:10-14 predicts. God maketh poor and He maketh rich in the spring of 1977 and 2013. In this case the rumor of war was Hal Lindsey and mine as being in December of 2011 and then in December of 2012 by then or then another rumor of war with Iran and ruler against ruler and war.

The two angels I saw on December 25, 2000 Christmas Day around 11 a.m. to 1 p.m. were the symbols of six wings of seraphim's and/or cherubim's and the 24 elders as six hours (–six wings) added to that time 24 (=cherubim's) hours before. December 25, 2000 was a Monday and the Chinese Dragon year. Add 12 years to that date and 24 hours before it and add six hours ahead of it equals Christmas Eve into Christmas day at 11 p.m. to 1 a.m. December 24-25, 2012 when angels are sent out and war with Iran happens and Auriga the Charioteer is over head at that time in the night exactly as the Bible's Psalms 68:17 predicted. That time is also the Chinese Year of the Dragon the same as December 25, 2000. December 24-25, 2012 is a Monday-Tuesday. The ending of the Moon day under the feet of the woman (=Israel) is the evening of Monday December 24, 2012. Then the starting of the day of Tuesday that is Latin for Mars the red planet, which is Leo that the sun rules, which the woman is clothed with in Revelation chapter 12. The great red dragon would be the Year 2012. The 12 stars of Revelation chapter 12 along with the chapter number could mean the 12th month, or our December. The reverse of the 12 to 21 and the moon equaling 2 plus zero equals 20-12 or 2012 December 21. Then adding three and a half days, as Revelation chapter 11 predicts, to December 21, 2012, is December 24-25, 2012 as the time when the great red Dragon Year pulls down stars (missiles- bombs) from heaven then or three and a half years from then in June 24-25, 2016, which Isaiah 40:2 predicts as double trouble for Israel in June of 2016 and in June of 1967 with the six day war. See my book 2012 for the documentation of these ancient prophecies. At that time is the end of Israel, not the world, which comes much later as that book predicts.

"The immediately after tribulation in those days shall the stars fall from heaven" might mean that wars, attacks, volcano eruptions, tidal waves and earthquakes happen in January of 2019 causing massive destruction and trouble then a greater troubles comes immediately after that in January of 2019 when the sun goes into a supernova causing pieces (stars) of it to rain down upon the earth destroying the earth completely. If you see an angel or person on the rooftop at this time run a way from Florida and the U.S. East Coast quickly. If you see armies in Jerusalem, Israel or Florida at this time of January of 2019 then run to the mountains east of Jerusalem, Israel or to Petra, Jordan. If you see a strange light by the sun and tidal waves or storms hitting the U.S. and prisons being flooded and the prisoners released at this time of January 2019 then those things could also be signs to run away and hide. For the end is near then or some other time when these same events happen. See Matthew chapter 24, Mark chapter 13, Luke chapters 17, 21.

Matthew 24:6-8, Luke 21:9-11 and Jeremiah 51:46 predictions of wars and rumors of wars and the end is not yet or by and by (two years), but then kingdom against kingdom and nation against nation and great earthquakes in diver places, famines and pestilence's might be backwards in orders. The kingdom against kingdom and nation against nation could mean the U.S. (Kingdom) and the United Kingdom (=England) along with many nations fight against Iraq in 1991 and 2003 until 2011. Then the Afghanistan war from 2001 to 2014 when its suppose to stop. Before each Iraq war there was a year before many rumors of wars and then the next year those wars came. This is the "beginning of sorrows" that Matthew 24:8 predicts. Then earthquakes in diver places (different places) came in Iran (2003), Asia-tidal waves (2004), Pakistan (2005), Haiti (2010), Japan (2011) and others along with famines and pestilence's. All these are the beginning of sorrows. Then in 2011 rumors of wars with Iran start and in 2012-2013 they happen, but that is not the end in 2012 or 2013. But when there is a sign by the sun or in the sun, a darkened sun, moon and stars (=Yellowstone or Canary Island eruption?) and waves roaring (tidal waves, Nor' Easters, hurricanes) and the stars from heaven start to fall to earth that is the end. See Matthew 24:29-33, Luke 21:19-28. The signs in the sun, moon and stars could be the solar flares in the sun and great Northern Lights seen farther south then ever in 2012 as a sign of war coming along with tidal waves and storms as the seas roaring as Luke 21:24-26 predicts. The sign in the stars that those same verses predicts could be an asteroid or comet said on the NBC evening news in March 2012 to be coming towards earth in 11 months (?) and could be a close to earth as the satellites and/or could hit the earth (?). Other signs in the stars could be the sun, moon, other moons and planets and other stars in other solar systems flare up seven times brighter as Isaiah predicted. It also could mean comet or asteroid impacts on earth, the moon or other moons and planets. Other strange events may happen at these times in the sun, moon and stars like supernovas in other solar systems. The sign in the moon could be a blood moon or lunar eclipse in 2012-2013, 2015-2016 or January 2019 or a asteroid or comet hit it or some other strange event happens to it.

In Daniel chapter 10 it predicts Israel to attack Iran (=Persia) then some three weeks later return to fight Iran (=Persia). Are the three weeks three years later starting from 2012-2013? That would equal 2015-2016. Will Israel attack Iran in 2012-2013 and then Iran waits three years to obtain a nuclear bomb or two or three nuclear bombs and attacks Israel then three years later? Then Israel responds with another attack on Iran (=Persia) just as Daniel chapter 10 predicted that Israel will return again to attack Iran (=Persia). Or is the three week delay in Daniel 10:4,13 three weeks from when Israel attacks Iran till Iran attacks Israel starting with Israel's attack first on Iran on December 3-4, November 28-30, 2012-2013 then 21 days later on December 20-22 or 24-25, 2012- 2013 Iran attacks Israel? Or is it 21 days from December 20- 22, or 24-25, 2012-2013 when Israel attacks Iran till Iran attacks Israel on January 10-12, 14-15, 2012-2013? Or are the first attacks delayed from December 2012 to January-February 2013? My book entitled 2012 as read earlier in this book predicts war in Israel and Iran in 2012-2013 or 2016. Will both come true as the 21 days or three weeks changed to years equals the time of wars with Israel and Iran. One attacks in December 2012-2013 another minor attacks in January 2012-2013 then Iran acquires nuclear bombs by 2015-2016 and then attacks Israel three years after it was attacked in 2012-2013.

Luke 21:9-11 predicts wars and rumors of wars then by and by but it is not the end. Was this predicting the rumors of wars with Iran in 2011-2012-2013 then wars, but the end is not by and by or two years later in 2014-2015 when Israel and/or the U.S. are destroyed and/or attacked or hit by earthquakes, volcanoes, tidal waves and storms, which makes many think the end has come, but as prophesied it is not yet. The wars and rumors of wars and the by and by and the end is not yet could also mean the 9-11-01 attacks then the second Iraq war in 2003 two years later as the by and by (2001+2=2003), but the end is not yet in 2003 exactly as prophesied.

Ecclesiastes 5:6 prediction of an angel people say is in error may have several meanings. One that the author is insane. Or that he is a heretic using new age, astrology and Chinese astrology knowledge forbidden by the Bible. Or he sets dates that Jesus said no one knows. How can you be ready if you don't know the time. Every time it mentions you can't know the time it is followed or preceded each place where it says that you can know the hour or day and should and be prepared and ready and watching. Did you know that? Matthew chapters 22 and 25 predict that if you don't know the day and hour and your caught sleeping in pajamas and the Lord comes you will be left behind and will not go into heaven with the bride and bridegroom when the two become one on a Sunday (=one) Monday (=2) January 20-21, 2019 at the month and sign of the door.

Also the preaching for money to give and get is also often followed or preceded by a verse saying its wrong to give to get or to give to prosper. Did you know that? See Luke chapter 6 and Matthew chapter 24. And that the prophecies of the one book of mine or the others didn't happen in 2011-2014 or 2015-2016, or that the book that predicts the prophecies for those years 2015-2016 misspells the word Prediction (Predicton) in the title and headings, thus in error. My book entitled Predictions for 2015 has all these things in them, but heed the warning of Ecclesiastes 5:6 that to tell the angel he is wrong about that book and my others that God could have wrath on you and destroy you and your works in a tidal wave and/or war or storm, unless they fail too or comes true not in 2015-2016, but in January of 2019. People would say he predicted a tidal wave in 2012-2013, 2015-2016 and nothing happened and begin to mock and celebrate Christmas and New Years then the end suddenly comes and takes them all by surprise.

Christmas Day 2060 Isaac Newton predicted 1260 days of Revelation chapter 12 added to Christmas Day 800 A.D., when Charlemagne was crown by the Pope as the Holy Roman Emperor. Adding the 1260 days as years to that date comes exactly to Christmas Day 2060 A.D. on Christmas Eve and Day which are a Friday evening and Saturday. Is that what Matthew 24:19-20 means by praying your flight be not on the Sabbath and not in winter? The Jewish Sabbath starts Friday evening and goes all day Saturday. Approximately December 7, 2060 is a full moon making December 21-22-23, 2060 a new moon. The Jews sometimes start their new moons a day to three days after ours in the U.S. making their new moon possibly being December 24-25, 2060 A.D. when the end come exactly as Isaac Newton predicted and Matthew 24:19-20, Colossians 2:16-17, Haggai 2:18-23 and Ecclesiastes 7:14 predicted. Matthew 11:11-12 predicted as the birthday of John the Baptist when the heavens and all the earth shake in a supernova and destroys the earth on that date of John the Baptist's birthday of December 24-25, 2060. Revelation chapters 12 predicts this time as a war in heaven (=sun=super-nova) and on the 12 month of our December on the 21st day, backwards of 12, plus three and a half days, as Revelation 11:11 predicts to when the end comes on a Dragon Year and by the dragon in the sun causing a sun supernova destroying all. The year 2060 A.D. is the Chinese Year of the Dragon the same as Christmas Day 800 A.D. when Charlemagne was crown ruler over the Holy Roman Empire, which is the great Roman Catholic Church and is the MYSTERY BABYLON THE GREAT MOTHER OF HARLOTS AND THE ABOMINATIONS OF THE EARTH. See Revelation chapter 17. The date December 21, 2060 plus three and a half days equals December 24-25, 2060 A.D. when the end comes. Haggai 2:18-23 predicts this date as a time when all blessing and good would come in the ninth month and 24th day, which to our calendar is December 24-25, 2060. That year Hanukah would be celebrated on is approximately December 17-25, 2060 A.D. Haggai's date has always been associated with the start of Hanukah that starts on a different dates each year and lasts eight days.

If the end comes then, and it may not, many will be mocking the Christians, Bible, churches and writers and teachers of Bible and Bible prophecy because all the great TV preachers that preached the end is near since 1949 are long dead and gone. A new bunch may replace them claiming the same thing but they will be mocked to as II Peter 3:2-18 predicts. And with Israel and possibly the U.S. completely or partially destroyed by wars, volcanoes, tidal waves and any other man made or natural disasters the world will even more mock and scoff Bible preachers, Christians, church and writers for long ago those things happened and no Rapture, no Second Coming of Christ and no end of the world. In fact if the U.S. and Israel are destroyed the world may go on with a Muslim super power and religion over all the world with or without the help of Russia and China. The Catholic Church may adopt them or turn to their religion and murder many who don't follow as they did already to Christians in the past 1600 years. That's why the woman of Revelation chapter 17 sits on seven hills of Rome where the Vatican is in or near and has a cup filled with the blood of true Saints and Christians. They are already trying for a Muslim Empire in the Mid East known to us as the Arab spring in which we actually helped some of them and the Christians and democratic super powers like Israel and the U.S are gone and they are being persecuted and killing Christians and Jews there and around the world. Italy is in the EU of Europe and might join up with Rome to one religion being Muslim. It maybe the fourth revived empire and fourth beast of Daniel chapters 2 and 7 predicted long ago. Daniel 11:1-8 predicts a fourth prince to come up out of Persia and be far worse then any others and as Revelation chapter 13 predicts speaks like a Dragon (=anti- Semitic). The currently President of Iran was born in Scorpio and in the Chinese Year of the Dragon he speaks great words against Israel and the U.S. and is trying to start a war with them so the last great evil or good leader comes to the great Muslims. If he does start this war before he leaves office or dies he would be the fourth leader out of Persia (=Iran) since 1979. The war he starts with Israel and the U.S. may have the weeds grow up to your knees in these desolate places just as Isaiah chapters 7, 13 and Nostradamus predicted. If Jesus doesn't return by 2060 all Christians and Jews may have been murdered by the Muslims and these wars. Europe may turn into a super power of Muslims and with the Mid East nations that are Muslims turn Asia and other parts of the world Muslim. Jesus predicted in Matthew 24:22 that if He delayed the very elect would be gone and John 16:1-2 predicts a time people kill Christians, Americans or Jews they will say they do God's (=Allah) service. And the Bible says woe unto them that teach children to sin. In a interview with Prime Minister of Israel in April of 2012 he was told that Palestinian children are taught from their youth to fight Jews and Israel. Russia, China and North Korea have done the same thing over the years against the U.S. and Americans. Are they the three nations that the antichrist subdues as Daniel 7:24 predicts and the 10 horns 10 nations that survive the disasters or wars in our future and are ruled by Muslims and/or the Pope and Communism. Are they also the three great nations the angel told George Washington about in the end that destroys the U.S. and/or the volcano eruptions come from that destroy the U.S. and/or the invading armies being the Canary Islands off the West Coast of Africa, Sicily, Italy and Asia? I am sorrow to report such horrible future that no one on earth has ever done as far as I know but the Bible clearly predicts it. It also predicts the opposite if we repent. That doesn't seem likely at this time. People are so arrogant and proud professing to be wise became fools and ever learning and never able to come to the light of the truth just as the Bible predicted for the last days. God will for this behavior withdraw his hand and let these wars and natural disasters happen to these two Christian nations of Israel and the U.S. Let's pray that He doesn't do that. And as one TV preacher teaches the Rapture isn't before the seven year period but at the very end of it, which I hold true too. But the seven year period may have already came true in WWII. And the end of Israel and the U.S. would leave Muslims in rule and they will deliver you up to kings and put you in prisons and torture you for 10 days (Revelation 2:10) or much longer even years but be patient and faithful until death and you will make it to heaven. See Luke 21:12-

19. The 1260 years maybe predicting the time of the Gentiles that Luke chapter 21 predicted when Muslims, Catholic and communism rule the world and kill many Christians, Jews and Americans as they can as Revelation chapter 17 predicts of the great mystery Babylon woman on seven hills would do and the other allies of it which may turn out to be communism, Muslims and Catholic. This may happen from Christmas Day 800 A.D. to Christmas Day 2060 A.D. when the times of the Gentiles is over and they kill the Saints (=Christians and Jews) no more. One TV preacher has taught already how the Vatican and the Pope in Rome on seven hills have tried to join its self with communism and Russia. See Irvin Baxter on TV and phone his ministry for DVD's on the Pope and Russia. Call 1-800-363-8463. After the great World War II the Catholic church helped many of or all Nazi war criminal leaders to escape through their churches as reported on in 60 Minutes in 2011-2012. And down through history priests and/or bishops that came to Rome came away thinking it was an open sewer of corruption and evil from the Pope down.

People who set dates at this time near 2060 will utterly be laugh at and be declared wrong and a false prophet. But as the Bible says no one knows the day and hour also it say for everyone to watch and be ready for in the night He will come. If you don't know the day and hour how can you stay up and watch for it? You can't unless you stay up every night which you can't so as Matthew 22:1-14,25:1-13 predicts be ready and watch on the dates given just in case.

Babylon the great as predicted in Revelation chapters 17 and 18 is predicted to be very rich as the Catholic church is already and may prosper the whole nation and Rome, but it predicts those riches come to naught in "one hour". See Revelation 18:19. Is the "one hour" that of 60 minutes or the 60th year from the year 2000 ending on Thursday June 21, 2001 as told of the time of Hosea 6:1-2 at the beginning of this chapter? That would give the date 2060 when the end comes. And is the "half hour" in Revelation 8:1 that of 30 minutes or 30 years in half when the final Harbinger happens to the U.S. with Yellowstone Park volcano erupting and/or other natural disasters or wars and attacks to finish off the great U.S.? Thirty minutes as 30 years added to the year 2000 equals 2030 when these or other events happen. In the quatrain C2:Q5 Nostradamus may predict this end time attack on Rome, Italy by submarine launch nuclear missile on it. Habakkuk 3:2 predicts in the midst of the years something will happen. Half of 60 years from 2060 equals 2030 when something may happened in the midst of the years. See Habakkuk 3:2. That same book predicts armies to go through a storm at sea as told of earlier in this book when Russia or 10 nations left from all the disasters from 2012-2019 and beyond happen that come to attack the U.S. My book *The Divine Code 2* chapter 4 describes this attack and war on America. See also Habukkuk 3:11 for this time when the sun and moon stand still, doesn't rotate and then starts at the sight of the arrows and glittering spears (nuclear missiles) they went forth.

On Christmas Day 2060 may just be the final harbinger for all the world. Isaiah 9:10 was used in the book *The Harbinger* by Jonathan Cahn, but verses six of that same chapter predicts Jesus' birth long ago in the Chinese Snake Year as 2013 A.D. is the Chinese Snake Year. Will the final Harbinger happen on Christmas Day when Christ was born on June 24-25, 2060-2061 or the day we celebrate Christmas Day on December 24-25, 2060 just as Isaiah 9:6 and 10 predicted? Remember Matthew 24:44-51 predicts people mock dates and go about celebrating Christmas Day then sudden destruction hits them when the are over eating, drinking and partying as Luke 21:34-36 also predicts. June is known as "the June Bride" more than any other month. Is June 24-25, 2060-2061 the time of the wedding of God at the end?

Chapter Thirty Two

Come to Christ

Forget about what the antichrist and false prophet say and write, which I showed in the first 14 chapters of my book *The Experiment in Philadelphia*, if they come. What they say will poison the mind. But fear God and keep His commandments just as Solomon wrote in Ecclesiastics 12:13-14. Jesus said if you love Him you will keep His commandments. See John 14:15. He also said He is the truth and the life and the only way to the Father and heaven. He is purely the Son of God and perfect in every way and righteous. All of us have failed in our life, some many times, and in many ways. Maintaining a balance of the two, as the antichrist may teach, is also wrong as Jesus taught in Revelation 3:16. He said, regarding those who are lukewarm (balance), that Jesus will vomit out of his mouth anyone and any church that is that way. Yet Jesus gives us a second chance at life. What a great and beautiful thing that is!

The second chance comes when you are ready to repent of your sins, ask Jesus into your heart and life and live His ways for the rest of your life. Say this simple prayer and mean it with all your heart:

> Dear Jesus: I repent of all my sins. Please forgive me for all the sins I have committed in my life. Come into my life and heart and be my Savior and Lord and I will live for you forever. Amen.

Imagine this: after you said that prayer all the mistakes you ever made in life are forgiven completely. There will be no more fear, shame or guilt or remembrance of them ever again. This is because the blood of Jesus dying on the cross has saved you and given you that new freedom from those things bothering you ever again. You have a new life in Jesus and can live and die knowing that and have no fear of past sins or death and hell. You are born again!

Change your lifestyle after you said that prayer and live for Jesus. Go to a Bible-based church every Sunday. Pray every day. Read the Bible everyday. Do not sin and keep all the laws of the land. When you get this second chance do not waste it or throw it away because it is precious. Love Jesus and worship Him every day and live for Him. Most of all, keep the two greatest commandments, which is to love God with all your mind, soul and heart and most of all love your neighbor as yourself. You will find a loving good friend in Jesus when these things are done. Pray for the baptism in the Holy Ghost and tell others of Jesus. Give copies of this book and my other books to others as witnessing tools. See the web site: WWW.Authorhouse.COM for all my books and future ones to come and it will tell you how to order them. Separate yourself from the world for the world is not friendly with the ways of God. And remember, no one or things can take your salvation away. God bless all of you now and forever. Amen.

A few things should be stated about Christianity today. Do not point the finger at other people's sins, point the finger at you. Judge yourselves and not others or people even those in authority. Judge not lest ye be judged. Examine yourselves and not others. See Luke 6:37, Jude 8-11 and Matthew

7:1-5. Sinners will see the positive light in you and follow Jesus. I know the Bible says to tell people of their sins, but it also says these things just mentioned. When Jesus was here He never judged the sinners, but judged very hard the religious leaders for their judgement of others over every little thing. The Holy Bible says not to bring up other people's sins. Jude says that even the archangel Michael didn't accused the Devil of anything when over a dispute over the body of Moses. If he doesn't judge the Devil himself how much more should we not judge people.

Do not give to get. That is the wrong way to teach people to give. I know the Bible verses that teach those things, but I also know the Bible says to give and not to expect back. See Luke 6:29-30 and Matthew 10:5-42. Freely you were given your gifts and freely you should give them to others not for money. See Matthew 10:5-42.

Do not come to Christ for prosperity, success, fame and power as many teach today. Come to Christ humbly and without these motivations or expectations. Christianity can be very difficult if followed correctly. See Matthew 10:5-42. Family and friends can turn against you. Living without the world as your god and all the sins it brings can be extremely difficult to give up. This is why James said be not friendly with the world because it is at enmity with God. See James 4:4.

Beware of Eastern religions and all other religions and spirituality movements no matter how good they sound for they are not from God, but are ancient Gentile gods who are devils as explained in my book *The Antichrist* as MYSTERY BABYLON. There were only Ten Commandments in the Bible and you know what the first one is? It's not do not murder, or do not steal, or do not commit adultery, as important as those commandments are and are of the ten. The first commandment was "to have no other gods before me (The Jewish God the one and only true God). God wouldn't of said that if there weren't other gods and wouldn't of put it at the beginning of the Ten Commandments if it were not very important. Look at all the trouble today in the world. The trouble is not true Christianity! Its other gods and other religions, which God explained in the Bible as devils (=gods). See my book *The Antichrist* for more details of those other gods.

People in this generation don't want to hear "the devil made me do it" or "the devil told me to do it" as it is so far and hard to believe these horrible killers telling us that is what really happened. Yet this generation loves to blame God for everything. The BTK serial killer claimed demons drove him to do it. And everyone mocked that answer. Another family member found several of his victims and he said when he found them brutally murdered he right then and there "lost his religion." Like God did it instead of demons. One famous hit song in the past was called "losing my religion." One person once said when trouble occurs it either drives people away from God or nearer to Him. And believing is everything. It's the mighty power in good and it is the mighty power in evil, just believing. Believing can change your life and keep you out of hell or it can bring you down to hell forever. That's why Jesus taught so much about faith and believing in the Bible. It is also why the Bible calls Christians believers and non Christians unbelievers.

In the past four decades we seen God, prayer, the Bible, Nativity scenes and Ten Commandments removed from our schools, public buildings and court houses. What have we seen ever since? A great murderous killings in schools, public buildings and courthouses. God is not mocked. He is not just sitting back while you take Him out of everything. If you don't want God in these places and things He will let the Devil and great lawlessness come in and that is exactly what happened. You got your wish of not having God in these places and now you have the Devil. But you say don't blame the Devil for those great murders, but you blame God. But you don't believe in God? What is your excuse then? This generation is like Romans 1:22 claims as "professing to be wise became fools."

Questions have raised as to whether the U.S. is a Christian nation and if Christianity should be allowed in any part of it especially public and federal buildings. The lawyers have gotten so many confused about this. A little girl was thrown out of school for saying grace. When Bibles or Jesus are not allowed to be read or spoken of to anyone or by anyone in public and federal places, is that freedom? That's a simple question. Is that freedom? Is it? NO!!! And we all will agree this nation was founded on just that--freedom. When you offend atheists by Nativity scenes, Bibles and Christianity and take them away what about the Christian's rights who you then offend?

Just Look at whom you elected President of the U.S.? You elected President Obama, who he and his wife are ashamed of the U.S. He goes over to Europe and makes friends with all of our enemies and blasts the U.S. for being proud. He, or one of his spokesmen, said the U.S. is not a Christian nation or founded on Christianity. Even a democratic news anchorperson said what would our enemies think of us with him saying such things? The latest poll in Israel says only eight percent of Israelis like President Obama. That makes 92 percent of Israelis who dislike him. He promise to be good friend with Israel before he was elected and the first day in office he gave an interview to an Arab TV network that shows captured Americans being beheaded by terrorist. President Obama refused nation prayer day to have any Christian preacher come into the White House to pray on a certain day which many U.S. Presidents have done on that day for decades. He never invited Billy Graham to the White House who's been in the audience of every U.S. President since the 1950's or 1960's. Yet on the Muslin Holy Day President Obama had a big party and celebration at the White House.

One neighbor I witness to about Jesus Christ said that if Jesus were born today He would be a bastard. I tried to tell them He was virgin born, but they mocked that. Such blasphemy! After I got done witnessing to them I said even if I am wrong do you want to take a chance on going to hell? Before I even finished the sentence he answered in a quick strong angry voice, Yes! Yes he will take the chance.

One man I was talking to about being born again said he liked a bumper sticker he saw that said: "I was born right the first time." I immediately thought of Paul's writing in the Bible that the preaching of the cross and salvation is utter foolishness to the unbeliever. You just can't understand why the whole world is foolish in Christianity and you are right can you?

One man I met once said he couldn't believe in a God that let his wife slip in and out of consciousness during Child labor. The man said that it is right there in the Bible that God would make women suffer during childbirth. And it is, but is that any reason to hate your creator or not to believe in Him?

Another man I met I said to him "have a Merry Christmas." Before I could even get the finished sentence out of my mouth he said back: "I'll have a merry Santa Claus Christmas!" He didn't even want the mention of Christmas just like many don't want Nativity scenes at Christmas time. What in God's name is the world coming to? These things are such hatred of God from this perverse and twisted generation. People quote Lennon the evil Russian leader, or Karl Marx, the founder of atheistic communism, long ago over his saying of how sickening religion is. And people today love *The Da Vinci Code* book that mocks and blasphemies God.

People who say the Bible is contradicting, vague and has inconsistencies are just ignorant. If they had any knowledge of it they wouldn't say those things. In one of my books remember me saying that I wondered at people who say things about the Bible and wonder how much research and study they did on it. The answers are always none. They say these things simply because they feel that way, not because of study and research. Let's throw our feelings out the window and look for solid truth to these things. Let's not base important things and decisions on feelings.

It is easy to knock something, but hard to prove it. I am sick of seeing Skeptic Magazine editor or owner on TV knocking prophecy. Anyone can do that. That is very easy. Why don't you try to prove it instead of saying it is vague and self- fulfilling prophecies when prophecy does come true? They all say the Bible is so vague or could be made to say anything and they put no stock into prophecy. Then when a detail prophecy comes true they say a coincidence or self fulfilling, meaning if you say you will get the flu on February 18 you will get the flu on that date because it's self fulfilling. Give me a break! You have no knowledge of prophecy so don't speak cause you ignorance shows. If you say enough times an earthquake is about to happen is that self-fulfilling? Then they say quickly "well there always been earthquakes." If a storm is prophesied and it happens is it a wild coincidence or self fulfilling because there always been storms? This type of thinking is not wise, but stupid. The study of Bible prophecy for the first Coming of Christ alone is amazing. All those details can't be vague or coincidence or self-fulfilling. See study Bibles in the rear for a list of those prophecies and Hal Lindsey's book The Late Great Planet Earth. Judas could of betrayed Jesus for any number of pieces of silver, but it was predicted 30. Jesus could have been born any other place, but Bethlehem, but was as predicted. His parents didn't even live in Bethlehem. You can go on and on about the many predicted events of Christ's first Coming. Read the list of them and their fulfillment's in those sources I just gave. You will be just amazed. See the Ryrie Study Bible pages 1879-1882.

Let me say something about TV preachers and your local preachers. And that is a few may be phonies and many may have sin in their life like we all do, but they are the only ones preaching Jesus Christ. They lead people to repent of their sins and accept Jesus Christ as Lord and Savior and to read the Bible, pray and go to Church. Do you do that? Does your family or friends do that? Do the people you watch or listen to on TV or radio or CD, movies, books or whatever do that? NO!!! If you took a survey of the people in all churches I think you will find a great many are there in church directly or indirectly by the TV preachers teaching them so. Jesus' Disciples came to Him one time and said they caught someone doing something in Jesus name and they forbid him not to do that. Jesus told them forbid them not for those who are with me are not against me.

Another note: The mystery Babylon as described in my other books as the birth of the Gentiles from women devils mating with Jewish men was true and not the antichrist writing. It is now made known as Romans 16:25-27 and Malachi 4:6 claimed for the obedience of faith for all. It was made known so the fathers (Jewish) love their sons (Gentiles) and the sons (Gentiles) love their fathers (Jewish) just as Malachi 4:6 predicted. So go in faith, obedience and love among all races both now and forever. See my other book The Antichrist.

A final note: At the end of this world and when the Second Coming of Christ happens there could be great storms, wars, volcanoes, earthquakes and other troubles happening in the world, but then it may not be. That year or two or three years before or a month or two before may see peace treaties, not many storms or earthquakes, a SDI system deployed, prosperity and many saying Peace, Peace and Peace and safety. Then one day many will be looking up to see a strange light by the Sun and soon after our Sun novas and the end. See Jeremiah chapter 6; I Thessalonians 5:3; Luke 21:25-36; Matthew 24:37-42. Is the saying of "Peace, Peace or Peace and safety" a prediction of two years of peace from 2012 or 2016, then a very great and sudden destruction? If President Obama reaches a Peace Treaty with Israel and the Palestinians between now and 2012-2013 or 2014-2016 then watch out for sudden destruction. The great antichrist was predicted to come and make peace then he starts an awful war. Was that prediction that of a Peace Treaty with the state of Israel and the Palestinians then war or sudden destruction? Or does it mean now with President Obama winning the Nobel Peace prize and then in 2010 attacks or helps Israel attack Iran then a tremendous war breaks out? That's exactly what the Bible predicted the antichrist to do all along. I don't think it is wrong for President Obama to help Israel to attack Iran, I think it is right. But what will happen after that attack is the big question. In these end times reverse is true of some things. You can do right and still be wrong and you can do wrong and be right. But as I said earlier the end time antichrist doesn't have to come cause all was fulfilled in WWII in Hitler.

Today many lay and wait for some TV preacher or local preacher or some Christian to fall to some sin and they then accuse them as being hypocrites and why they don't follow Christ and Christianity.

That's just the point! Follow Christ and not Christians, men, women and children. If you put your trust in them they are sure to fall. But if you put your trust in Christ He will never fall. Read the four gospels of the New Testament and see for yourself how perfect Christ was His whole life. People will always let you down, but Christ will never let you down. Put your trust in His righteousness and not in peoples' righteousness.

But remember Jesus Christ is the true meaning of life and not vanity or emptiness. He loves you deeply and wants you to accept Him as Lord and savior. Come to Christ…

Amen!

About the Author:

Kurt Brian Bakley was born 8:11 p.m. Friday evening October 15, 1954 at Cooper Hospital in Camden, New Jersey across the river from Philadelphia during Hurricane Hazel. He grew up hating books, reading and writing because of his eye problems and learning disabilities and dropped out of high school. Then one Saturday night when he was 21 years old, after partying that night, he woke up early Sunday morning with massive amount of knowledge and yearning to read, write and research all kinds of knowledge. He went out first thing that Sunday morning to the mall and waited till noon for the bookstore to open. He immediately went in and bought several books and began his reading, writing and researching to this day. That was on August 29 of 1976 and today (2012) he is still reading, writing and researching information on prophecy and Christianity. He has over 50,000 hours of research and writing from then to now (2012), his 36th year of doing so. His fourteen books from 2001 that he's written are: *The Nativity*; *The Antichrist*; *The Experiment in Philadelphia: Did Einstein discover God?*; *The boy who could predict earthquakes*; *2012: The two earthquakes and God's two witnesses*; *Prophecies that have, will, or didn't happen*; *The balanced life*; and then the *The Life of Kurt B. Bakley* and then *The Divine Code 2*, then the *The Divine Code* and then the *Predictions for 2013-2014*, then the *Predictions for 2015* and then *Predictions for 2011-2019*, *The Divine Code 3 and End Time Signs*. All are available now (September 2012). All 14 books are available at this web site: WWW. authorhouse.Com. now (September of 2012). Read them in this order, first, *The Nativity*, then *The Antichrist*, then the next, *The Experiment at Philadelphia*, then *The boy who could predict earthquakes*, then *2012: The two earthquakes and God's two witnesses*, then the *Prophecies that have, will, or didn't happen*, then *The balanced life* and then *The Life of Kurt B. Bakley* and then *The Divine Code 2 and The Divine Code* and then *Predictions for 2013-2014* and then *Predictions for 2015* and then *Predictions for 2011-2019* and then *The Divine Code 3* and then *End Time Signs*. After you read them once read them through the second time slowly. When you read them in that order read them from cover to cover, start with the rear cover then the introduction and all the way through. Do not skip round or you will get confused. Don't stop because you have a question or don't understand or want to look up documentation. They are all a hard read but bare with them. You can look up documentation on the second round through when you read them for the second time. Revelation chapter 5 predicts these books are the seven eyes and seven horns that go around the world on the World Wide Web (WWW). The seven horns and seven eyes are seven plus seven, which equal 14, which are the fourteen books I written minus the four that were canceled. Is the satellite that powers the world wide web 10 by 20 cubits as Zechariah 5:1-2 predicted for a great flying (satellite) roll (a round satellite-ancient book) that size? On the web site: WWW. Authorhouse.com just type in my name Kurt B. Bakley in the search box and then click the go or search and all or most of my books will come up. Type Kurt Bakley for my other books. *The Divine Code* first published in January 26, 2001, not available any more predicts planes flying into buildings in New York City on September 15-17, 2001. Five or six days off but still an amazing prophecy. That same book predicted the new millenium to start June 21, 2001. My book *Prophecies that have, will, and didn't happen* show that certain ancient Bible prophecies are detailed and correct, but fail to happen. This book *The Divine Code* along with the first The Divine Code 3, The mystery of good and evil, The mystery of God and The Mayan Code are all expired, canceled and not live or available any more. But most of them are included in these other 14 books. They being The mystery of good and evil, The Mayan Code and The mystery of God. My book *The Divine Code 2* documented how the Bible predicted a vile person to come to power in Russia born in the Taurus sign and start a war and invade the Middle East, Israel and Florida. Such a person ran for President of Russia in 1996 born in the Taurus sign and promised to invade the Middle East, but he failed to be elected. The book *The Divine Code 2* shows prophecies of TWA flight 800 explosion and crash off of Long Island near a place called Babylon. It tells of ancient prophecies that gives the place and attitude and what caused it to explode. Look at the copyright page of each of my books to see when they were published so you can't say they were written after the fact. Do what ever the angel tells you. If the Authorhouse web site changes call 1-888-519-5121 and ask them for the new web site or order all these books above by phone at that number and extension 5022 or the extension the operator tells you for ordering books. If you can't find them type in the title of the book. Keep trying till you get through by either internet or by phone. The web site and phone lines may be jam for all the orders and it may take several hours or days or weeks or months to get through. If you can't get through try Amazon.Com or Barnes & Noble. Com. Remember what the angel tells you to do the one time it appears or the two times it appears to you.